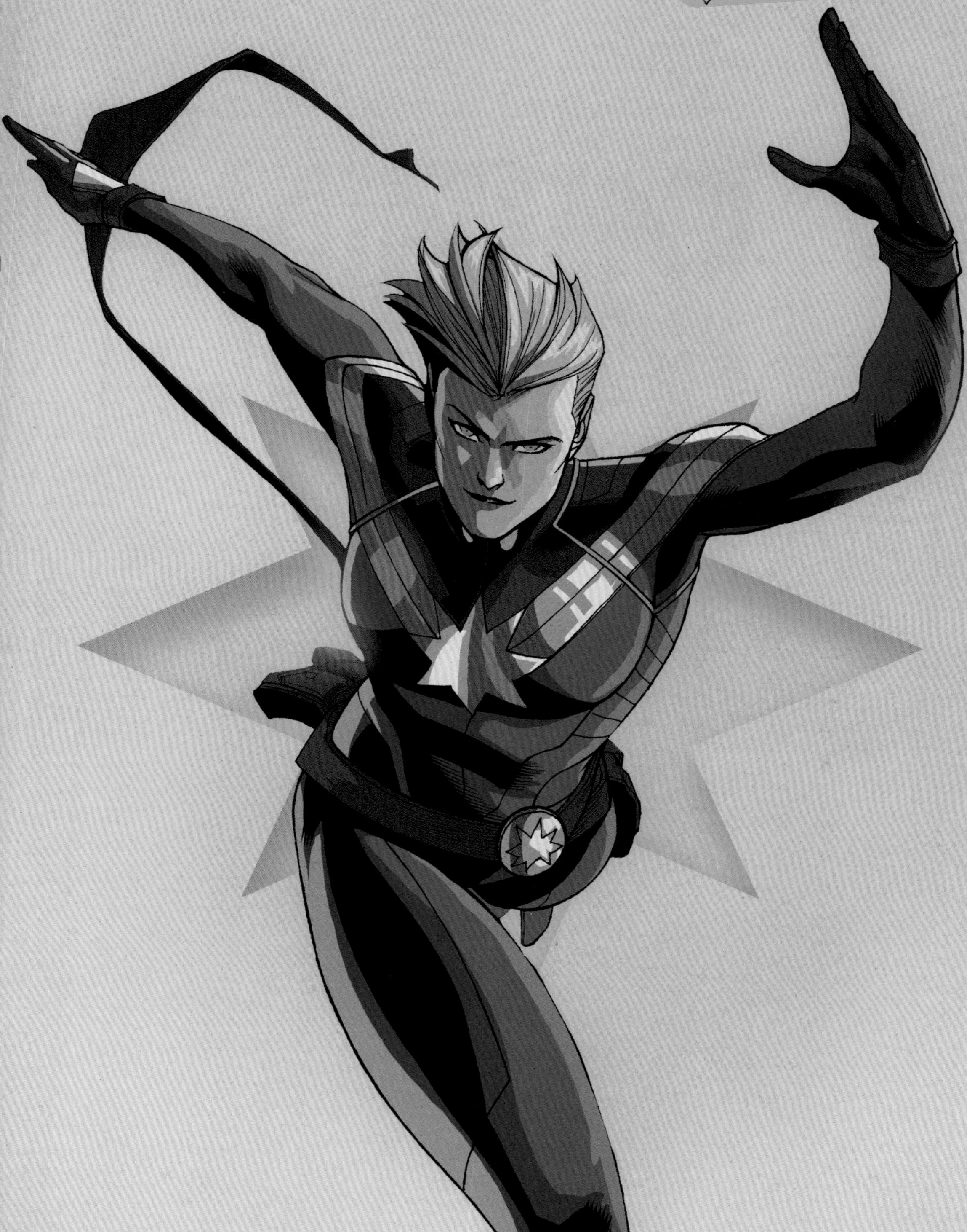

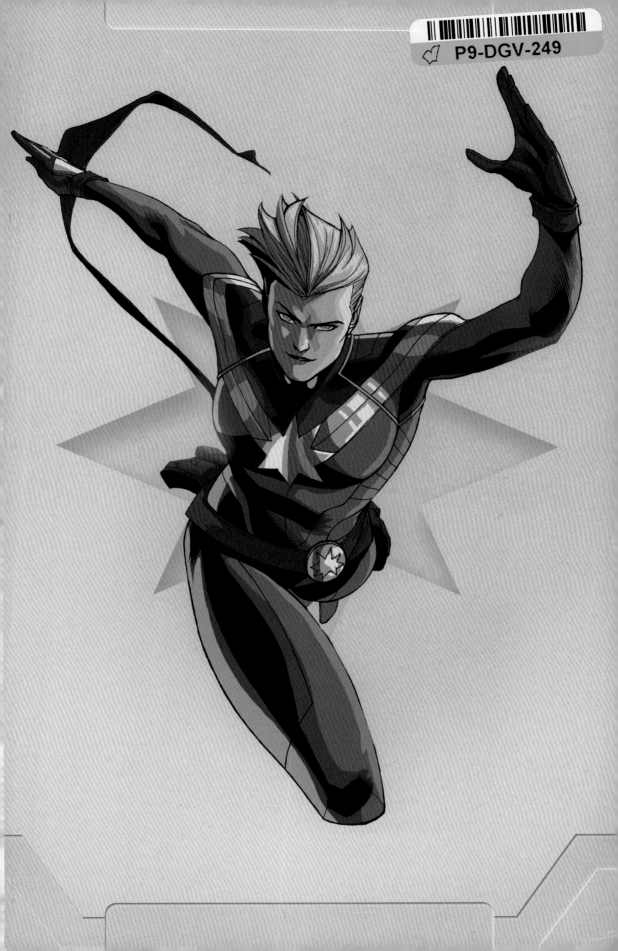

WHEN FORMER U.S. AIR FORCE PILOT **CAROL DANVERS**
WAS CAUGHT IN THE EXPLOSION OF AN ALIEN DEVICE,
SHE WAS IMBUED WITH SUPERHUMAN POWERS. AS AN
AVENGER, SHE USED HER GIFTS TO PROTECT THE PLANET.
NOW A NEW CHAPTER AWAITS, YET SHE IS AND
ALWAYS WILL BE EARTH'S MIGHTIEST HERO. SHE IS...

CAPTAIN MARVEL

CIVIL WAR II

**RUTH FLETCHER GAGE
& CHRISTOS GAGE**
WRITERS

KRIS ANKA (#6, #8),
MARCO FAILLA (#7)
& THONY SILAS (#9-10)
ARTISTS

ANDY OWENS
ADDITIONAL INKS, #8

MATTHEW WILSON
COLOR ARTIST

VC's JOE CARAMAGNA
LETTERER

KRIS ANKA
COVER ART

CHARLES BEACHAM
ASSISTANT EDITOR

SANA AMANAT
EDITOR

JENNIFER GRÜNWALD
COLLECTION EDITOR

KATERI WOODY
ASSOCIATE MANAGING EDITOR

MARK D. BEAZLEY
EDITOR, SPECIAL PROJECTS

JEFF YOUNGQUIST
VP PRODUCTION & SPECIAL PROJECTS

DAVID GABRIEL
SVP PRINT, SALES & MARKETING

JAY BOWEN & ADAM DEL RE
BOOK DESIGNERS

AXEL ALONSO
EDITOR IN CHIEF

JOE QUESADA
CHIEF CREATIVE OFFICER

DAN BUCKLEY
PUBLISHER

ALAN FINE
EXECUTIVE PRODUCER

CAPTAIN MARVEL VOL. 2: CIVIL WAR II. Contains material originally published in magazine form as CAPTAIN MARVEL #6-10. First printing 2017.
ISBN# 978-0-7851-9643-3. Published by MARVEL WORLDWIDE, INC., a subsidiary of MARVEL ENTERTAINMENT, LLC. OFFICE OF PUBLICATION: 135
West 50th Street, New York, NY 10020. Copyright © 2017 MARVEL No similarity between any of the names, characters, persons, and/or institutions
in this magazine with those of any living or dead person or institution is intended, and any such similarity which may exist is purely coincidental.
Printed in Canada. ALAN FINE, President, Marvel Entertainment; **DAN BUCKLEY,** President, TV, Publishing & Brand Management; **JOE QUESADA,**
Chief Creative Officer; **TOM BREVOORT,** SVP of Publishing; **DAVID BOGART,** SVP of Business Affairs & Operations, Publishing & Partnership;
C.B. CEBULSKI, VP of Brand Management & Development, Asia; **DAVID GABRIEL,** SVP of Sales & Marketing, Publishing; **JEFF YOUNGQUIST,** VP
of Production & Special Projects; **DAN CARR,** Executive Director of Publishing Technology; **ALEX MORALES,** Director of Publishing Operations;
SUSAN CRESPI, Production Manager; **STAN LEE,** Chairman Emeritus. For information regarding advertising in Marvel Comics or on Marvel.com,
please contact Vit DeBellis, Integrated Sales Manager, at vdebellis@marvel.com. For Marvel subscription inquiries, please call 888-511-5480.
Manufactured between 12/9/2016 and 1/16/2017 by SOLISCO PRINTERS, SCOTT, QC, CANADA.
10 9 8 7 6 5 4 3 2 1

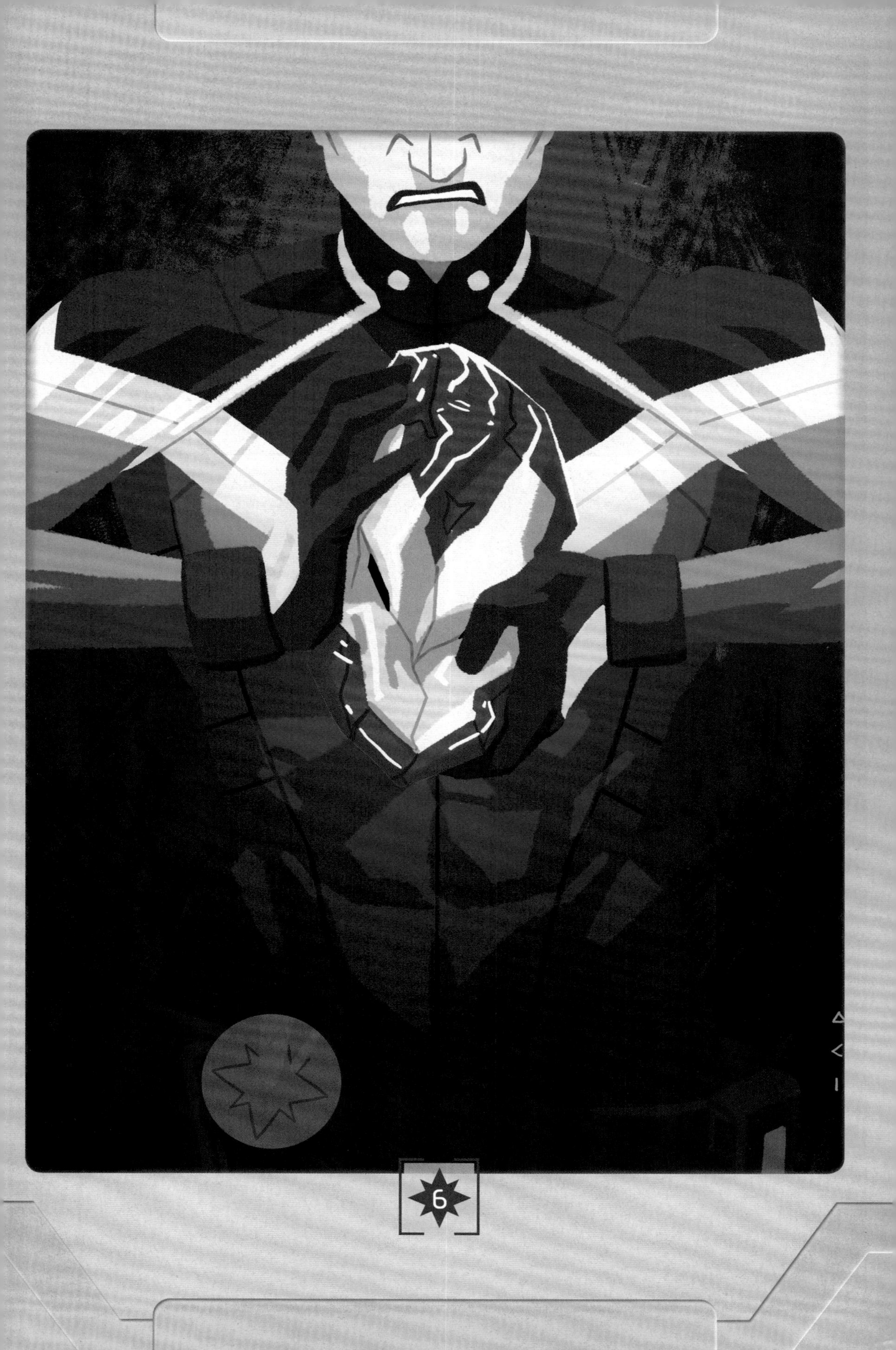

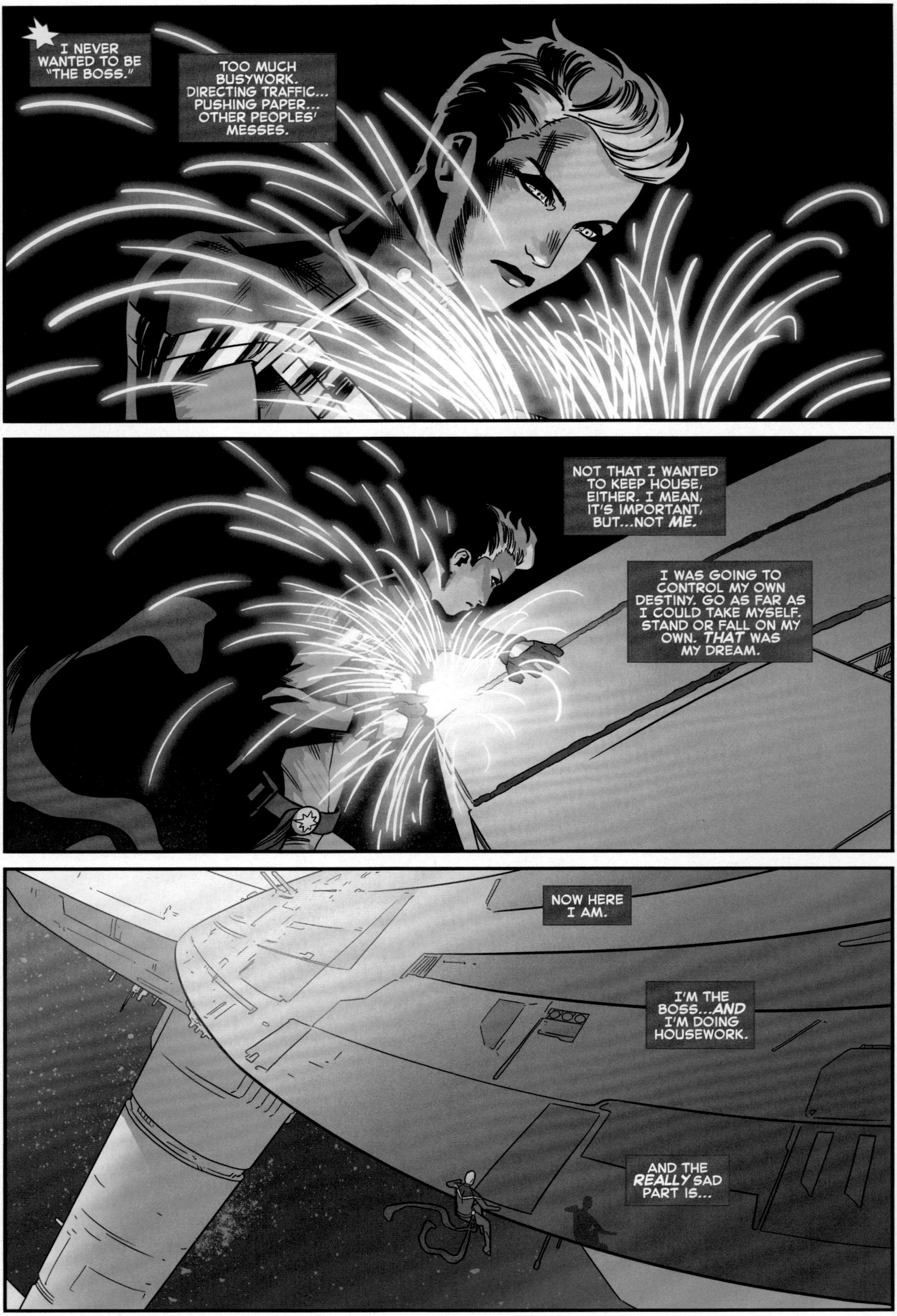
I NEVER WANTED TO BE "THE BOSS."
TOO MUCH BUSYWORK. DIRECTING TRAFFIC... PUSHING PAPER... OTHER PEOPLES' MESSES.
NOT THAT I WANTED TO KEEP HOUSE, EITHER. I MEAN, IT'S IMPORTANT, BUT...NOT *ME.*
I WAS GOING TO CONTROL MY OWN DESTINY. GO AS FAR AS I COULD TAKE MYSELF. STAND OR FALL ON MY OWN. *THAT* WAS MY DREAM.
NOW HERE I AM.
I'M THE BOSS...*AND* I'M DOING HOUSEWORK.
AND THE *REALLY* SAD PART IS...

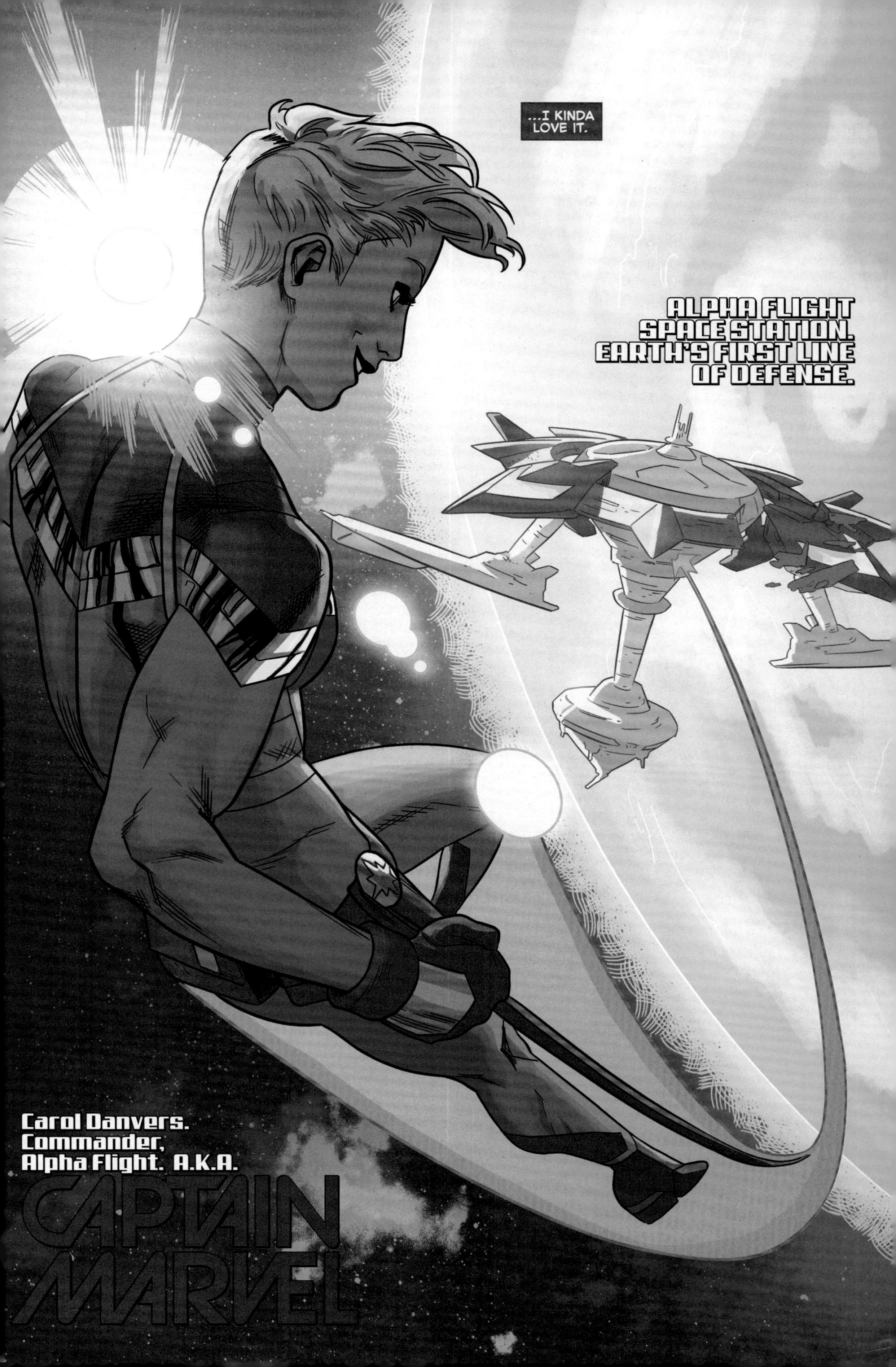
...I KINDA LOVE IT.
ALPHA FLIGHT SPACE STATION. EARTH'S FIRST LINE OF DEFENSE.
Carol Danvers. Commander, Alpha Flight. A.K.A.
CAPTAIN MARVEL

CIVIL WAR II

CAPTAIN MARVEL

RECENTLY, CAPTAIN MARVEL WAS APPOINTED
COMMANDER OF ALPHA FLIGHT SPACE STATION,
AN INTERPLANETARY VENTURE CREATED TO
BE EARTH'S FIRST LINE OF DEFENSE AGAINST
EXTRATERRESTRIAL THREATS. NOT SURE SHE
WAS UP TO THE TASK OF LEADING, CAROL
ACCEPTED THE JOB WITH SOME UNCERTAINTY.

THOUGH THEIR FIRST MISSION NEARLY SAW THE
SPACE STATION DESTROYED, CAPTAIN MARVEL
AND HER CREW FORGED AN UNBREAKABLE BOND
— MAKING CAPTAIN MARVEL CONFIDENT THAT
THEY CAN HANDLE ANYTHING THE UNIVERSE
THROWS AT THEM.

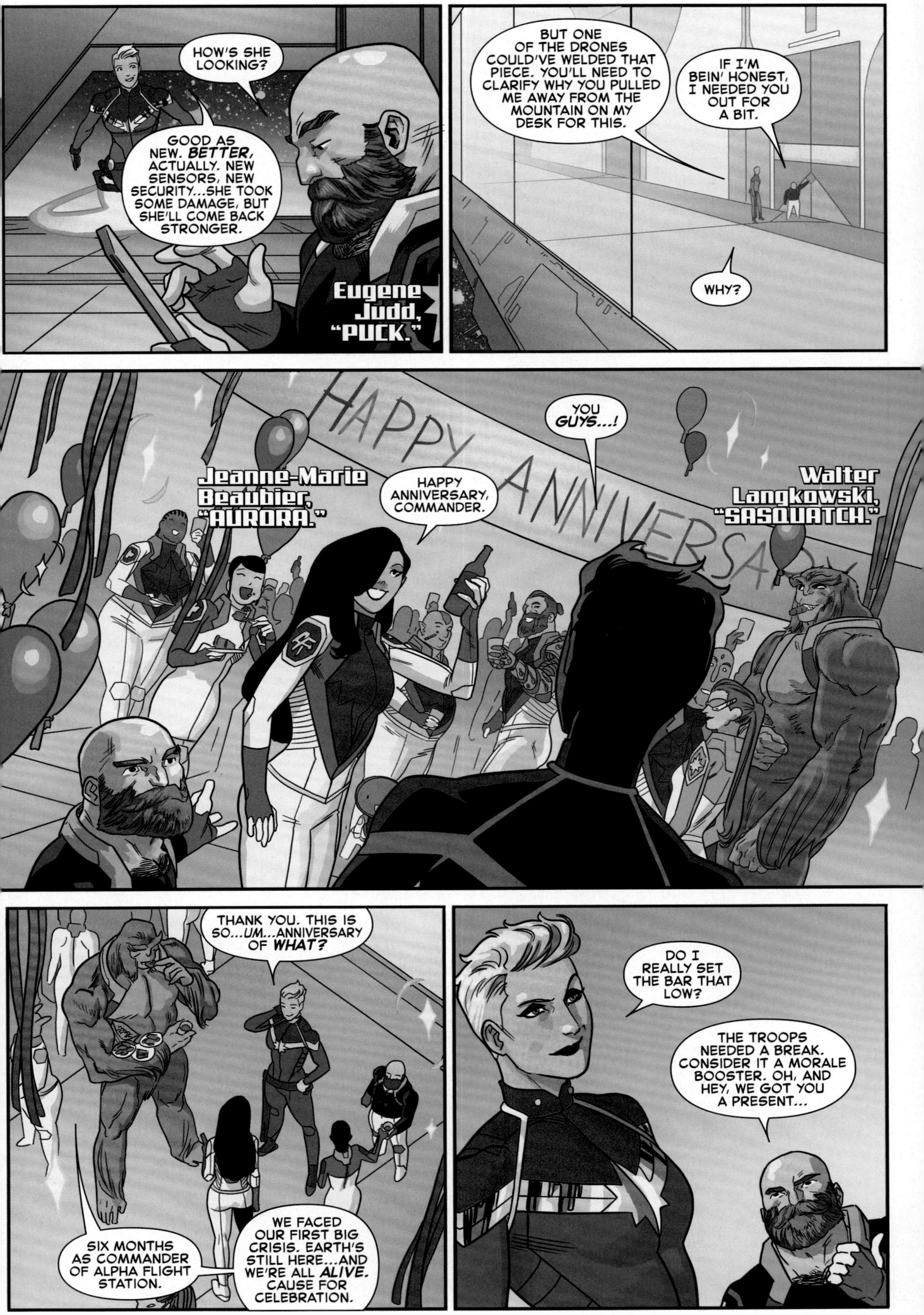

HOW'S SHE LOOKING?
GOOD AS NEW. BETTER, ACTUALLY. NEW SENSORS, NEW SECURITY...SHE TOOK SOME DAMAGE, BUT SHE'LL COME BACK STRONGER.
Eugene Judd, "PUCK."
BUT ONE OF THE DRONES COULD'VE WELDED THAT PIECE. YOU'LL NEED TO CLARIFY WHY YOU PULLED ME AWAY FROM THE MOUNTAIN ON MY DESK FOR THIS.
IF I'M BEIN' HONEST, I NEEDED YOU OUT FOR A BIT.
WHY?
HAPPY ANNIVERSARY
Jeanne-Marie Beaubier, "AURORA."
HAPPY ANNIVERSARY, COMMANDER.
YOU GUYS...!
Walter Langkowski, "SASQUATCH."
THANK YOU. THIS IS SO...UM...ANNIVERSARY OF WHAT?
SIX MONTHS AS COMMANDER OF ALPHA FLIGHT STATION.
WE FACED OUR FIRST BIG CRISIS. EARTH'S STILL HERE...AND WE'RE ALL ALIVE. CAUSE FOR CELEBRATION.
DO I REALLY SET THE BAR THAT LOW?
THE TROOPS NEEDED A BREAK. CONSIDER IT A MORALE BOOSTER. OH, AND HEY, WE GOT YOU A PRESENT...

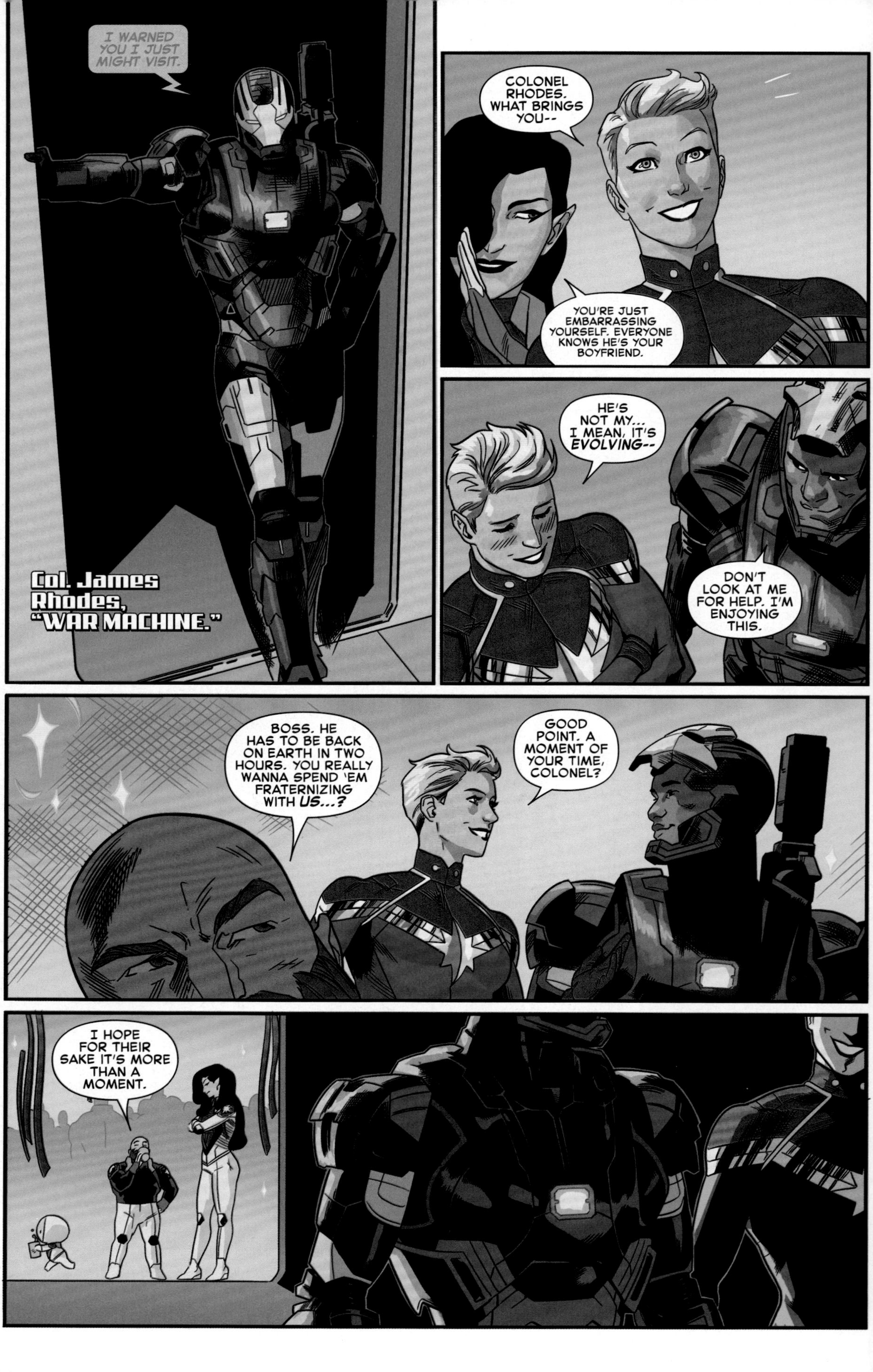
I WARNED YOU I JUST MIGHT VISIT.
Col. James Rhodes, "WAR MACHINE."
COLONEL RHODES. WHAT BRINGS YOU--
YOU'RE JUST EMBARRASSING YOURSELF. EVERYONE KNOWS HE'S YOUR BOYFRIEND.
HE'S NOT MY... I MEAN, IT'S *EVOLVING--*
DON'T LOOK AT ME FOR HELP. I'M ENJOYING THIS.
BOSS. HE HAS TO BE BACK ON EARTH IN TWO HOURS. YOU REALLY WANNA SPEND 'EM FRATERNIZING WITH *US...?*
GOOD POINT. A MOMENT OF YOUR TIME, COLONEL?
I HOPE FOR THEIR SAKE IT'S MORE THAN A MOMENT.

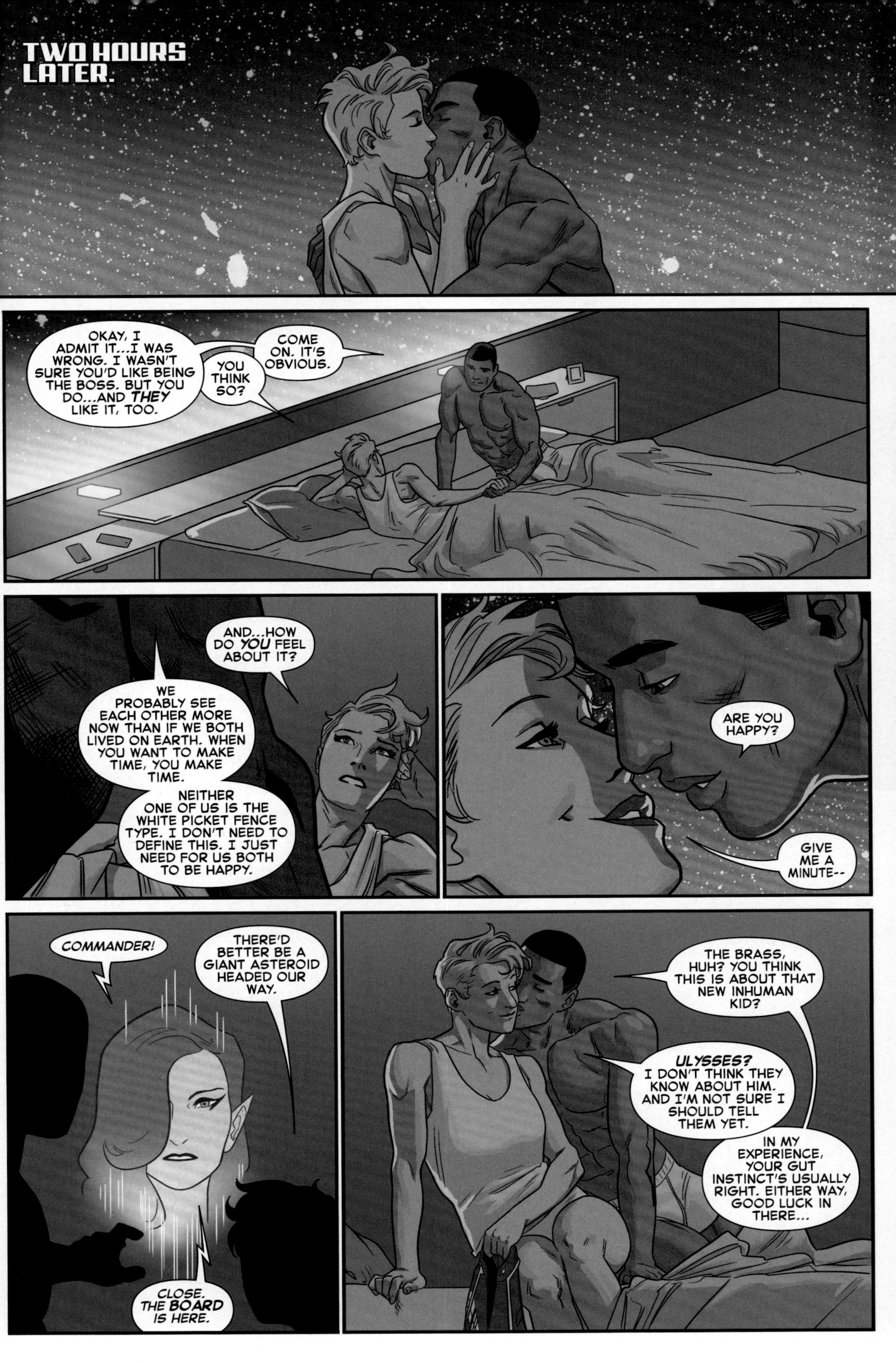
TWO HOURS LATER.
OKAY, I ADMIT IT...I WAS WRONG. I WASN'T SURE YOU'D LIKE BEING THE BOSS. BUT YOU DO...AND THEY LIKE IT, TOO.
YOU THINK SO?
COME ON. IT'S OBVIOUS.
AND...HOW DO YOU FEEL ABOUT IT?
WE PROBABLY SEE EACH OTHER MORE NOW THAN IF WE BOTH LIVED ON EARTH. WHEN YOU WANT TO MAKE TIME, YOU MAKE TIME.
NEITHER ONE OF US IS THE WHITE PICKET FENCE TYPE. I DON'T NEED TO DEFINE THIS. I JUST NEED FOR US BOTH TO BE HAPPY.
ARE YOU HAPPY?
GIVE ME A MINUTE--
COMMANDER!
THERE'D BETTER BE A GIANT ASTEROID HEADED OUR WAY.
CLOSE. THE BOARD IS HERE.
THE BRASS, HUH? YOU THINK THIS IS ABOUT THAT NEW INHUMAN KID?
ULYSSES? I DON'T THINK THEY KNOW ABOUT HIM. AND I'M NOT SURE I SHOULD TELL THEM YET.
IN MY EXPERIENCE, YOUR GUT INSTINCT'S USUALLY RIGHT. EITHER WAY, GOOD LUCK IN THERE...

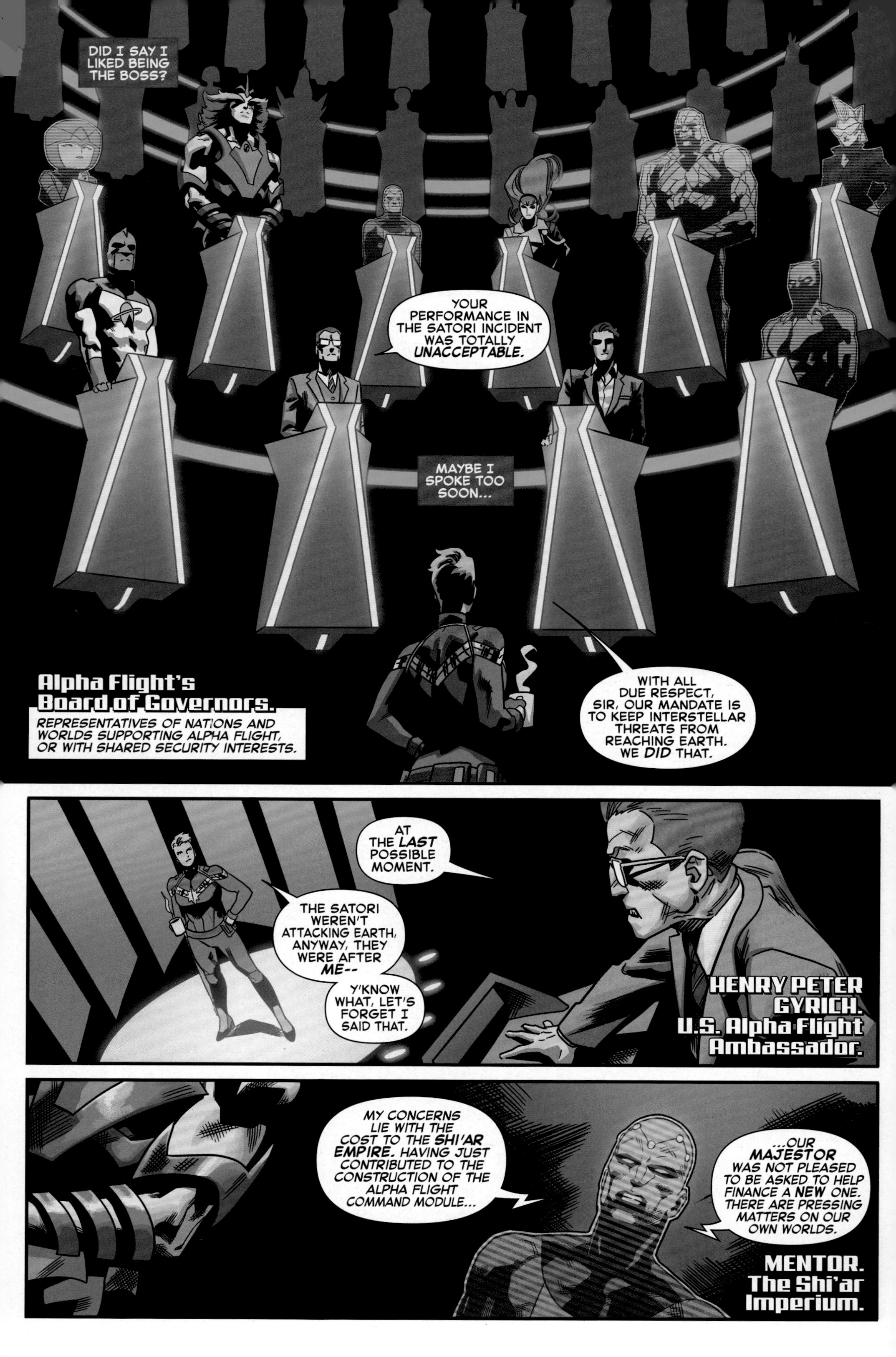
DID I SAY I LIKED BEING THE BOSS?
YOUR PERFORMANCE IN THE SATORI INCIDENT WAS TOTALLY *UNACCEPTABLE.*
MAYBE I SPOKE TOO SOON...
Alpha Flight's Board of Governors.
REPRESENTATIVES OF NATIONS AND WORLDS SUPPORTING ALPHA FLIGHT, OR WITH SHARED SECURITY INTERESTS.
WITH ALL DUE RESPECT, SIR, OUR MANDATE IS TO KEEP INTERSTELLAR THREATS FROM REACHING EARTH. WE *DID* THAT.
AT THE *LAST* POSSIBLE MOMENT.
THE SATORI WEREN'T ATTACKING EARTH, ANYWAY, THEY WERE AFTER *ME--*
Y'KNOW WHAT, LET'S FORGET I SAID THAT.
HENRY PETER GYRICH. U.S. Alpha Flight Ambassador.
MY CONCERNS LIE WITH THE COST TO THE *SHI'AR EMPIRE.* HAVING JUST CONTRIBUTED TO THE CONSTRUCTION OF THE ALPHA FLIGHT COMMAND MODULE...
...OUR *MAJESTOR* WAS NOT PLEASED TO BE ASKED TO HELP FINANCE A *NEW* ONE. THERE ARE PRESSING MATTERS ON OUR OWN WORLDS.
MENTOR. The Shi'ar Imperium.

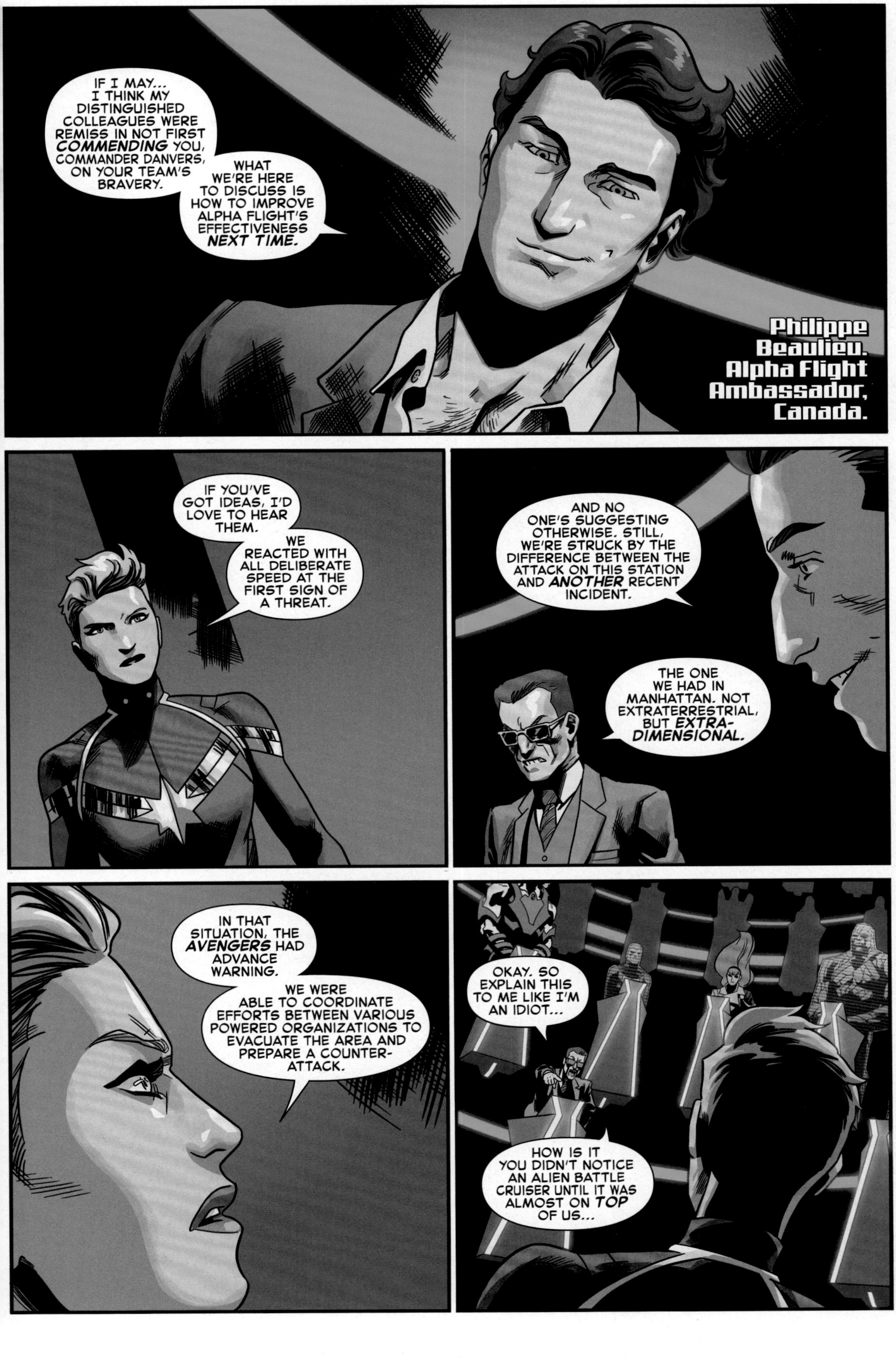
IF I MAY... I THINK MY DISTINGUISHED COLLEAGUES WERE REMISS IN NOT FIRST COMMENDING YOU, COMMANDER DANVERS, ON YOUR TEAM'S BRAVERY.
WHAT WE'RE HERE TO DISCUSS IS HOW TO IMPROVE ALPHA FLIGHT'S EFFECTIVENESS NEXT TIME.
Philippe Beaulieu. Alpha Flight Ambassador, Canada.
IF YOU'VE GOT IDEAS, I'D LOVE TO HEAR THEM.
WE REACTED WITH ALL DELIBERATE SPEED AT THE FIRST SIGN OF A THREAT.
AND NO ONE'S SUGGESTING OTHERWISE. STILL, WE'RE STRUCK BY THE DIFFERENCE BETWEEN THE ATTACK ON THIS STATION AND ANOTHER RECENT INCIDENT.
THE ONE WE HAD IN MANHATTAN. NOT EXTRATERRESTRIAL, BUT EXTRA-DIMENSIONAL.
IN THAT SITUATION, THE AVENGERS HAD ADVANCE WARNING.
WE WERE ABLE TO COORDINATE EFFORTS BETWEEN VARIOUS POWERED ORGANIZATIONS TO EVACUATE THE AREA AND PREPARE A COUNTER-ATTACK.
OKAY. SO EXPLAIN THIS TO ME LIKE I'M AN IDIOT...
HOW IS IT YOU DIDN'T NOTICE AN ALIEN BATTLE CRUISER UNTIL IT WAS ALMOST ON TOP OF US...

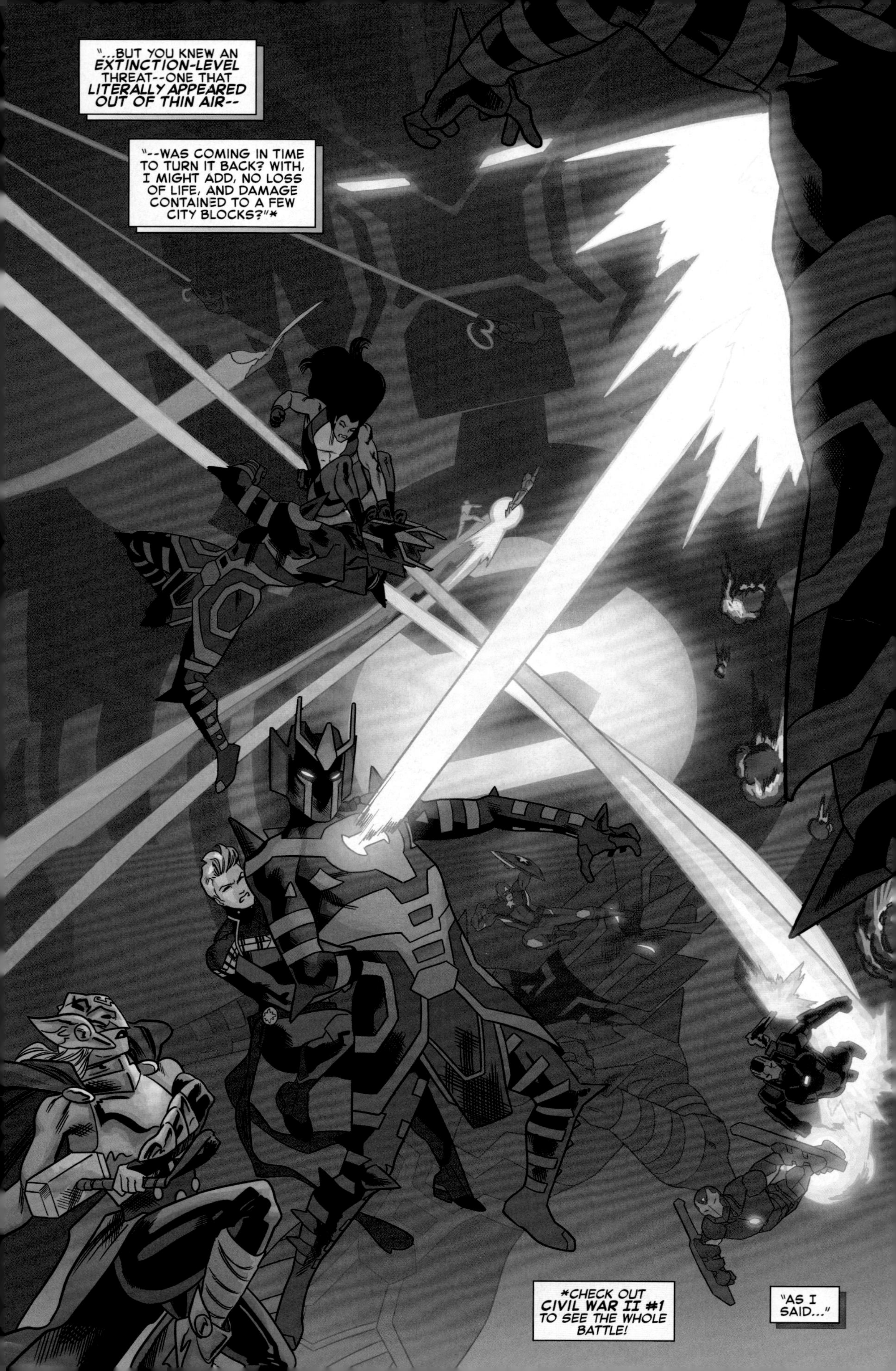
"...BUT YOU KNEW AN EXTINCTION-LEVEL THREAT--ONE THAT LITERALLY APPEARED OUT OF THIN AIR--
"--WAS COMING IN TIME TO TURN IT BACK? WITH, I MIGHT ADD, NO LOSS OF LIFE, AND DAMAGE CONTAINED TO A FEW CITY BLOCKS?"*
*CHECK OUT CIVIL WAR II #1 TO SEE THE WHOLE BATTLE!
"AS I SAID..."

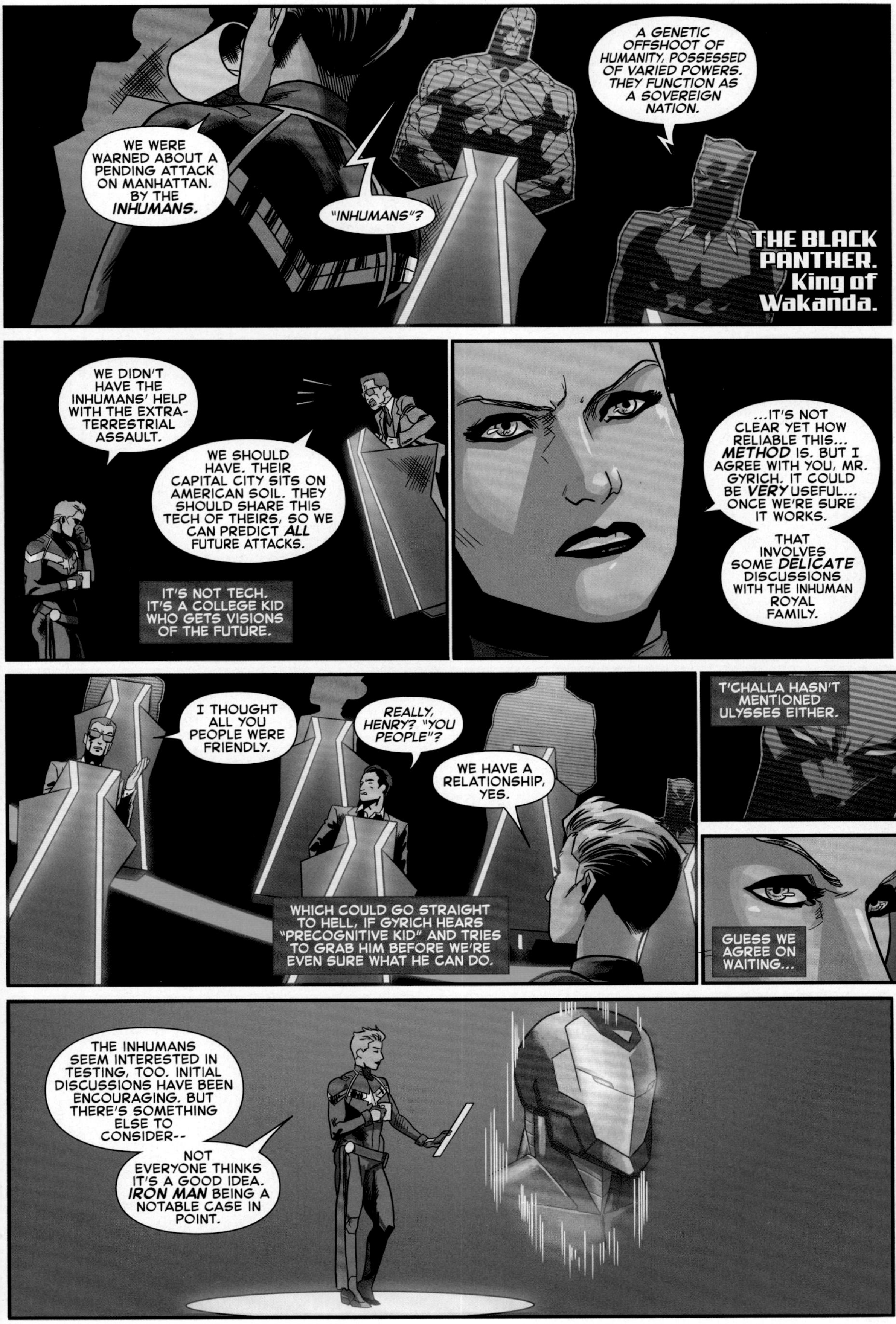
WE WERE WARNED ABOUT A PENDING ATTACK ON MANHATTAN. BY THE *INHUMANS.*
"INHUMANS"?
A GENETIC OFFSHOOT OF HUMANITY, POSSESSED OF VARIED POWERS. THEY FUNCTION AS A SOVEREIGN NATION.
THE BLACK PANTHER. King of Wakanda.
WE DIDN'T HAVE THE INHUMANS' HELP WITH THE EXTRA-TERRESTRIAL ASSAULT.
WE SHOULD HAVE. THEIR CAPITAL CITY SITS ON AMERICAN SOIL. THEY SHOULD SHARE THIS TECH OF THEIRS, SO WE CAN PREDICT *ALL* FUTURE ATTACKS.
IT'S NOT TECH. IT'S A COLLEGE KID WHO GETS VISIONS OF THE FUTURE.
...IT'S NOT CLEAR YET HOW RELIABLE THIS... *METHOD* IS. BUT I AGREE WITH YOU, MR. GYRICH. IT COULD BE *VERY* USEFUL... ONCE WE'RE SURE IT WORKS.
THAT INVOLVES SOME *DELICATE* DISCUSSIONS WITH THE INHUMAN ROYAL FAMILY.
I THOUGHT ALL YOU PEOPLE WERE FRIENDLY.
REALLY, HENRY? "YOU PEOPLE"?
WE HAVE A RELATIONSHIP, YES.
WHICH COULD GO STRAIGHT TO HELL, IF GYRICH HEARS "PRECOGNITIVE KID" AND TRIES TO GRAB HIM BEFORE WE'RE EVEN SURE WHAT HE CAN DO.
T'CHALLA HASN'T MENTIONED ULYSSES EITHER.
GUESS WE AGREE ON WAITING...
THE INHUMANS SEEM INTERESTED IN TESTING, TOO. INITIAL DISCUSSIONS HAVE BEEN ENCOURAGING. BUT THERE'S SOMETHING ELSE TO CONSIDER--
NOT EVERYONE THINKS IT'S A GOOD IDEA. *IRON MAN* BEING A NOTABLE CASE IN POINT.

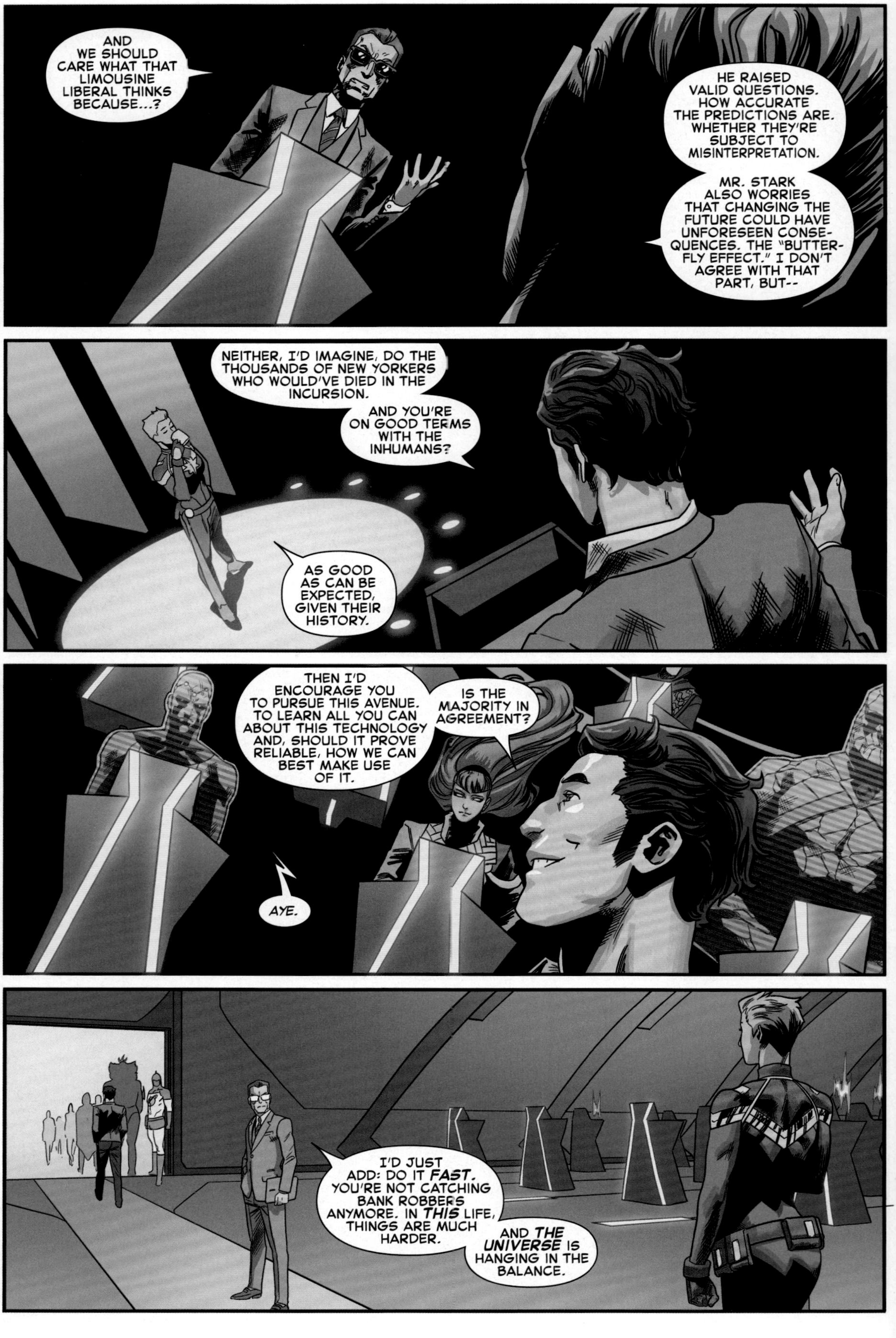
AND WE SHOULD CARE WHAT THAT LIMOUSINE LIBERAL THINKS BECAUSE...?
HE RAISED VALID QUESTIONS. HOW ACCURATE THE PREDICTIONS ARE. WHETHER THEY'RE SUBJECT TO MISINTERPRETATION.
MR. STARK ALSO WORRIES THAT CHANGING THE FUTURE COULD HAVE UNFORESEEN CONSE-QUENCES. THE "BUTTER-FLY EFFECT." I DON'T AGREE WITH THAT PART, BUT--
NEITHER, I'D IMAGINE, DO THE THOUSANDS OF NEW YORKERS WHO WOULD'VE DIED IN THE INCURSION.
AND YOU'RE ON GOOD TERMS WITH THE INHUMANS?
AS GOOD AS CAN BE EXPECTED, GIVEN THEIR HISTORY.
THEN I'D ENCOURAGE YOU TO PURSUE THIS AVENUE. TO LEARN ALL YOU CAN ABOUT THIS TECHNOLOGY AND, SHOULD IT PROVE RELIABLE, HOW WE CAN BEST MAKE USE OF IT.
IS THE MAJORITY IN AGREEMENT?
AYE.
I'D JUST ADD: DO IT FAST. YOU'RE NOT CATCHING BANK ROBBERS ANYMORE. IN THIS LIFE, THINGS ARE MUCH HARDER.
AND THE UNIVERSE IS HANGING IN THE BALANCE.

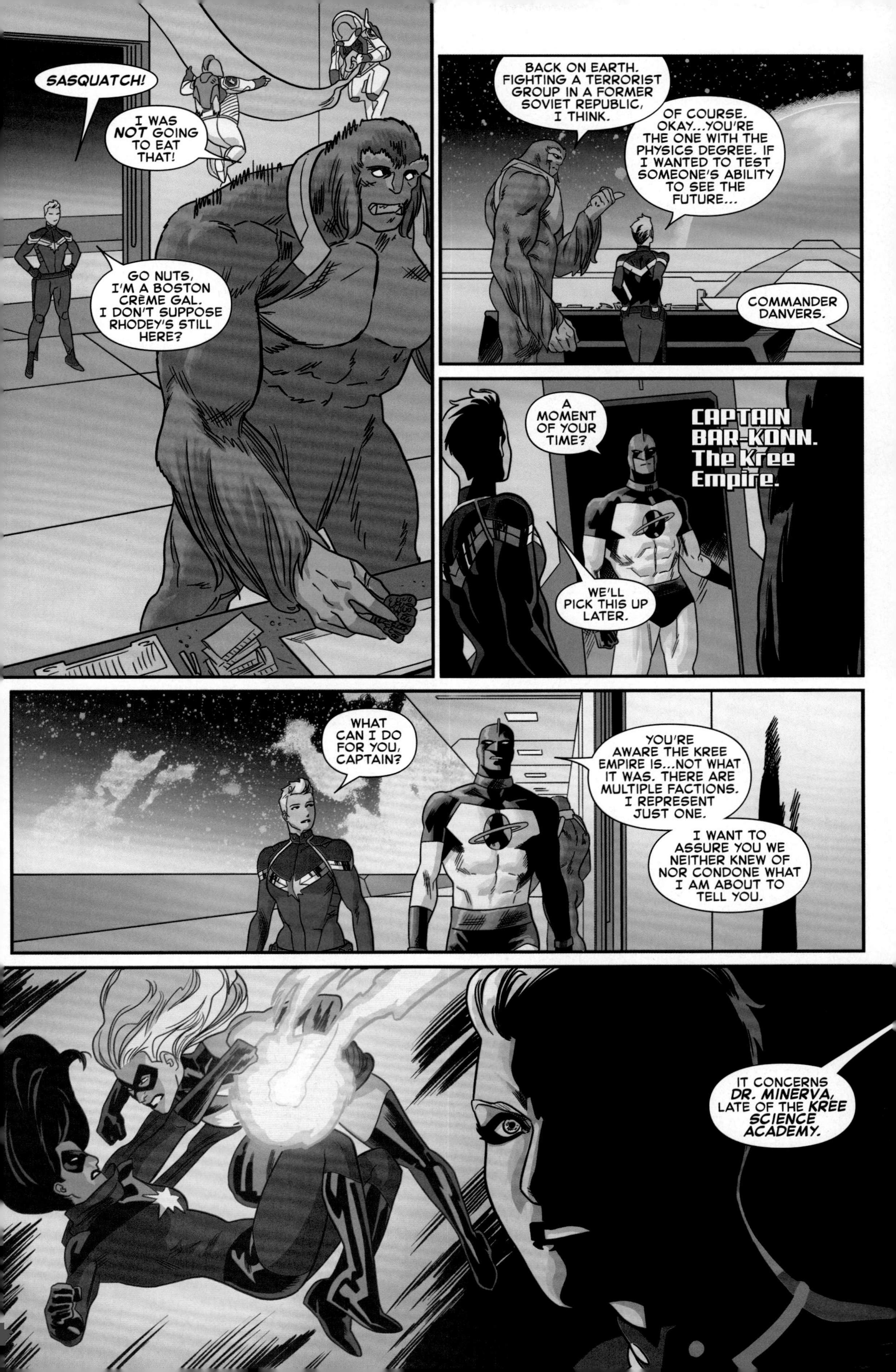
SASQUATCH!
I WAS NOT GOING TO EAT THAT!
GO NUTS, I'M A BOSTON CRÈME GAL. I DON'T SUPPOSE RHODEY'S STILL HERE?
BACK ON EARTH. FIGHTING A TERRORIST GROUP IN A FORMER SOVIET REPUBLIC, I THINK.
OF COURSE. OKAY...YOU'RE THE ONE WITH THE PHYSICS DEGREE. IF I WANTED TO TEST SOMEONE'S ABILITY TO SEE THE FUTURE...
COMMANDER DANVERS.
A MOMENT OF YOUR TIME?
CAPTAIN BAR-KONN. The Kree Empire.
WE'LL PICK THIS UP LATER.
WHAT CAN I DO FOR YOU, CAPTAIN?
YOU'RE AWARE THE KREE EMPIRE IS...NOT WHAT IT WAS. THERE ARE MULTIPLE FACTIONS. I REPRESENT JUST ONE.
I WANT TO ASSURE YOU WE NEITHER KNEW OF NOR CONDONE WHAT I AM ABOUT TO TELL YOU.
IT CONCERNS DR. MINERVA, LATE OF THE KREE SCIENCE ACADEMY.

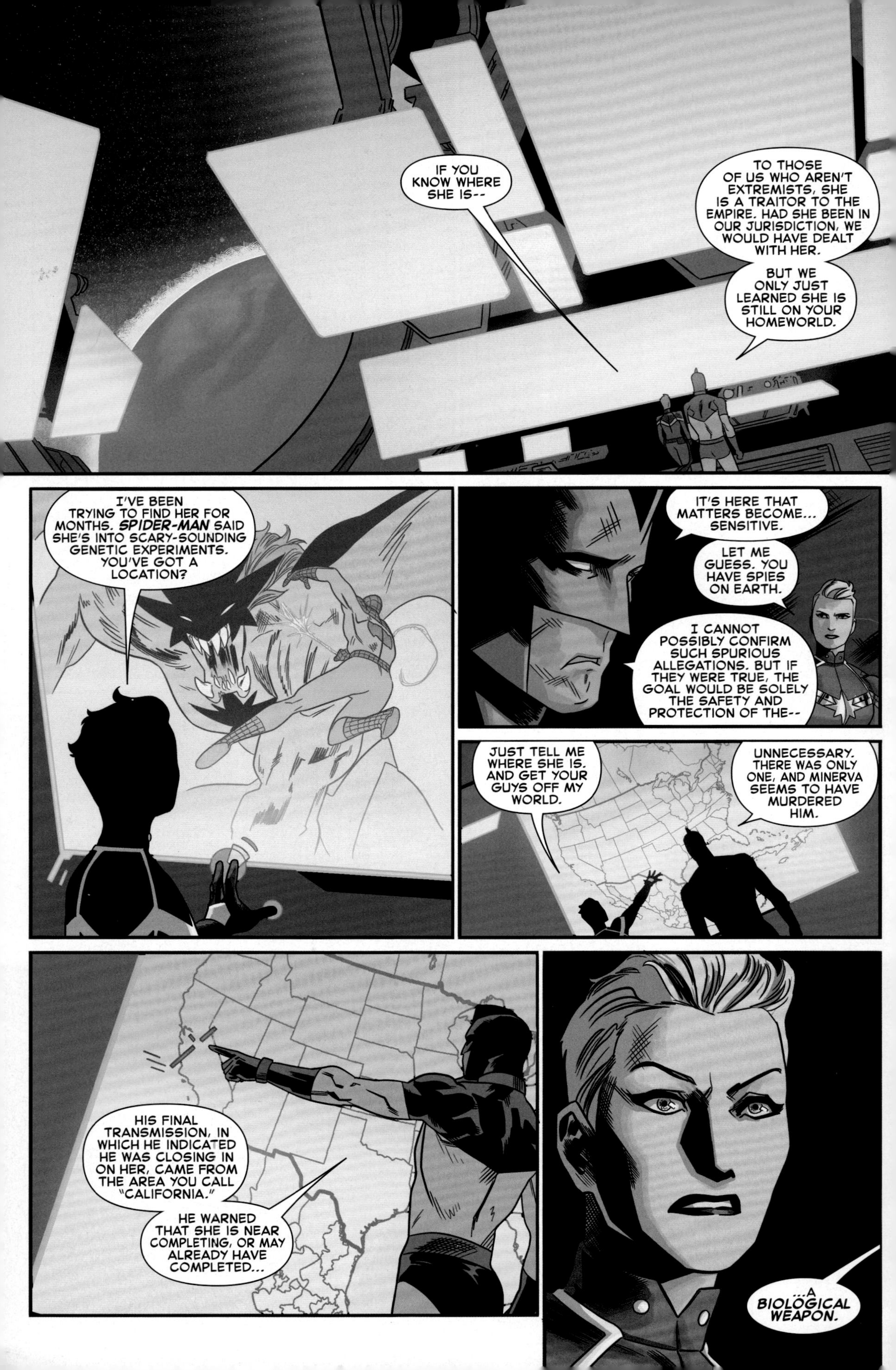
IF YOU KNOW WHERE SHE IS--
TO THOSE OF US WHO AREN'T EXTREMISTS, SHE IS A TRAITOR TO THE EMPIRE. HAD SHE BEEN IN OUR JURISDICTION, WE WOULD HAVE DEALT WITH HER.
BUT WE ONLY JUST LEARNED SHE IS STILL ON YOUR HOMEWORLD.
I'VE BEEN TRYING TO FIND HER FOR MONTHS. SPIDER-MAN SAID SHE'S INTO SCARY-SOUNDING GENETIC EXPERIMENTS. YOU'VE GOT A LOCATION?
IT'S HERE THAT MATTERS BECOME... SENSITIVE.
LET ME GUESS. YOU HAVE SPIES ON EARTH.
I CANNOT POSSIBLY CONFIRM SUCH SPURIOUS ALLEGATIONS. BUT IF THEY WERE TRUE, THE GOAL WOULD BE SOLELY THE SAFETY AND PROTECTION OF THE--
JUST TELL ME WHERE SHE IS. AND GET YOUR GUYS OFF MY WORLD.
UNNECESSARY. THERE WAS ONLY ONE, AND MINERVA SEEMS TO HAVE MURDERED HIM.
HIS FINAL TRANSMISSION, IN WHICH HE INDICATED HE WAS CLOSING IN ON HER, CAME FROM THE AREA YOU CALL "CALIFORNIA."
HE WARNED THAT SHE IS NEAR COMPLETING, OR MAY ALREADY HAVE COMPLETED...
...A BIOLOGICAL WEAPON.

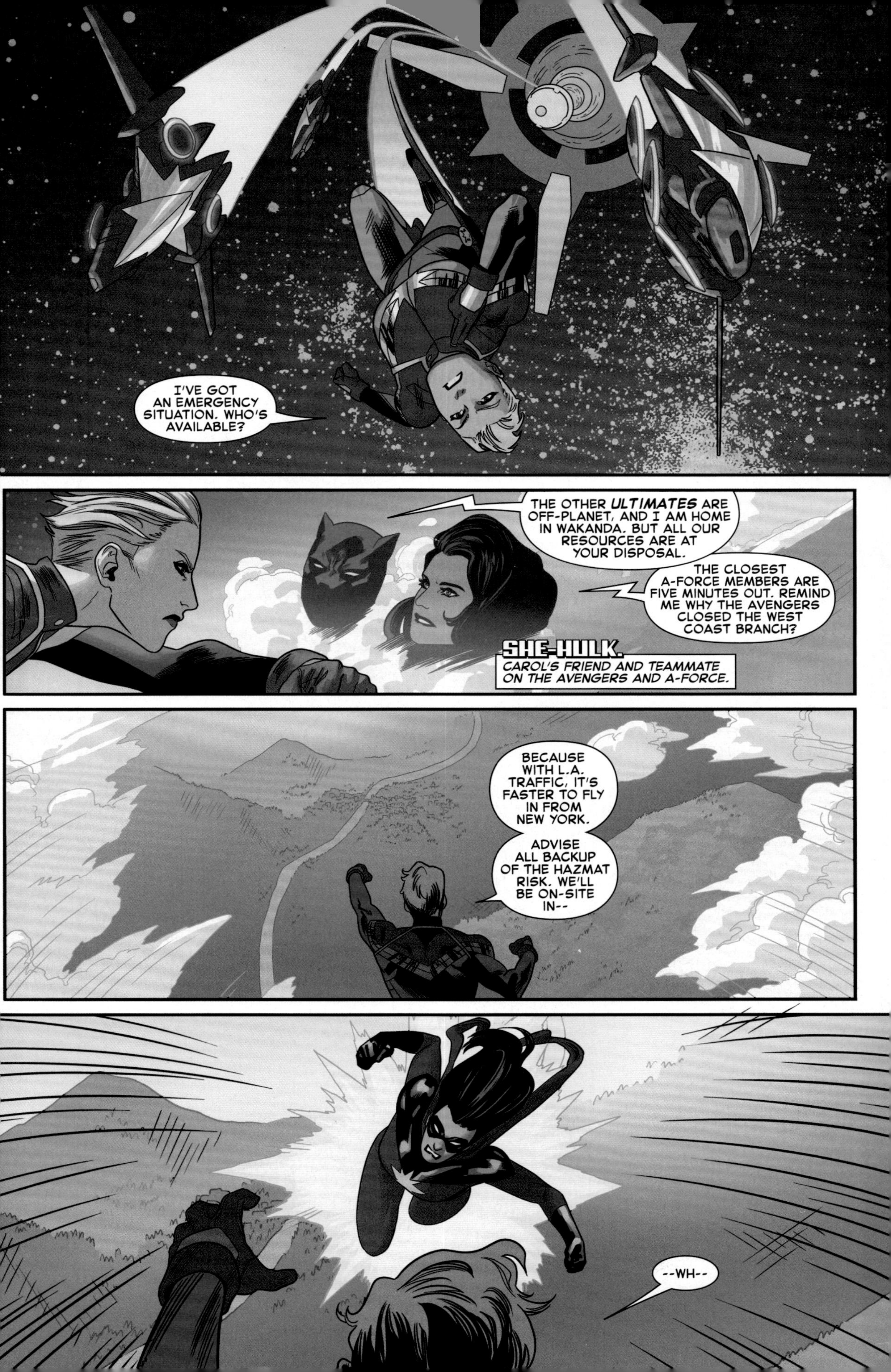

I'VE GOT AN EMERGENCY SITUATION. WHO'S AVAILABLE?
THE OTHER *ULTIMATES* ARE OFF-PLANET, AND I AM HOME IN WAKANDA. BUT ALL OUR RESOURCES ARE AT YOUR DISPOSAL.
THE CLOSEST A-FORCE MEMBERS ARE FIVE MINUTES OUT. REMIND ME WHY THE AVENGERS CLOSED THE WEST COAST BRANCH?
SHE-HULK.
CAROL'S FRIEND AND TEAMMATE ON THE AVENGERS AND A-FORCE.
BECAUSE WITH L.A. TRAFFIC, IT'S FASTER TO FLY IN FROM NEW YORK.
ADVISE ALL BACKUP OF THE HAZMAT RISK. WE'LL BE ON-SITE IN--
--WH--

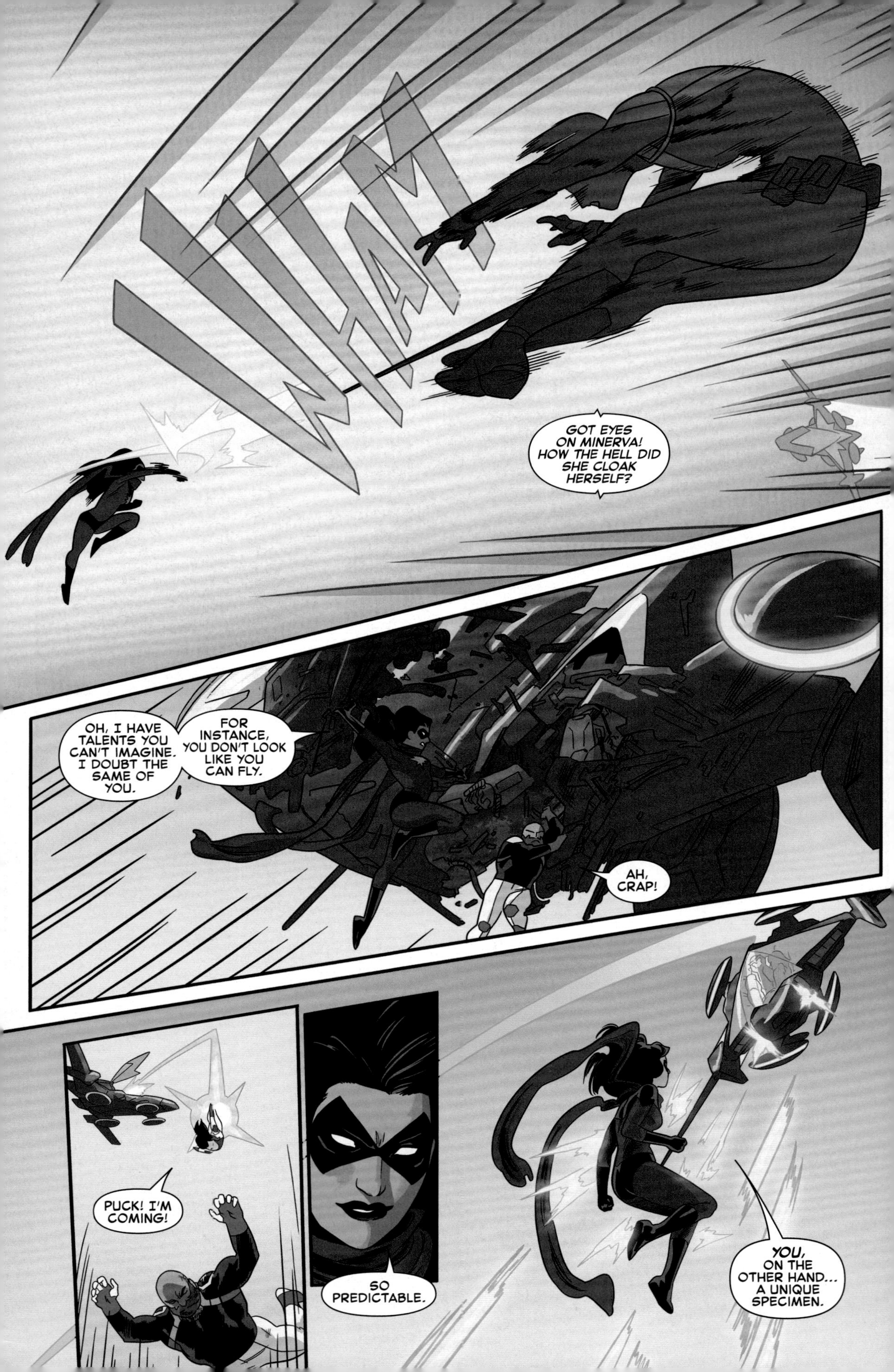
WHAM
GOT EYES ON MINERVA! HOW THE HELL DID SHE CLOAK HERSELF?
OH, I HAVE TALENTS YOU CAN'T IMAGINE. I DOUBT THE SAME OF YOU.
FOR INSTANCE, YOU DON'T LOOK LIKE YOU CAN FLY.
AH, CRAP!
PUCK! I'M COMING!
SO PREDICTABLE.
YOU, ON THE OTHER HAND... A UNIQUE SPECIMEN.

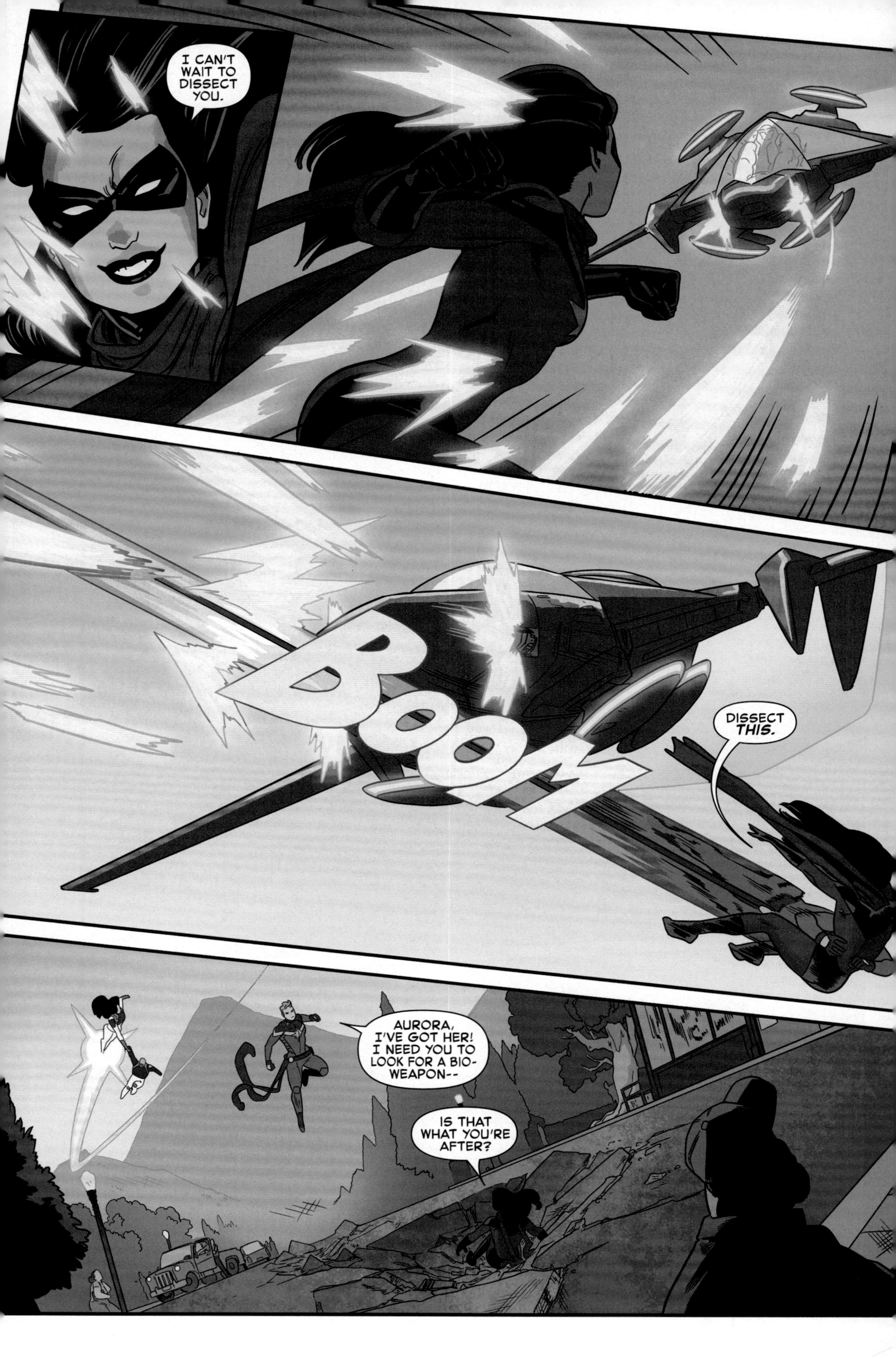
I CAN'T WAIT TO DISSECT YOU.
BOOM
DISSECT THIS.
AURORA, I'VE GOT HER! I NEED YOU TO LOOK FOR A BIO-WEAPON--
IS THAT WHAT YOU'RE AFTER?

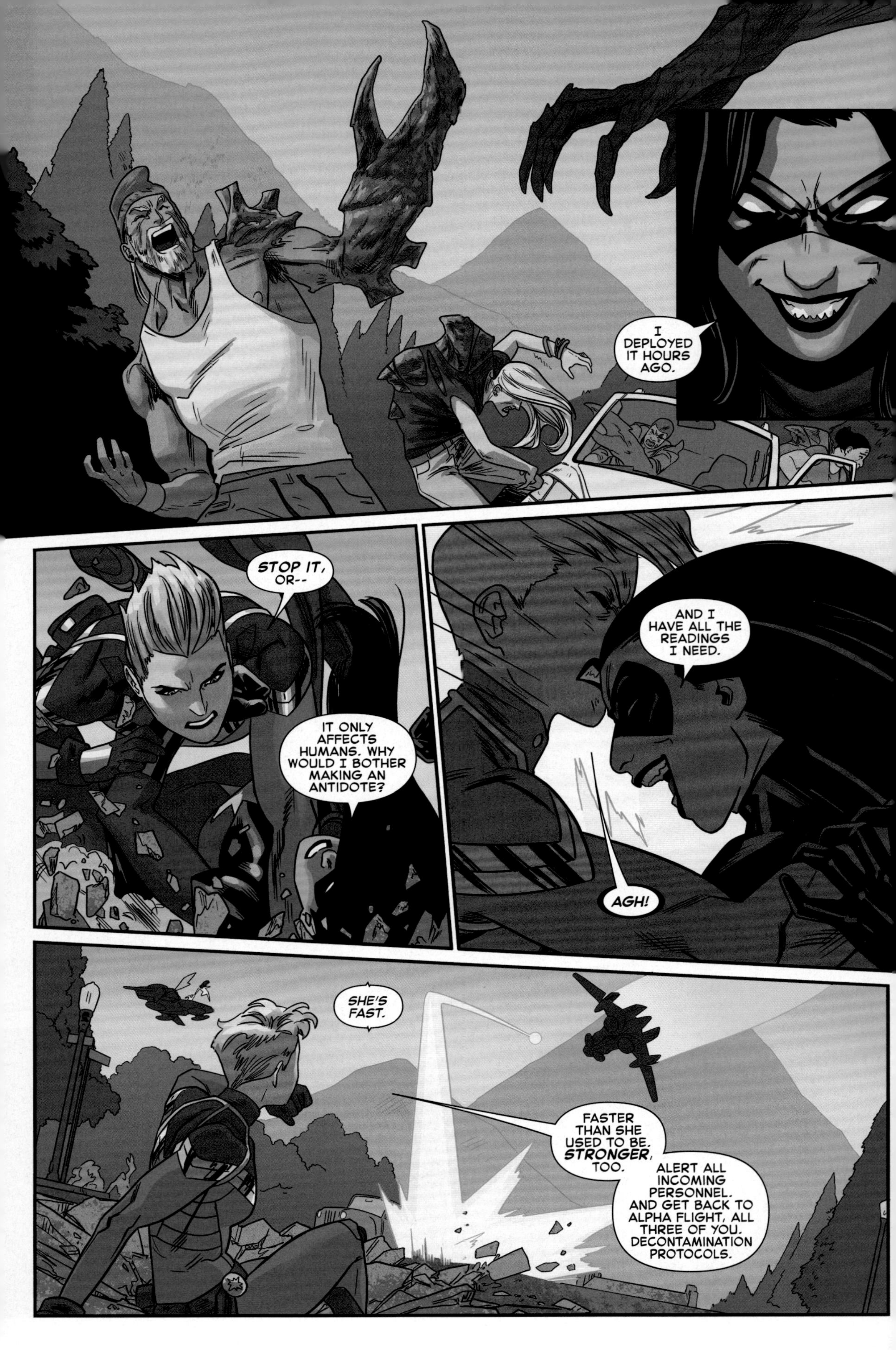
I DEPLOYED IT HOURS AGO.
STOP IT, OR--
IT ONLY AFFECTS HUMANS. WHY WOULD I BOTHER MAKING AN ANTIDOTE?
AND I HAVE ALL THE READINGS I NEED.
AGH!
SHE'S FAST.
FASTER THAN SHE USED TO BE. STRONGER, TOO.
ALERT ALL INCOMING PERSONNEL. AND GET BACK TO ALPHA FLIGHT, ALL THREE OF YOU. DECONTAMINATION PROTOCOLS.

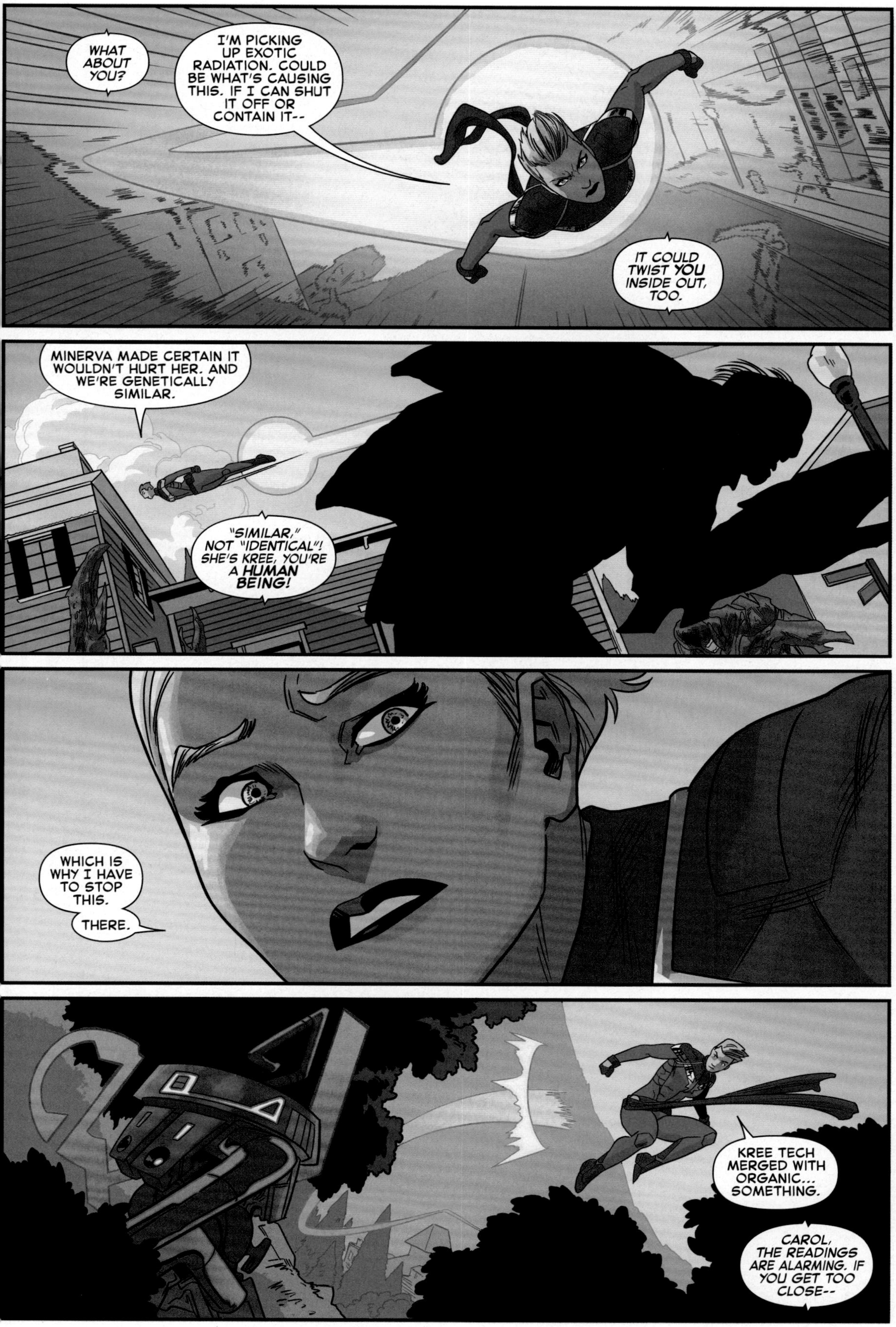

WHAT ABOUT YOU?
I'M PICKING UP EXOTIC RADIATION. COULD BE WHAT'S CAUSING THIS. IF I CAN SHUT IT OFF OR CONTAIN IT--
IT COULD TWIST YOU INSIDE OUT, TOO.
MINERVA MADE CERTAIN IT WOULDN'T HURT HER. AND WE'RE GENETICALLY SIMILAR.
"SIMILAR," NOT "IDENTICAL"! SHE'S KREE, YOU'RE A HUMAN BEING!
WHICH IS WHY I HAVE TO STOP THIS.
THERE.
KREE TECH MERGED WITH ORGANIC... SOMETHING.
CAROL, THE READINGS ARE ALARMING. IF YOU GET TOO CLOSE--

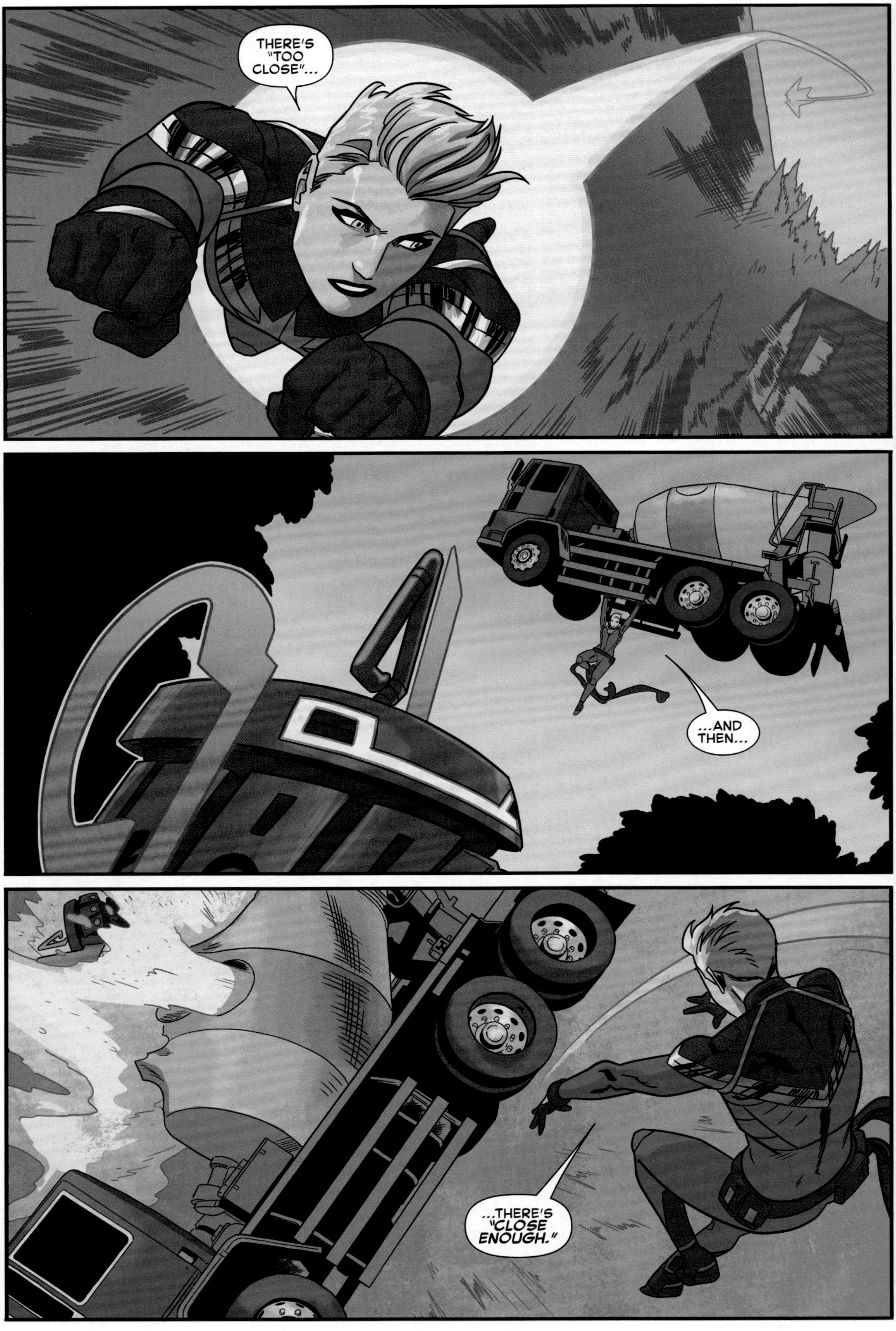
THERE'S "TOO CLOSE"...
...AND THEN...
...THERE'S "CLOSE ENOUGH."

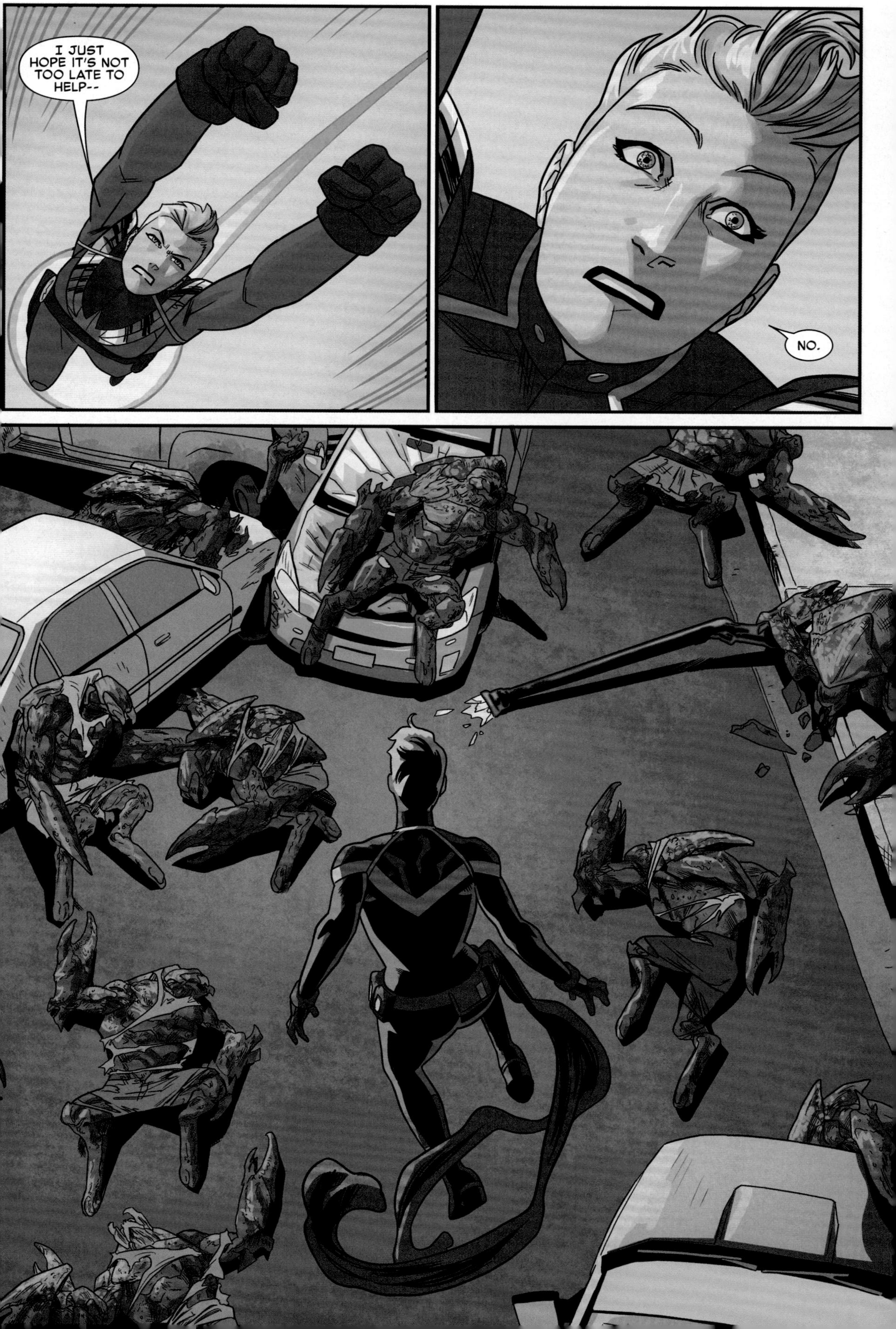
I JUST HOPE IT'S NOT TOO LATE TO HELP--
NO.

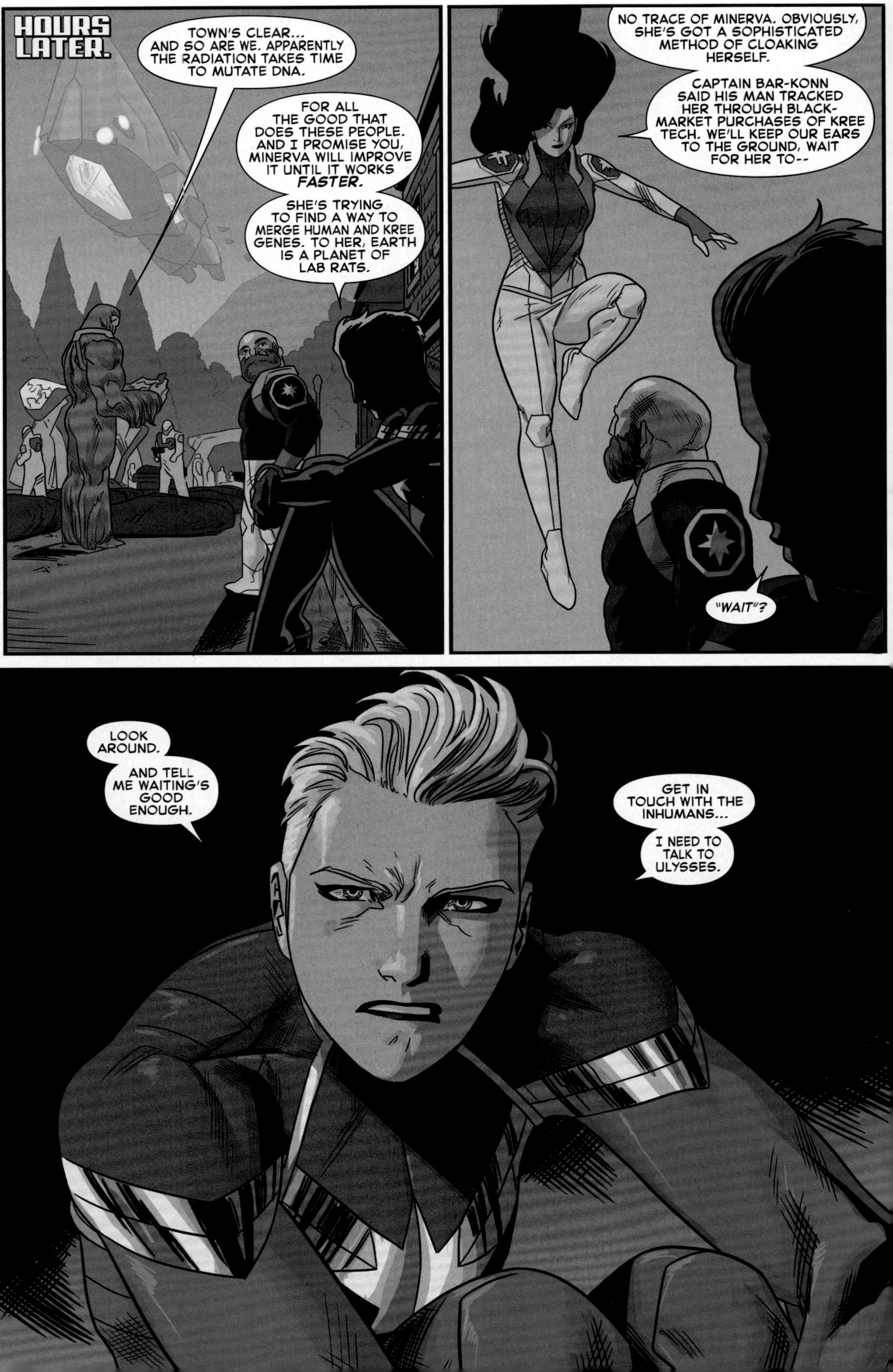
HOURS LATER.
TOWN'S CLEAR... AND SO ARE WE. APPARENTLY THE RADIATION TAKES TIME TO MUTATE DNA.
FOR ALL THE GOOD THAT DOES THESE PEOPLE. AND I PROMISE YOU, MINERVA WILL IMPROVE IT UNTIL IT WORKS FASTER.
SHE'S TRYING TO FIND A WAY TO MERGE HUMAN AND KREE GENES. TO HER, EARTH IS A PLANET OF LAB RATS.
NO TRACE OF MINERVA. OBVIOUSLY, SHE'S GOT A SOPHISTICATED METHOD OF CLOAKING HERSELF.
CAPTAIN BAR-KONN SAID HIS MAN TRACKED HER THROUGH BLACK-MARKET PURCHASES OF KREE TECH. WE'LL KEEP OUR EARS TO THE GROUND, WAIT FOR HER TO--
"WAIT"?
LOOK AROUND.
AND TELL ME WAITING'S GOOD ENOUGH.
GET IN TOUCH WITH THE INHUMANS...
I NEED TO TALK TO ULYSSES.

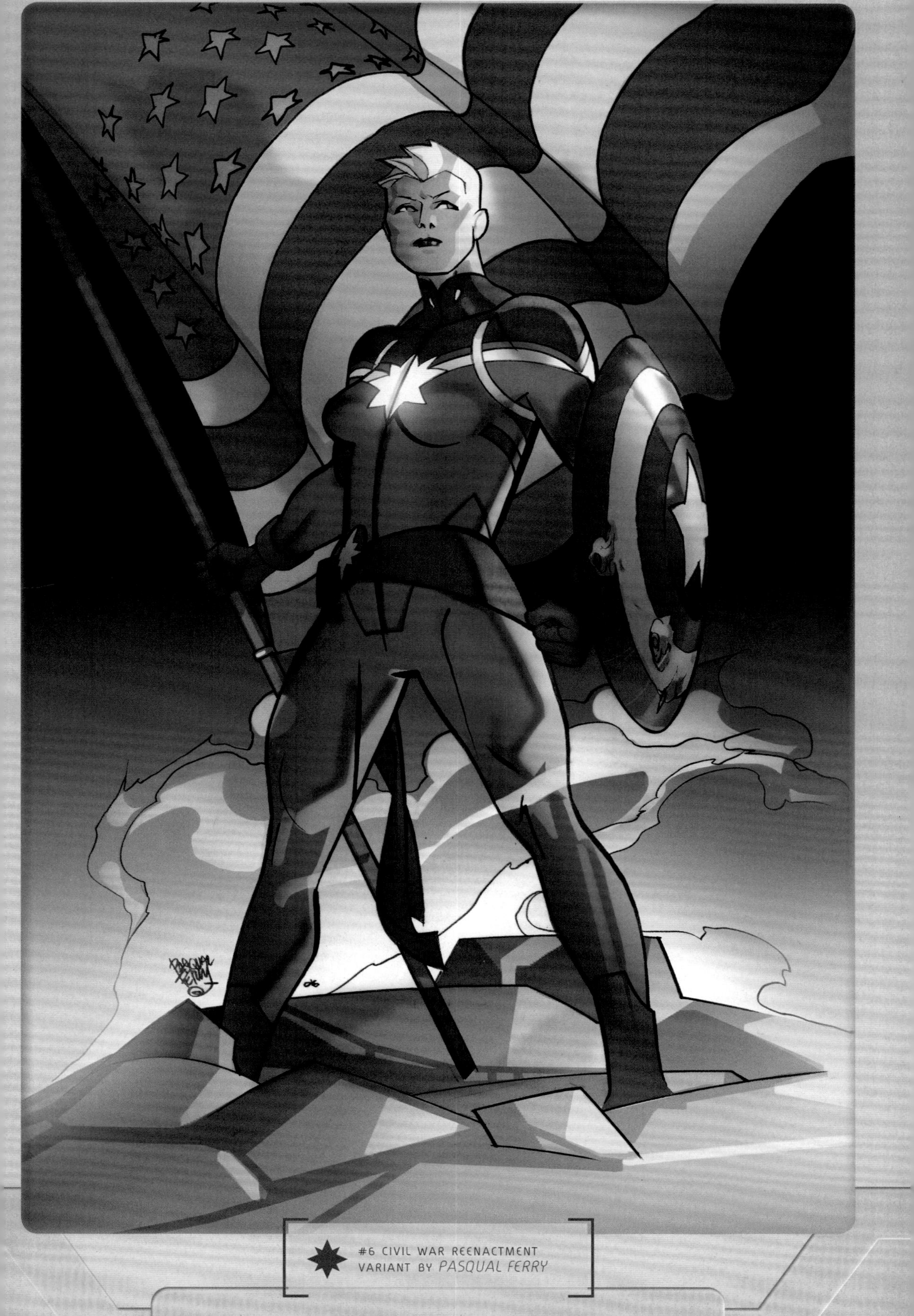

#6 CIVIL WAR REENACTMENT
VARIANT BY *PASQUAL FERRY*

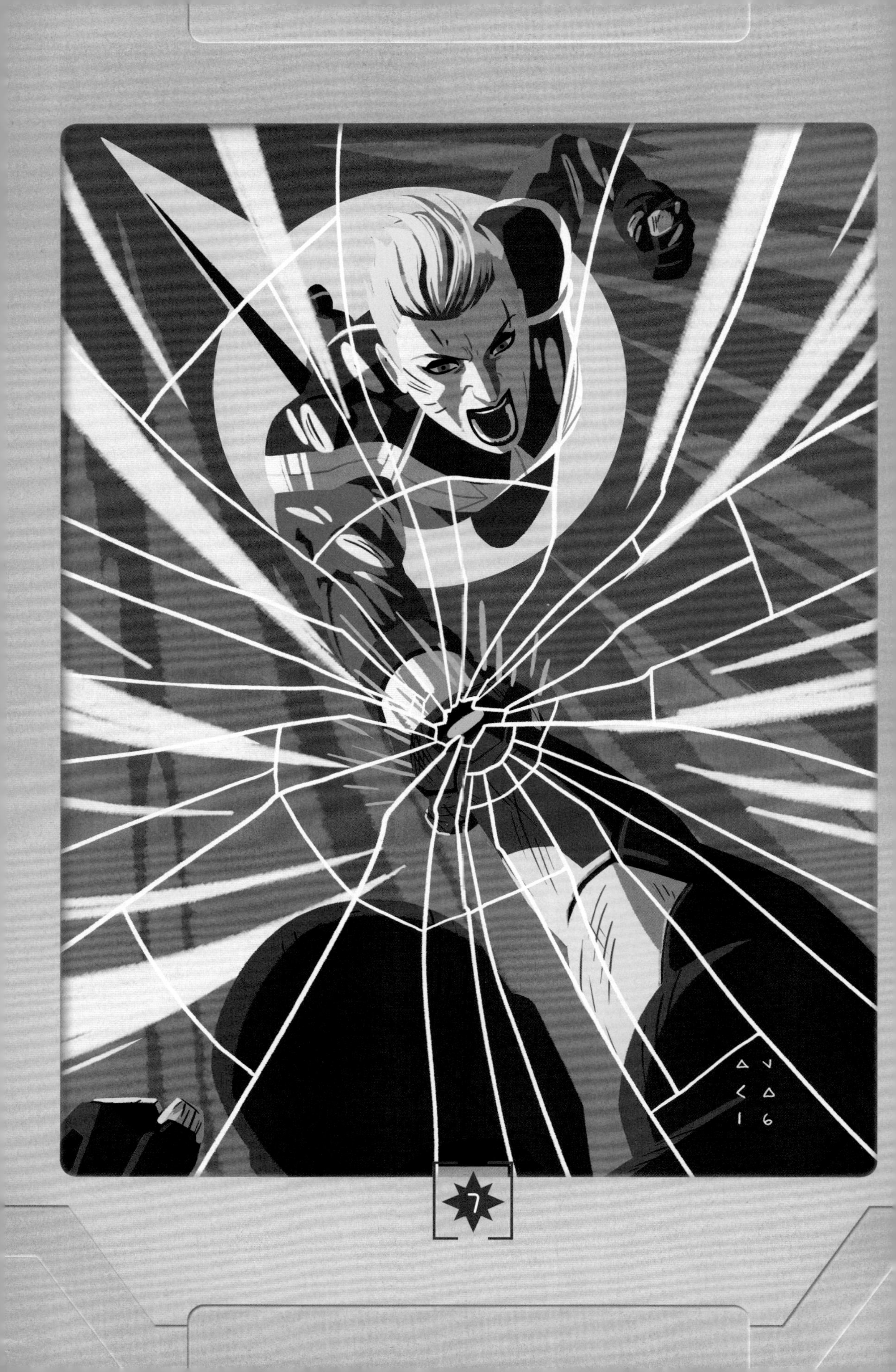

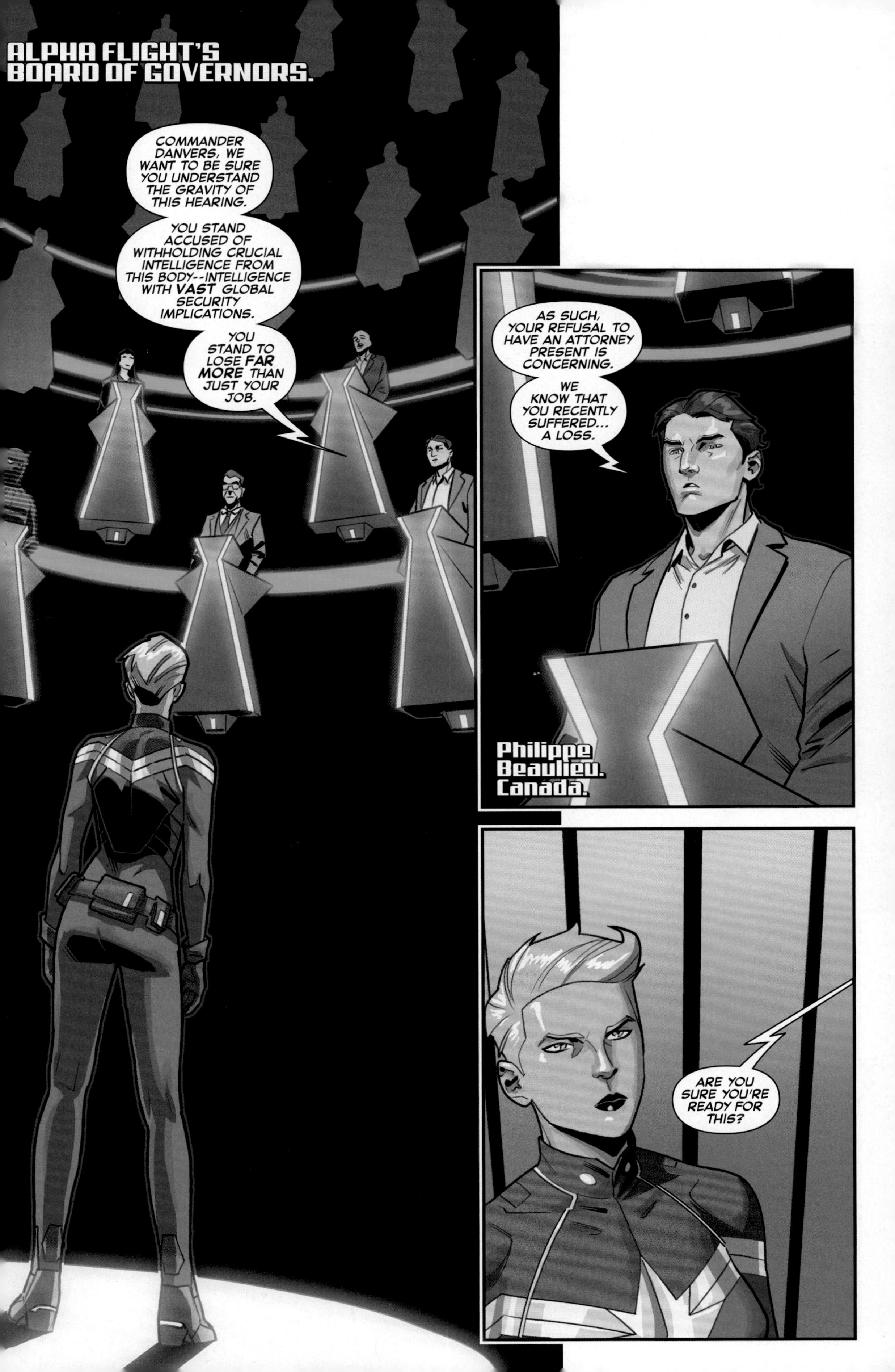
ALPHA FLIGHT'S BOARD OF GOVERNORS.
COMMANDER DANVERS, WE WANT TO BE SURE YOU UNDERSTAND THE GRAVITY OF THIS HEARING.
YOU STAND ACCUSED OF WITHHOLDING CRUCIAL INTELLIGENCE FROM THIS BODY--INTELLIGENCE WITH VAST GLOBAL SECURITY IMPLICATIONS.
YOU STAND TO LOSE FAR MORE THAN JUST YOUR JOB.
AS SUCH, YOUR REFUSAL TO HAVE AN ATTORNEY PRESENT IS CONCERNING.
WE KNOW THAT YOU RECENTLY SUFFERED... A LOSS.
Philippe Beaulieu. Canada.
ARE YOU SURE YOU'RE READY FOR THIS?

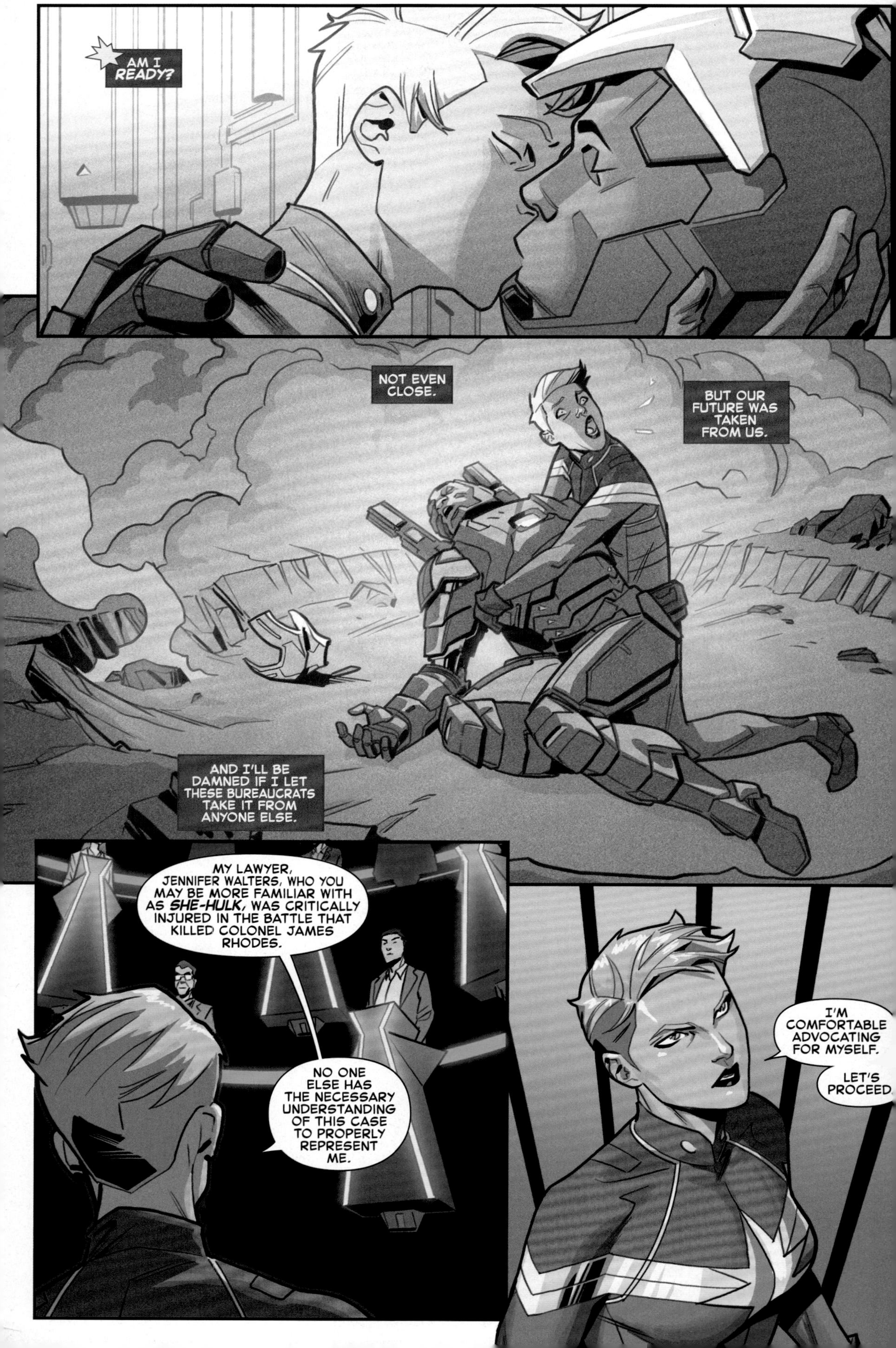

AM I READY?
NOT EVEN CLOSE.
BUT OUR FUTURE WAS TAKEN FROM US.
AND I'LL BE DAMNED IF I LET THESE BUREAUCRATS TAKE IT FROM ANYONE ELSE.
MY LAWYER, JENNIFER WALTERS, WHO YOU MAY BE MORE FAMILIAR WITH AS SHE-HULK, WAS CRITICALLY INJURED IN THE BATTLE THAT KILLED COLONEL JAMES RHODES.
NO ONE ELSE HAS THE NECESSARY UNDERSTANDING OF THIS CASE TO PROPERLY REPRESENT ME.
I'M COMFORTABLE ADVOCATING FOR MYSELF.
LET'S PROCEED.

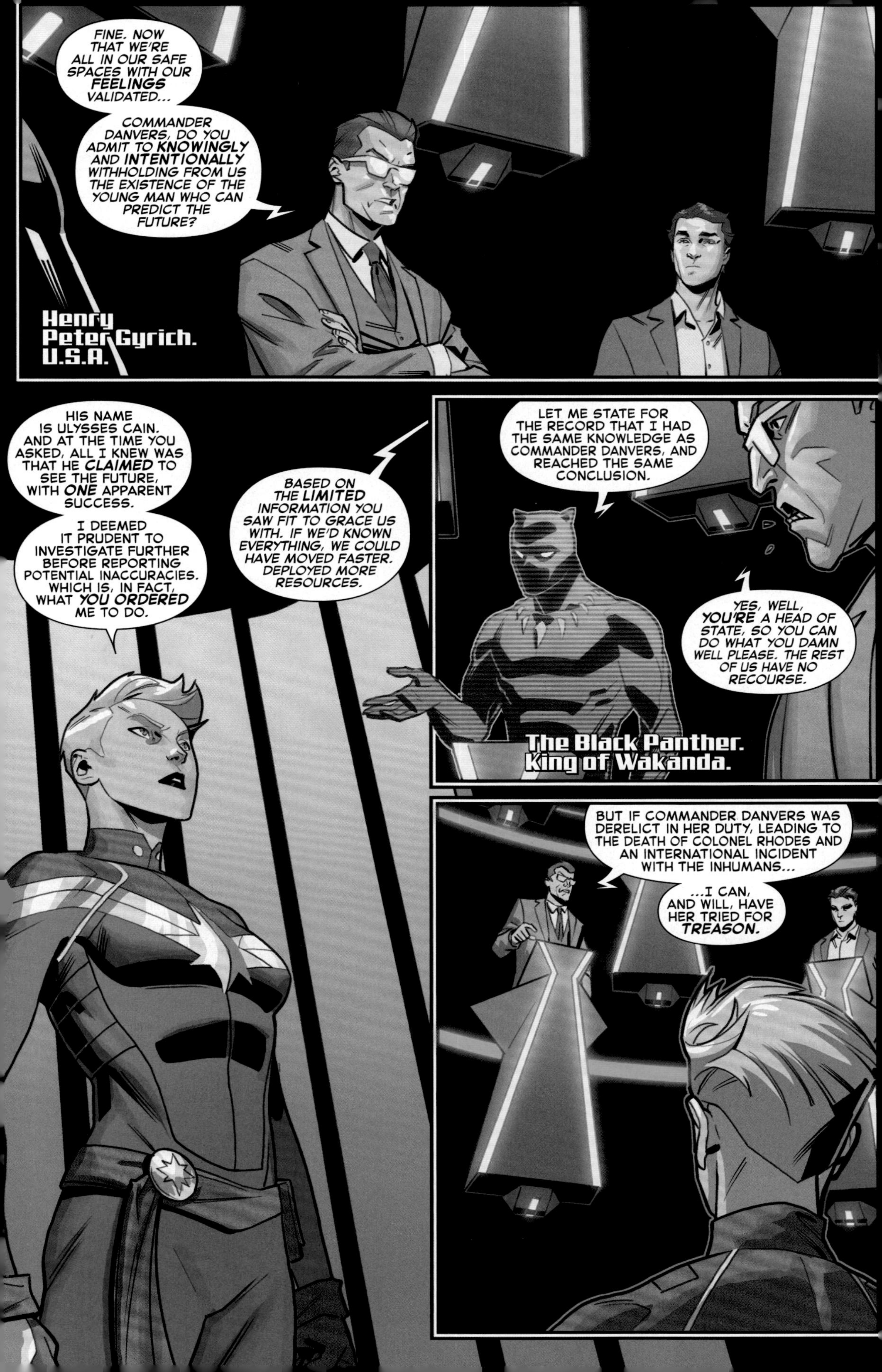

FINE. NOW THAT WE'RE ALL IN OUR SAFE SPACES WITH OUR FEELINGS VALIDATED...
COMMANDER DANVERS, DO YOU ADMIT TO KNOWINGLY AND INTENTIONALLY WITHHOLDING FROM US THE EXISTENCE OF THE YOUNG MAN WHO CAN PREDICT THE FUTURE?
Henry Peter Gyrich. U.S.A.
HIS NAME IS ULYSSES CAIN. AND AT THE TIME YOU ASKED, ALL I KNEW WAS THAT HE CLAIMED TO SEE THE FUTURE, WITH ONE APPARENT SUCCESS.
I DEEMED IT PRUDENT TO INVESTIGATE FURTHER BEFORE REPORTING POTENTIAL INACCURACIES. WHICH IS, IN FACT, WHAT YOU ORDERED ME TO DO.
BASED ON THE LIMITED INFORMATION YOU SAW FIT TO GRACE US WITH. IF WE'D KNOWN EVERYTHING, WE COULD HAVE MOVED FASTER. DEPLOYED MORE RESOURCES.
LET ME STATE FOR THE RECORD THAT I HAD THE SAME KNOWLEDGE AS COMMANDER DANVERS, AND REACHED THE SAME CONCLUSION.
YES, WELL, YOU'RE A HEAD OF STATE, SO YOU CAN DO WHAT YOU DAMN WELL PLEASE. THE REST OF US HAVE NO RECOURSE.
The Black Panther. King of Wakanda.
BUT IF COMMANDER DANVERS WAS DERELICT IN HER DUTY, LEADING TO THE DEATH OF COLONEL RHODES AND AN INTERNATIONAL INCIDENT WITH THE INHUMANS...
...I CAN, AND WILL, HAVE HER TRIED FOR TREASON.

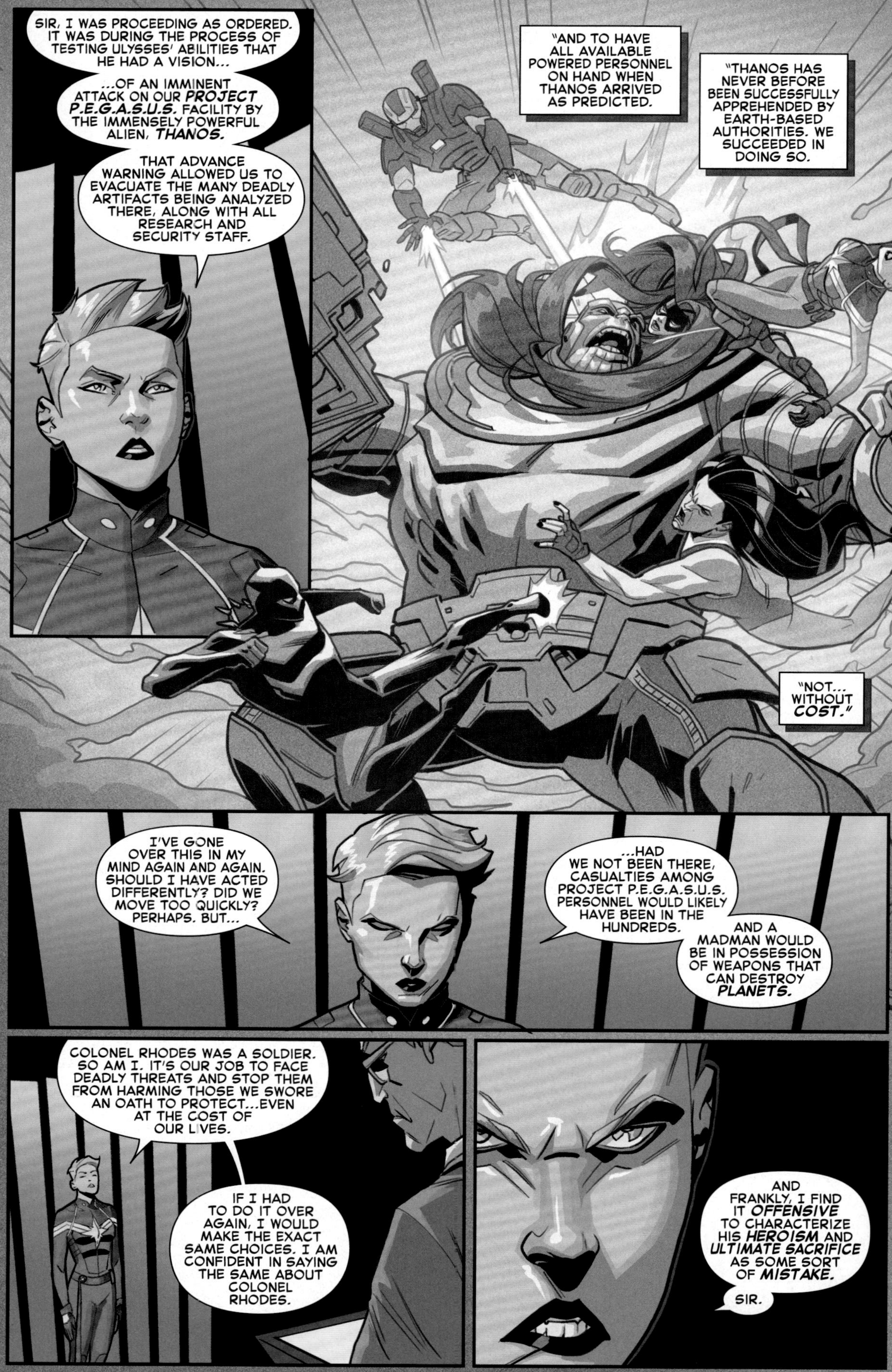
SIR, I WAS PROCEEDING AS ORDERED. IT WAS DURING THE PROCESS OF TESTING ULYSSES' ABILITIES THAT HE HAD A VISION...
...OF AN IMMINENT ATTACK ON OUR PROJECT P.E.G.A.S.U.S. FACILITY BY THE IMMENSELY POWERFUL ALIEN, THANOS.
THAT ADVANCE WARNING ALLOWED US TO EVACUATE THE MANY DEADLY ARTIFACTS BEING ANALYZED THERE, ALONG WITH ALL RESEARCH AND SECURITY STAFF.
"AND TO HAVE ALL AVAILABLE POWERED PERSONNEL ON HAND WHEN THANOS ARRIVED AS PREDICTED.
"THANOS HAS NEVER BEFORE BEEN SUCCESSFULLY APPREHENDED BY EARTH-BASED AUTHORITIES. WE SUCCEEDED IN DOING SO.
"NOT... WITHOUT COST."
I'VE GONE OVER THIS IN MY MIND AGAIN AND AGAIN. SHOULD I HAVE ACTED DIFFERENTLY? DID WE MOVE TOO QUICKLY? PERHAPS. BUT...
...HAD WE NOT BEEN THERE, CASUALTIES AMONG PROJECT P.E.G.A.S.U.S. PERSONNEL WOULD LIKELY HAVE BEEN IN THE HUNDREDS.
AND A MADMAN WOULD BE IN POSSESSION OF WEAPONS THAT CAN DESTROY PLANETS.
COLONEL RHODES WAS A SOLDIER. SO AM I. IT'S OUR JOB TO FACE DEADLY THREATS AND STOP THEM FROM HARMING THOSE WE SWORE AN OATH TO PROTECT...EVEN AT THE COST OF OUR LIVES.
IF I HAD TO DO IT OVER AGAIN, I WOULD MAKE THE EXACT SAME CHOICES. I AM CONFIDENT IN SAYING THE SAME ABOUT COLONEL RHODES.
AND FRANKLY, I FIND IT OFFENSIVE TO CHARACTERIZE HIS HEROISM AND ULTIMATE SACRIFICE AS SOME SORT OF MISTAKE.
SIR.

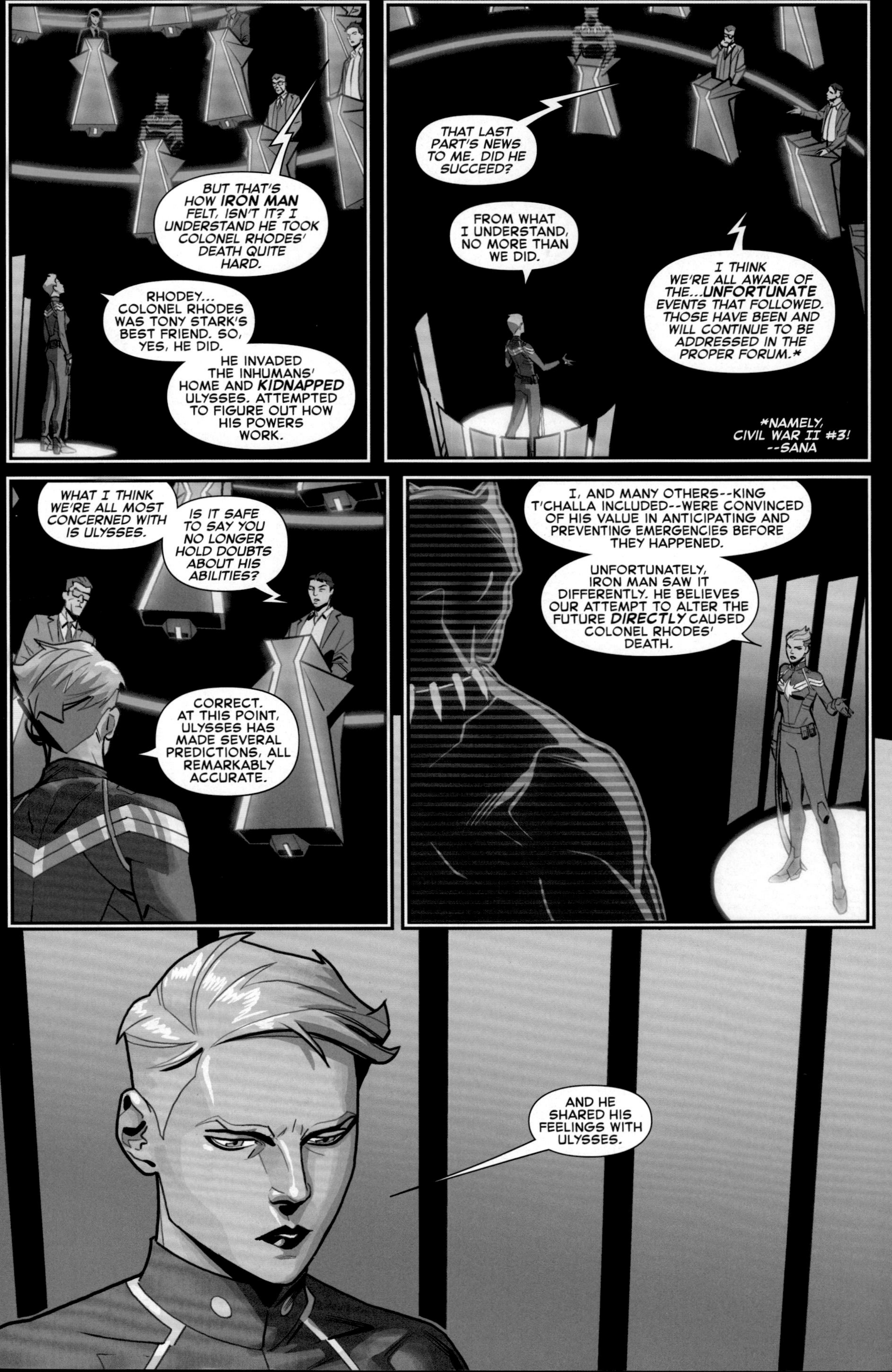
BUT THAT'S HOW IRON MAN FELT, ISN'T IT? I UNDERSTAND HE TOOK COLONEL RHODES' DEATH QUITE HARD.
RHODEY... COLONEL RHODES WAS TONY STARK'S BEST FRIEND. SO, YES, HE DID.
HE INVADED THE INHUMANS' HOME AND KIDNAPPED ULYSSES. ATTEMPTED TO FIGURE OUT HOW HIS POWERS WORK.
THAT LAST PART'S NEWS TO ME. DID HE SUCCEED?
FROM WHAT I UNDERSTAND, NO MORE THAN WE DID.
I THINK WE'RE ALL AWARE OF THE...UNFORTUNATE EVENTS THAT FOLLOWED. THOSE HAVE BEEN AND WILL CONTINUE TO BE ADDRESSED IN THE PROPER FORUM.*
*NAMELY, CIVIL WAR II #3! --SANA
WHAT I THINK WE'RE ALL MOST CONCERNED WITH IS ULYSSES.
IS IT SAFE TO SAY YOU NO LONGER HOLD DOUBTS ABOUT HIS ABILITIES?
CORRECT. AT THIS POINT, ULYSSES HAS MADE SEVERAL PREDICTIONS, ALL REMARKABLY ACCURATE.
I, AND MANY OTHERS--KING T'CHALLA INCLUDED--WERE CONVINCED OF HIS VALUE IN ANTICIPATING AND PREVENTING EMERGENCIES BEFORE THEY HAPPENED.
UNFORTUNATELY, IRON MAN SAW IT DIFFERENTLY. HE BELIEVES OUR ATTEMPT TO ALTER THE FUTURE DIRECTLY CAUSED COLONEL RHODES' DEATH.
AND HE SHARED HIS FEELINGS WITH ULYSSES.

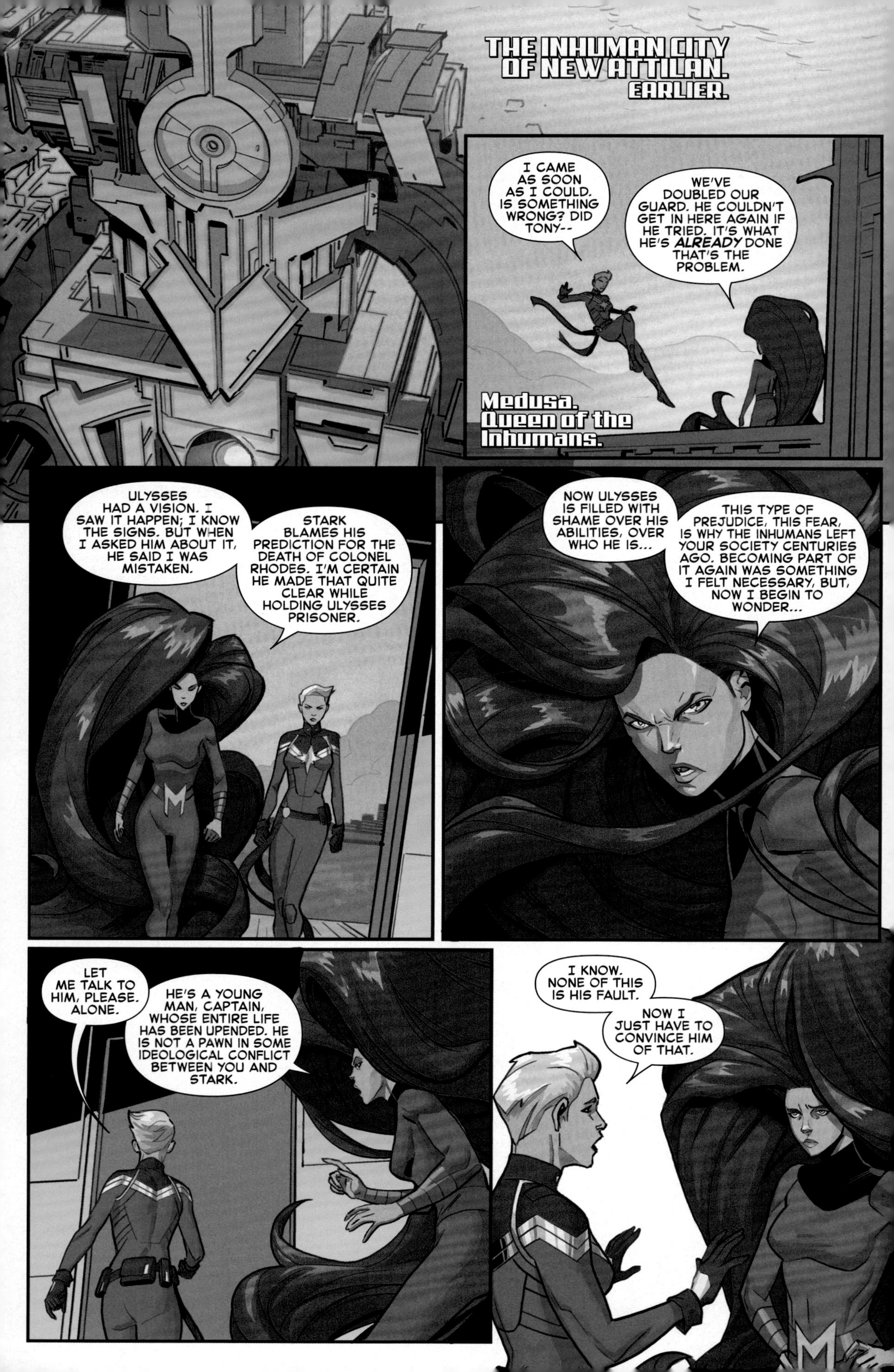
THE INHUMAN CITY OF NEW ATTILAN. EARLIER.
I CAME AS SOON AS I COULD. IS SOMETHING WRONG? DID TONY--
WE'VE DOUBLED OUR GUARD. HE COULDN'T GET IN HERE AGAIN IF HE TRIED. IT'S WHAT HE'S *ALREADY* DONE THAT'S THE PROBLEM.
Medusa. Queen of the Inhumans.
ULYSSES HAD A VISION. I SAW IT HAPPEN; I KNOW THE SIGNS. BUT WHEN I ASKED HIM ABOUT IT, HE SAID I WAS MISTAKEN.
STARK BLAMES HIS PREDICTION FOR THE DEATH OF COLONEL RHODES. I'M CERTAIN HE MADE THAT QUITE CLEAR WHILE HOLDING ULYSSES PRISONER.
NOW ULYSSES IS FILLED WITH SHAME OVER HIS ABILITIES, OVER WHO HE IS...
THIS TYPE OF PREJUDICE, THIS FEAR, IS WHY THE INHUMANS LEFT YOUR SOCIETY CENTURIES AGO. BECOMING PART OF IT AGAIN WAS SOMETHING I FELT NECESSARY, BUT, NOW I BEGIN TO WONDER...
LET ME TALK TO HIM, PLEASE. ALONE.
HE'S A YOUNG MAN, CAPTAIN, WHOSE ENTIRE LIFE HAS BEEN UPENDED. HE IS NOT A PAWN IN SOME IDEOLOGICAL CONFLICT BETWEEN YOU AND STARK.
I KNOW. NONE OF THIS IS HIS FAULT.
NOW I JUST HAVE TO CONVINCE HIM OF THAT.

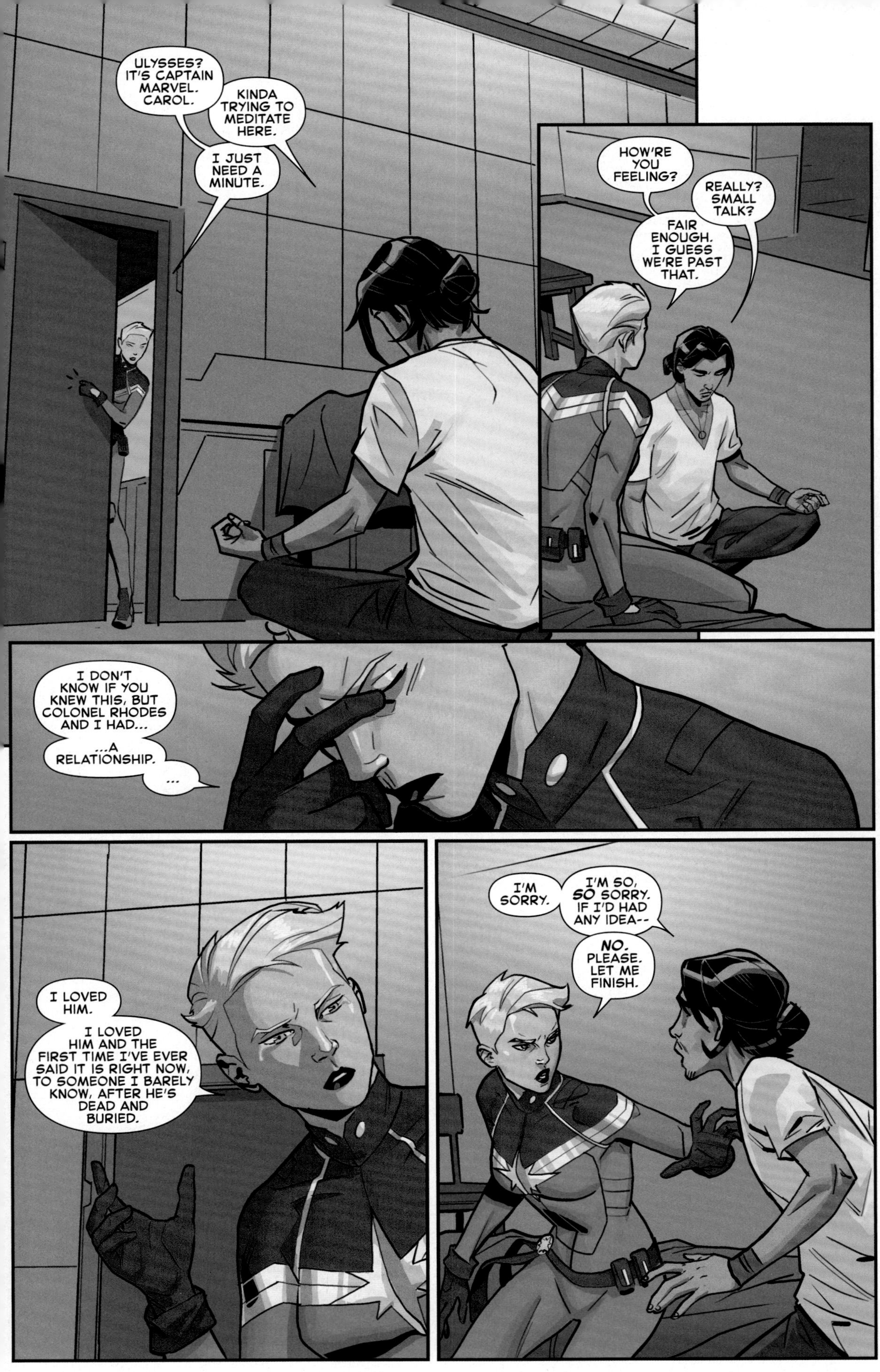
ULYSSES? IT'S CAPTAIN MARVEL. CAROL.
KINDA TRYING TO MEDITATE HERE.
I JUST NEED A MINUTE.
HOW'RE YOU FEELING?
REALLY? SMALL TALK?
FAIR ENOUGH. I GUESS WE'RE PAST THAT.
I DON'T KNOW IF YOU KNEW THIS, BUT COLONEL RHODES AND I HAD...
...A RELATIONSHIP.
...
I LOVED HIM.
I LOVED HIM AND THE FIRST TIME I'VE EVER SAID IT IS RIGHT NOW, TO SOMEONE I BARELY KNOW, AFTER HE'S DEAD AND BURIED.
I'M SORRY.
I'M SO, SO SORRY. IF I'D HAD ANY IDEA--
NO. PLEASE. LET ME FINISH.

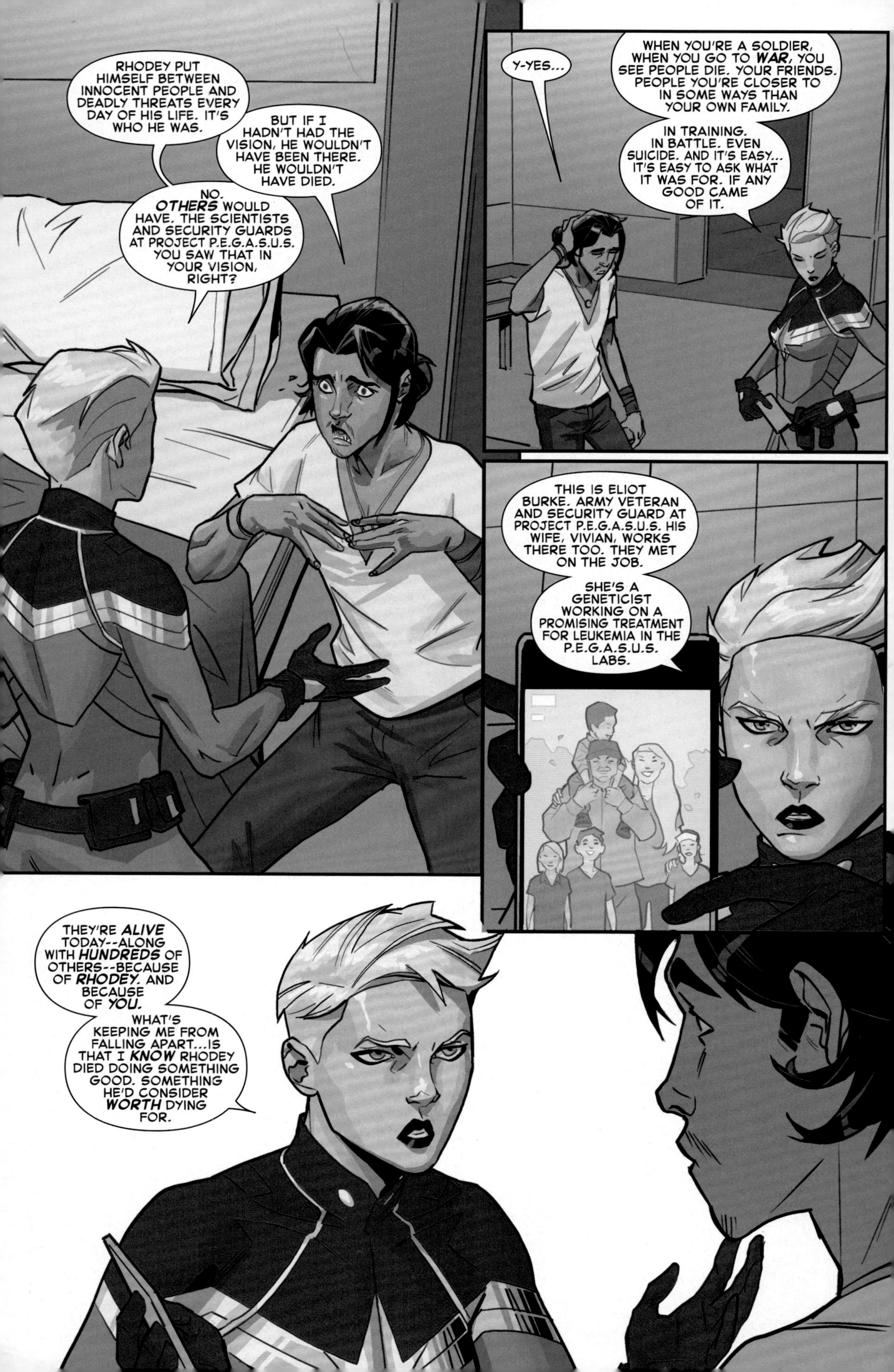
RHODEY PUT HIMSELF BETWEEN INNOCENT PEOPLE AND DEADLY THREATS EVERY DAY OF HIS LIFE. IT'S WHO HE WAS.
BUT IF I HADN'T HAD THE VISION, HE WOULDN'T HAVE BEEN THERE. HE WOULDN'T HAVE DIED.
NO. OTHERS WOULD HAVE. THE SCIENTISTS AND SECURITY GUARDS AT PROJECT P.E.G.A.S.U.S. YOU SAW THAT IN YOUR VISION, RIGHT?
Y-YES...
WHEN YOU'RE A SOLDIER, WHEN YOU GO TO WAR, YOU SEE PEOPLE DIE. YOUR FRIENDS. PEOPLE YOU'RE CLOSER TO IN SOME WAYS THAN YOUR OWN FAMILY.
IN TRAINING. IN BATTLE. EVEN SUICIDE. AND IT'S EASY... IT'S EASY TO ASK WHAT IT WAS FOR. IF ANY GOOD CAME OF IT.
THIS IS ELIOT BURKE. ARMY VETERAN AND SECURITY GUARD AT PROJECT P.E.G.A.S.U.S. HIS WIFE, VIVIAN, WORKS THERE TOO. THEY MET ON THE JOB.
SHE'S A GENETICIST WORKING ON A PROMISING TREATMENT FOR LEUKEMIA IN THE P.E.G.A.S.U.S. LABS.
THEY'RE ALIVE TODAY--ALONG WITH HUNDREDS OF OTHERS--BECAUSE OF RHODEY. AND BECAUSE OF YOU.
WHAT'S KEEPING ME FROM FALLING APART...IS THAT I KNOW RHODEY DIED DOING SOMETHING GOOD. SOMETHING HE'D CONSIDER WORTH DYING FOR.

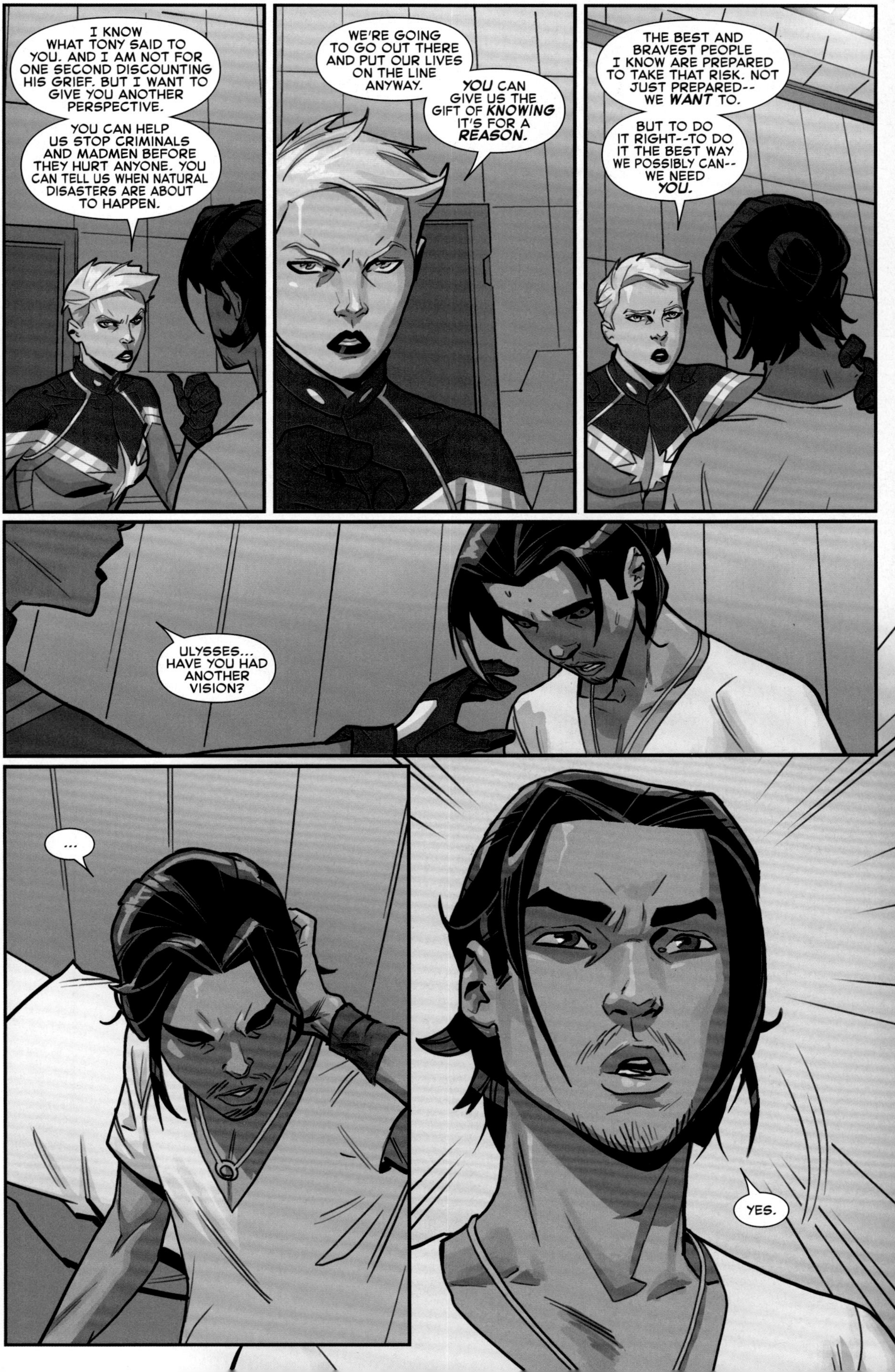

I KNOW WHAT TONY SAID TO YOU. AND I AM NOT FOR ONE SECOND DISCOUNTING HIS GRIEF. BUT I WANT TO GIVE YOU ANOTHER PERSPECTIVE.
YOU CAN HELP US STOP CRIMINALS AND MADMEN BEFORE THEY HURT ANYONE. YOU CAN TELL US WHEN NATURAL DISASTERS ARE ABOUT TO HAPPEN.
WE'RE GOING TO GO OUT THERE AND PUT OUR LIVES ON THE LINE ANYWAY.
YOU CAN GIVE US THE GIFT OF KNOWING IT'S FOR A REASON.
THE BEST AND BRAVEST PEOPLE I KNOW ARE PREPARED TO TAKE THAT RISK. NOT JUST PREPARED-- WE WANT TO.
BUT TO DO IT RIGHT--TO DO IT THE BEST WAY WE POSSIBLY CAN-- WE NEED YOU.
ULYSSES... HAVE YOU HAD ANOTHER VISION?
...
YES.

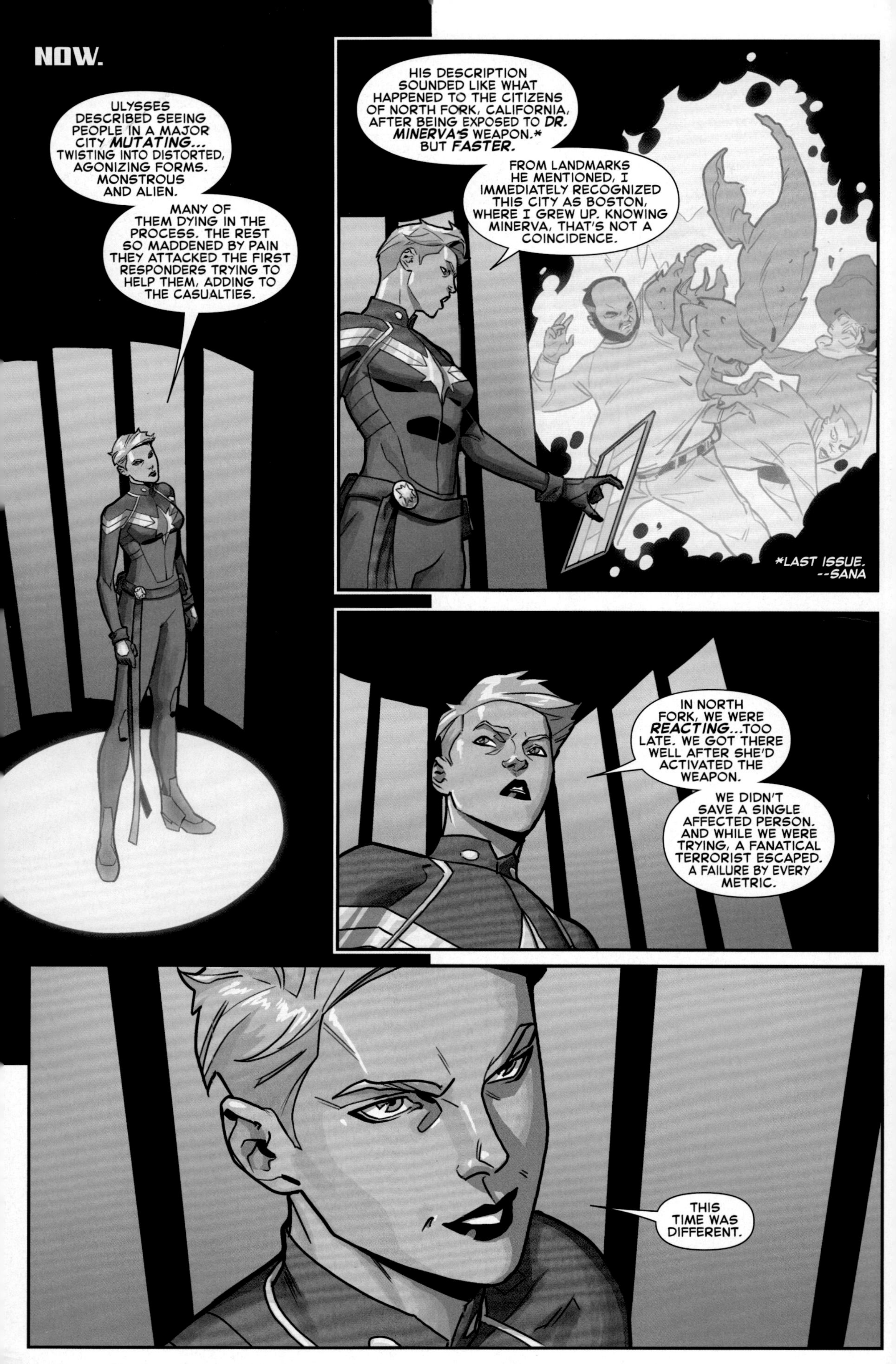
NOW.
ULYSSES DESCRIBED SEEING PEOPLE IN A MAJOR CITY MUTATING... TWISTING INTO DISTORTED, AGONIZING FORMS. MONSTROUS AND ALIEN.
MANY OF THEM DYING IN THE PROCESS. THE REST SO MADDENED BY PAIN THEY ATTACKED THE FIRST RESPONDERS TRYING TO HELP THEM, ADDING TO THE CASUALTIES.
HIS DESCRIPTION SOUNDED LIKE WHAT HAPPENED TO THE CITIZENS OF NORTH FORK, CALIFORNIA, AFTER BEING EXPOSED TO DR. MINERVA'S WEAPON.* BUT FASTER.
FROM LANDMARKS HE MENTIONED, I IMMEDIATELY RECOGNIZED THIS CITY AS BOSTON, WHERE I GREW UP. KNOWING MINERVA, THAT'S NOT A COINCIDENCE.
*LAST ISSUE. --SANA
IN NORTH FORK, WE WERE REACTING...TOO LATE. WE GOT THERE WELL AFTER SHE'D ACTIVATED THE WEAPON.
WE DIDN'T SAVE A SINGLE AFFECTED PERSON. AND WHILE WE WERE TRYING, A FANATICAL TERRORIST ESCAPED. A FAILURE BY EVERY METRIC.
THIS TIME WAS DIFFERENT.

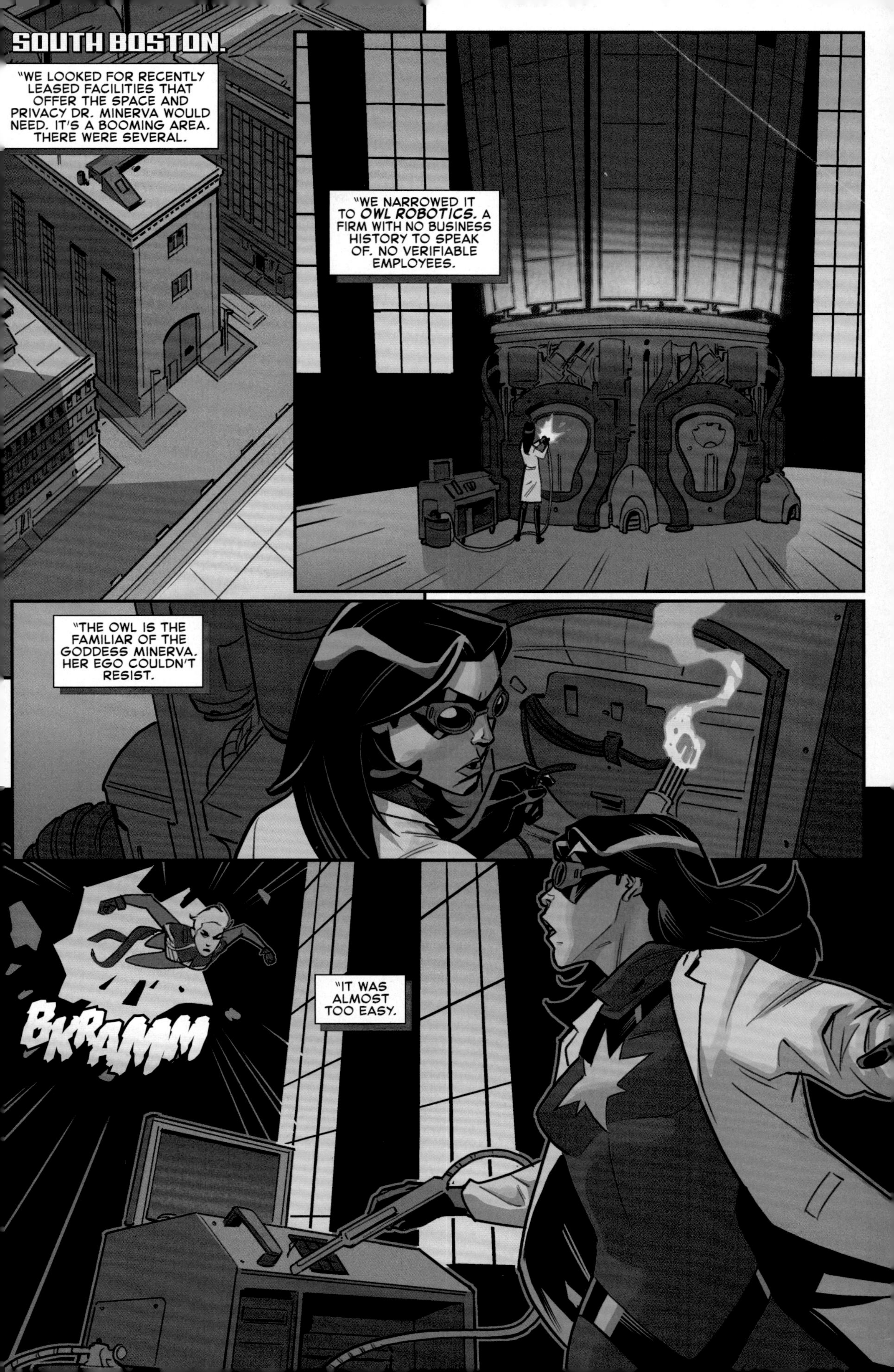
SOUTH BOSTON.
"WE LOOKED FOR RECENTLY LEASED FACILITIES THAT OFFER THE SPACE AND PRIVACY DR. MINERVA WOULD NEED. IT'S A BOOMING AREA. THERE WERE SEVERAL.
"WE NARROWED IT TO *OWL ROBOTICS.* A FIRM WITH NO BUSINESS HISTORY TO SPEAK OF. NO VERIFIABLE EMPLOYEES.
"THE OWL IS THE FAMILIAR OF THE GODDESS MINERVA. HER EGO COULDN'T RESIST.
BKRAMM
"IT WAS ALMOST TOO EASY.

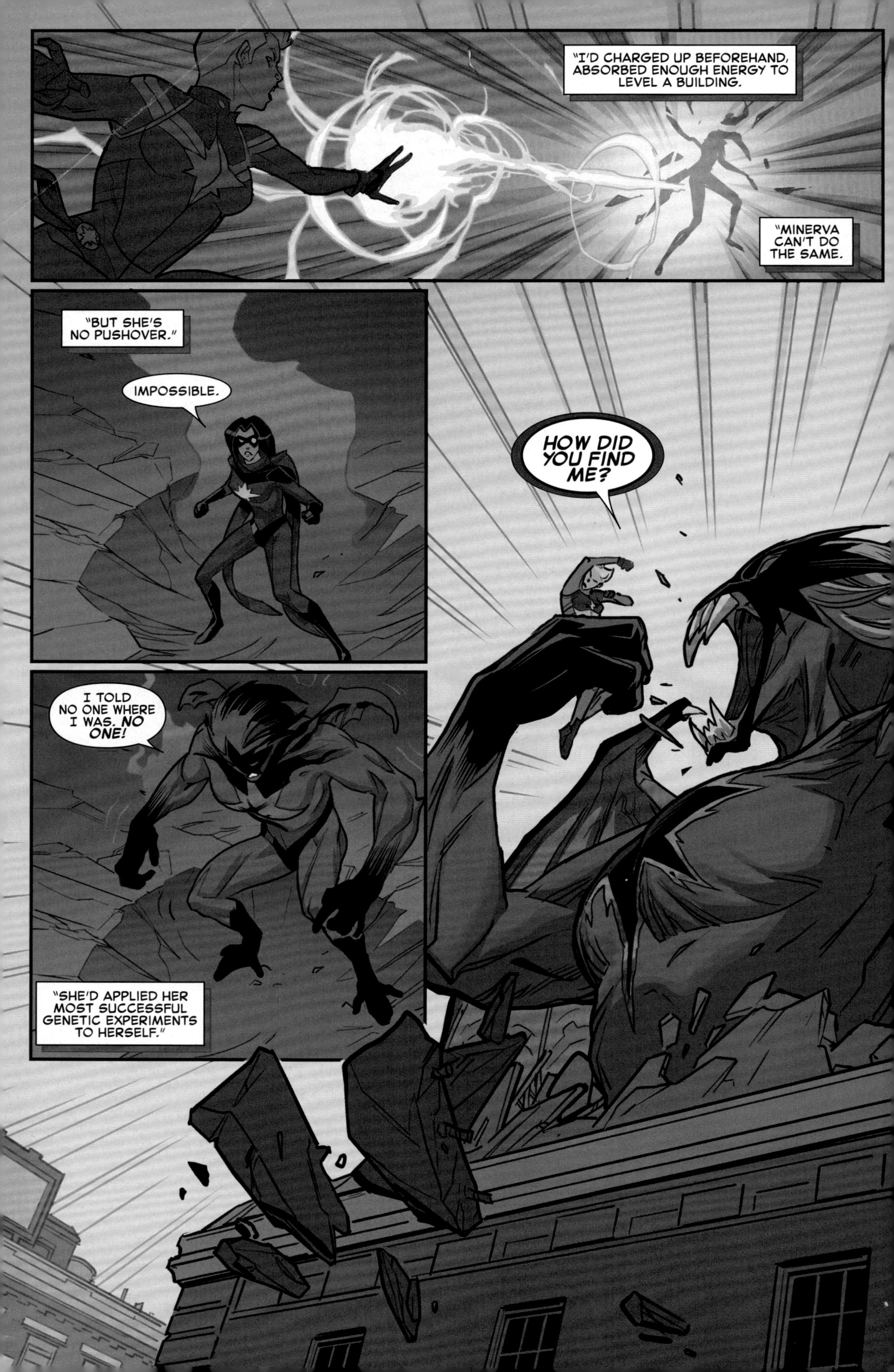
"I'D CHARGED UP BEFOREHAND, ABSORBED ENOUGH ENERGY TO LEVEL A BUILDING.
"MINERVA CAN'T DO THE SAME.
"BUT SHE'S NO PUSHOVER."
IMPOSSIBLE.
HOW DID YOU FIND ME?
I TOLD NO ONE WHERE I WAS. NO ONE!
"SHE'D APPLIED HER MOST SUCCESSFUL GENETIC EXPERIMENTS TO HERSELF."

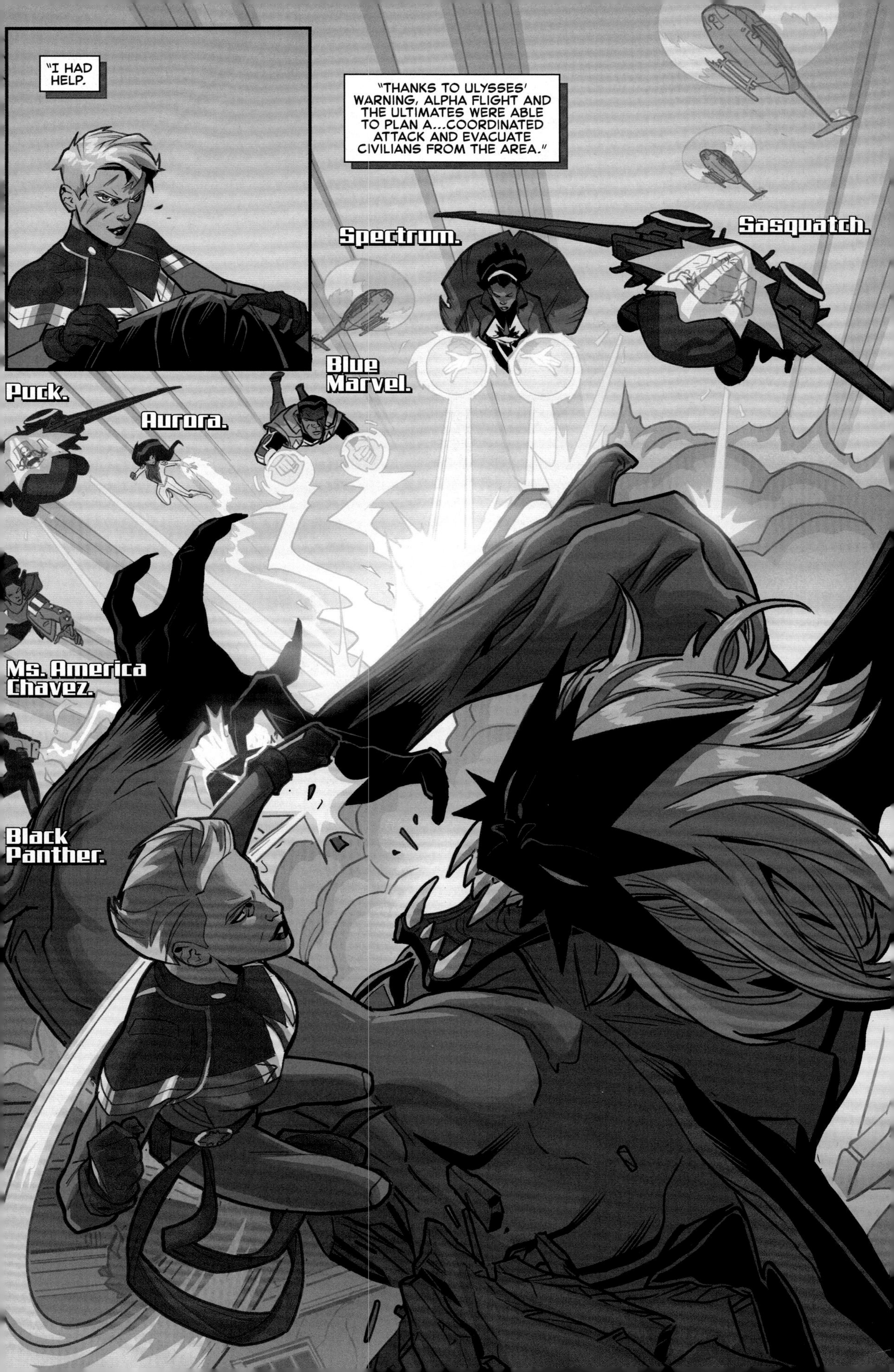

"I HAD HELP.
"THANKS TO ULYSSES' WARNING, ALPHA FLIGHT AND THE ULTIMATES WERE ABLE TO PLAN A...COORDINATED ATTACK AND EVACUATE CIVILIANS FROM THE AREA."
Spectrum.
Sasquatch.
Blue Marvel.
Puck.
Aurora.
Ms. America Chavez.
Black Panther.

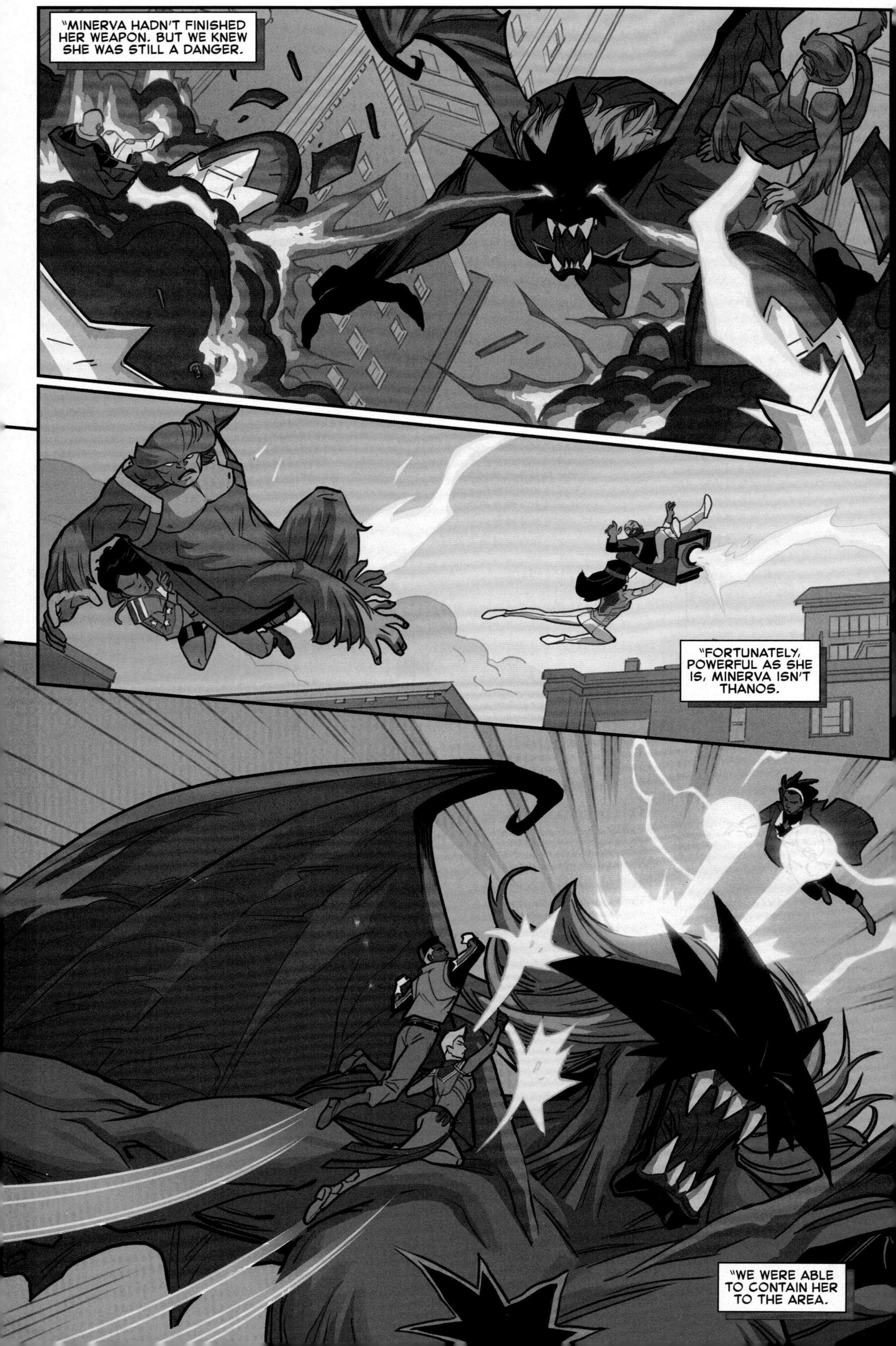
"MINERVA HADN'T FINISHED HER WEAPON. BUT WE KNEW SHE WAS STILL A DANGER.
"FORTUNATELY, POWERFUL AS SHE IS, MINERVA ISN'T THANOS.
"WE WERE ABLE TO CONTAIN HER TO THE AREA.

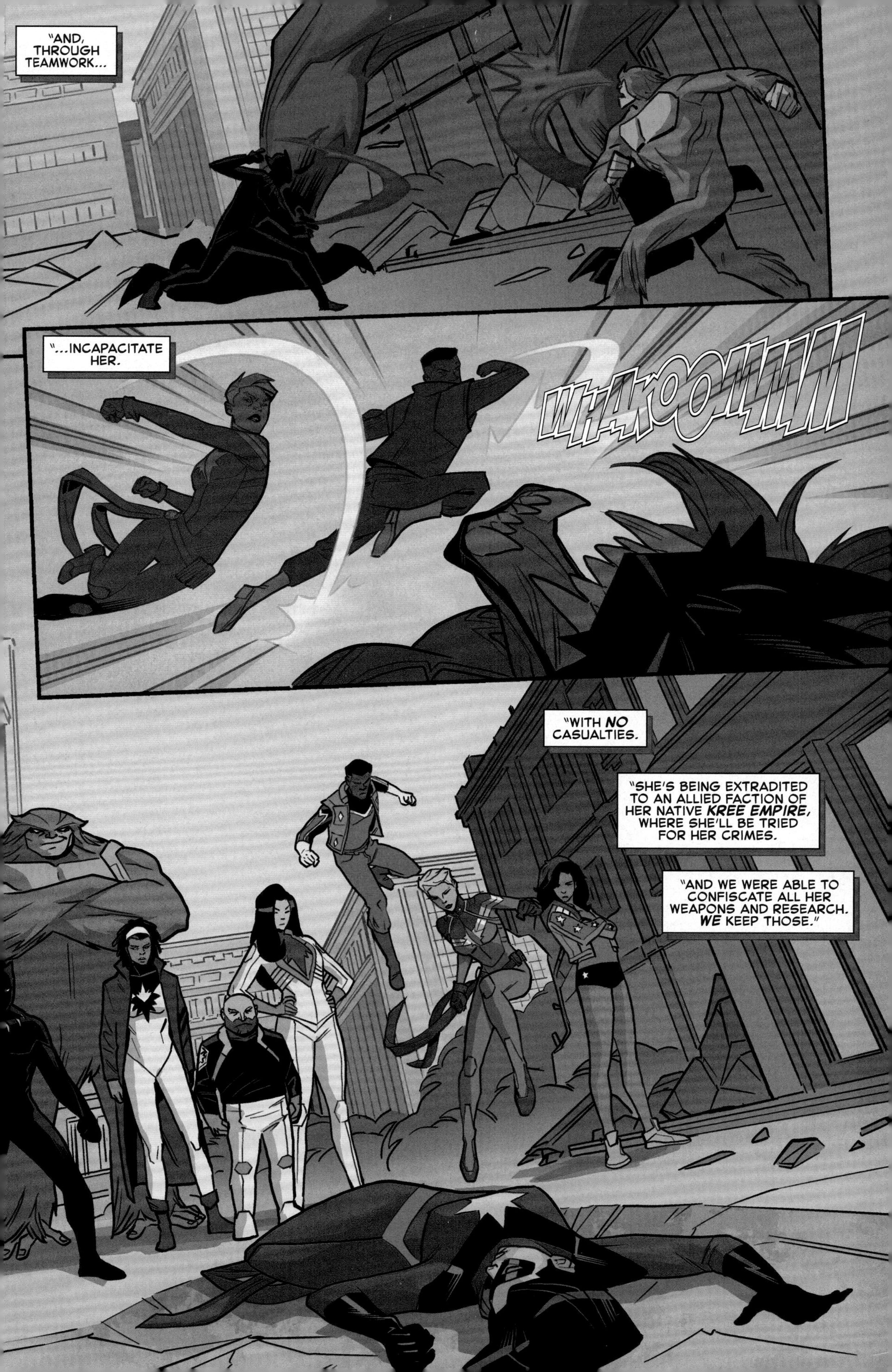
"AND, THROUGH TEAMWORK...
"...INCAPACITATE HER.
WHAKOOMMM
"WITH NO CASUALTIES.
"SHE'S BEING EXTRADITED TO AN ALLIED FACTION OF HER NATIVE KREE EMPIRE, WHERE SHE'LL BE TRIED FOR HER CRIMES.
"AND WE WERE ABLE TO CONFISCATE ALL HER WEAPONS AND RESEARCH. WE KEEP THOSE."

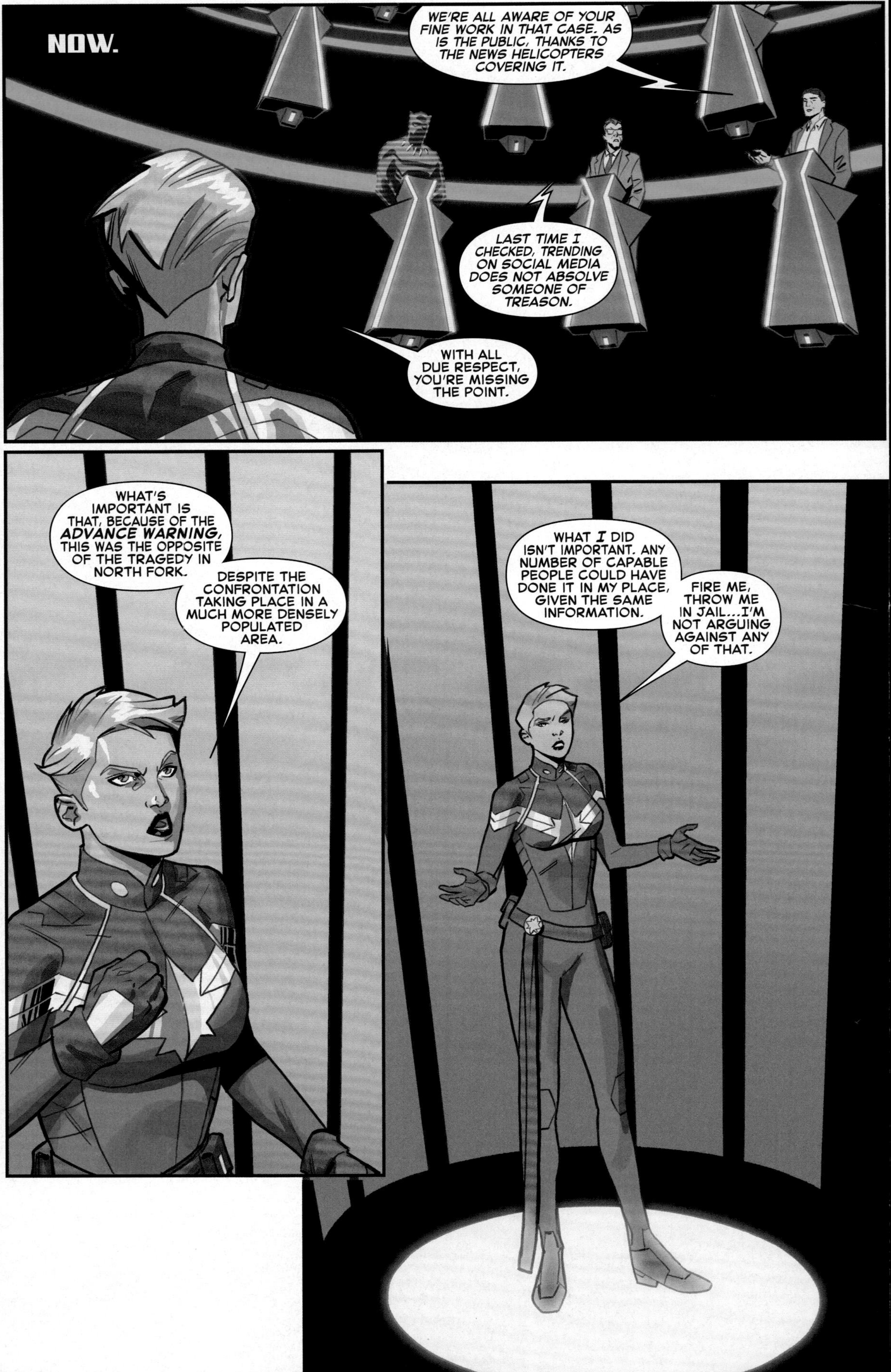
NOW.
WE'RE ALL AWARE OF YOUR FINE WORK IN THAT CASE. AS IS THE PUBLIC, THANKS TO THE NEWS HELICOPTERS COVERING IT.
LAST TIME I CHECKED, TRENDING ON SOCIAL MEDIA DOES NOT ABSOLVE SOMEONE OF TREASON.
WITH ALL DUE RESPECT, YOU'RE MISSING THE POINT.
WHAT'S IMPORTANT IS THAT, BECAUSE OF THE ***ADVANCE WARNING,*** THIS WAS THE OPPOSITE OF THE TRAGEDY IN NORTH FORK.
DESPITE THE CONFRONTATION TAKING PLACE IN A MUCH MORE DENSELY POPULATED AREA.
WHAT ***I*** DID ISN'T IMPORTANT. ANY NUMBER OF CAPABLE PEOPLE COULD HAVE DONE IT IN MY PLACE, GIVEN THE SAME INFORMATION.
FIRE ME, THROW ME IN JAIL...I'M NOT ARGUING AGAINST ANY OF THAT.

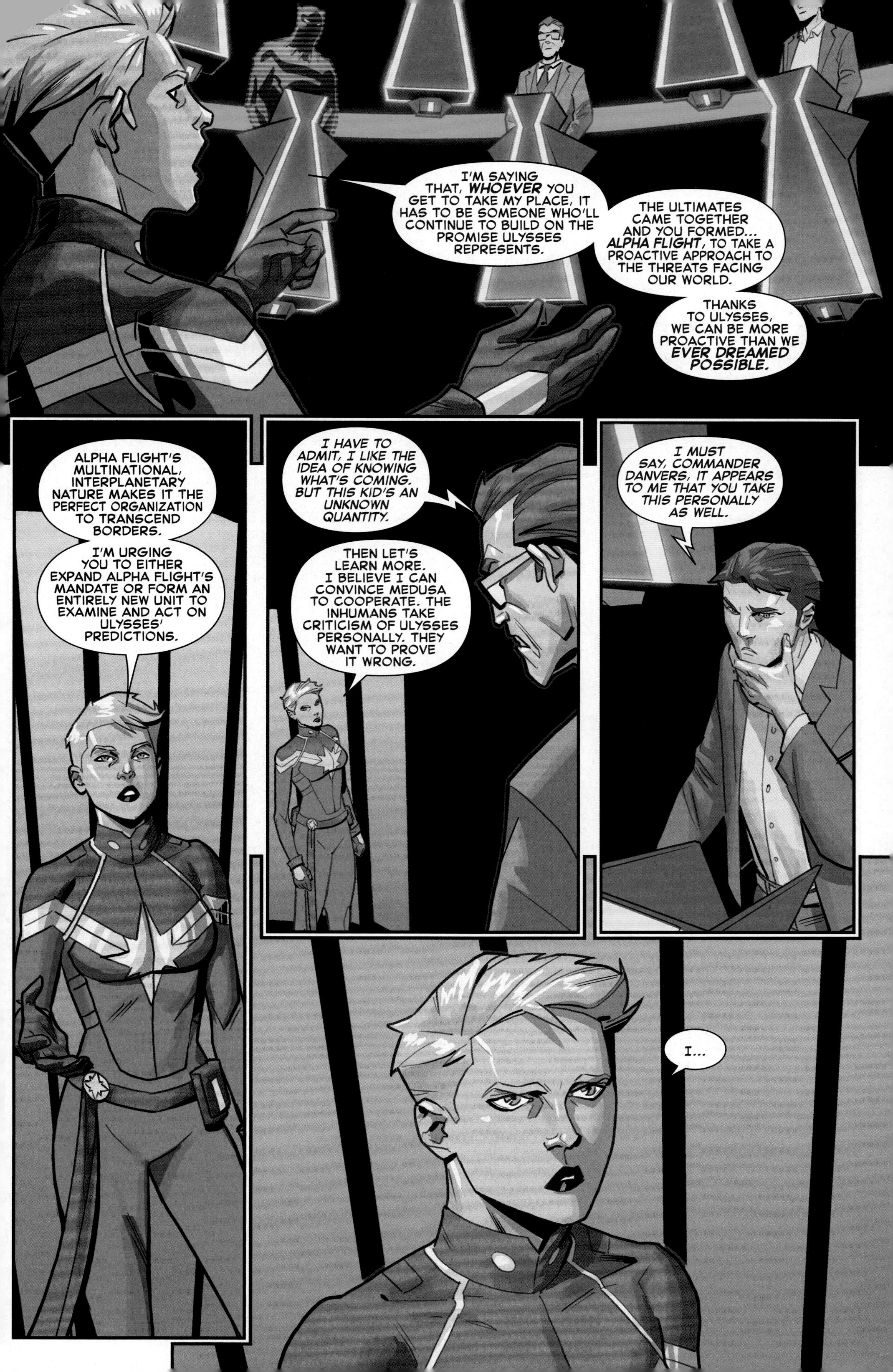
I'M SAYING THAT, WHOEVER YOU GET TO TAKE MY PLACE, IT HAS TO BE SOMEONE WHO'LL CONTINUE TO BUILD ON THE PROMISE ULYSSES REPRESENTS.
THE ULTIMATES CAME TOGETHER AND YOU FORMED... ALPHA FLIGHT, TO TAKE A PROACTIVE APPROACH TO THE THREATS FACING OUR WORLD.
THANKS TO ULYSSES, WE CAN BE MORE PROACTIVE THAN WE EVER DREAMED POSSIBLE.
ALPHA FLIGHT'S MULTINATIONAL, INTERPLANETARY NATURE MAKES IT THE PERFECT ORGANIZATION TO TRANSCEND BORDERS.
I'M URGING YOU TO EITHER EXPAND ALPHA FLIGHT'S MANDATE OR FORM AN ENTIRELY NEW UNIT TO EXAMINE AND ACT ON ULYSSES' PREDICTIONS.
I HAVE TO ADMIT, I LIKE THE IDEA OF KNOWING WHAT'S COMING. BUT THIS KID'S AN UNKNOWN QUANTITY.
THEN LET'S LEARN MORE. I BELIEVE I CAN CONVINCE MEDUSA TO COOPERATE. THE INHUMANS TAKE CRITICISM OF ULYSSES PERSONALLY. THEY WANT TO PROVE IT WRONG.
I MUST SAY, COMMANDER DANVERS, IT APPEARS TO ME THAT YOU TAKE THIS PERSONALLY AS WELL.
I...

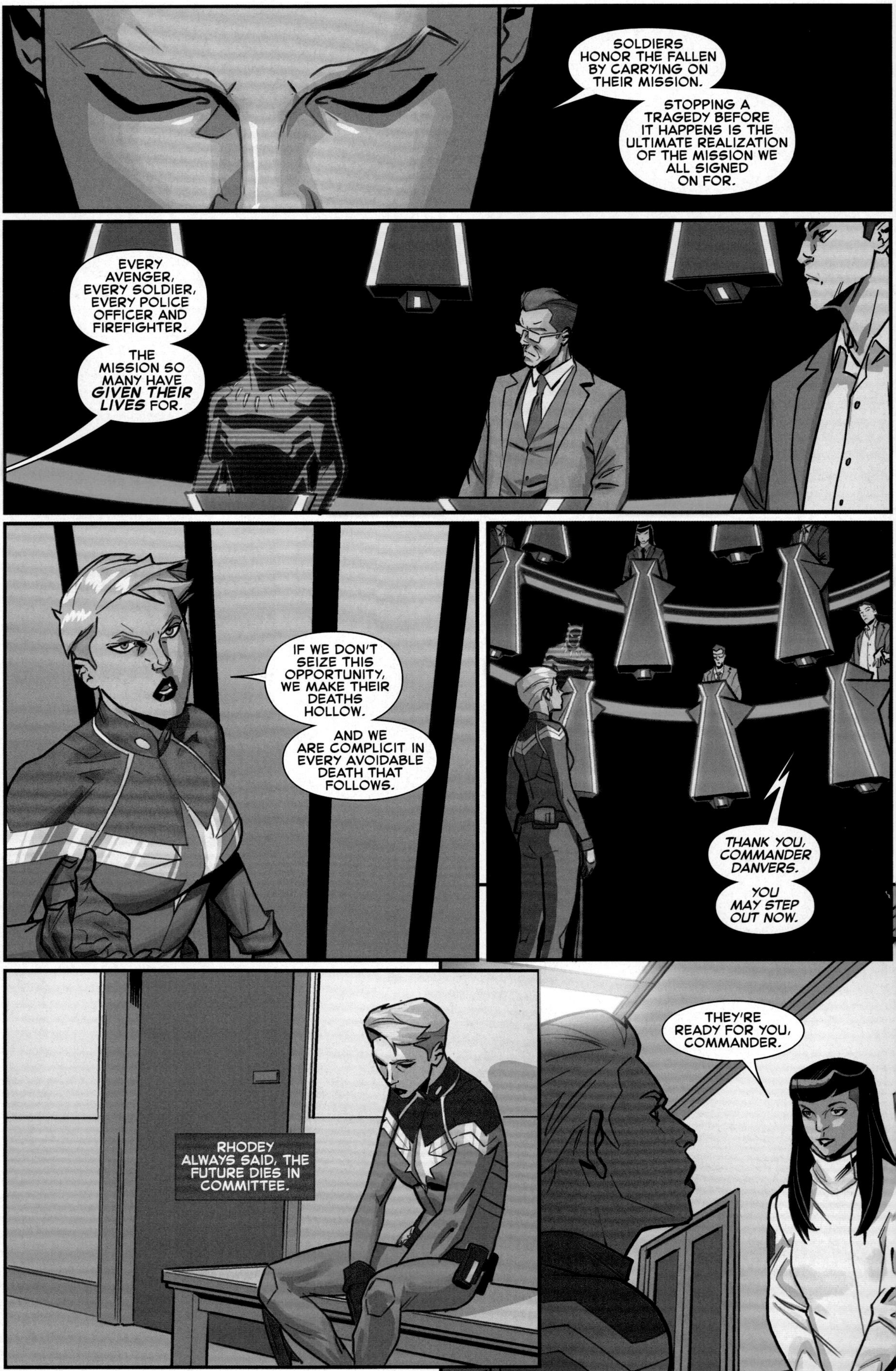
SOLDIERS HONOR THE FALLEN BY CARRYING ON THEIR MISSION.
STOPPING A TRAGEDY BEFORE IT HAPPENS IS THE ULTIMATE REALIZATION OF THE MISSION WE ALL SIGNED ON FOR.
EVERY AVENGER, EVERY SOLDIER, EVERY POLICE OFFICER AND FIREFIGHTER.
THE MISSION SO MANY HAVE *GIVEN THEIR LIVES* FOR.
IF WE DON'T SEIZE THIS OPPORTUNITY, WE MAKE THEIR DEATHS HOLLOW.
AND WE ARE COMPLICIT IN EVERY AVOIDABLE DEATH THAT FOLLOWS.
THANK YOU, COMMANDER DANVERS.
YOU MAY STEP OUT NOW.
THEY'RE READY FOR YOU, COMMANDER.
RHODEY ALWAYS SAID, THE FUTURE DIES IN COMMITTEE.

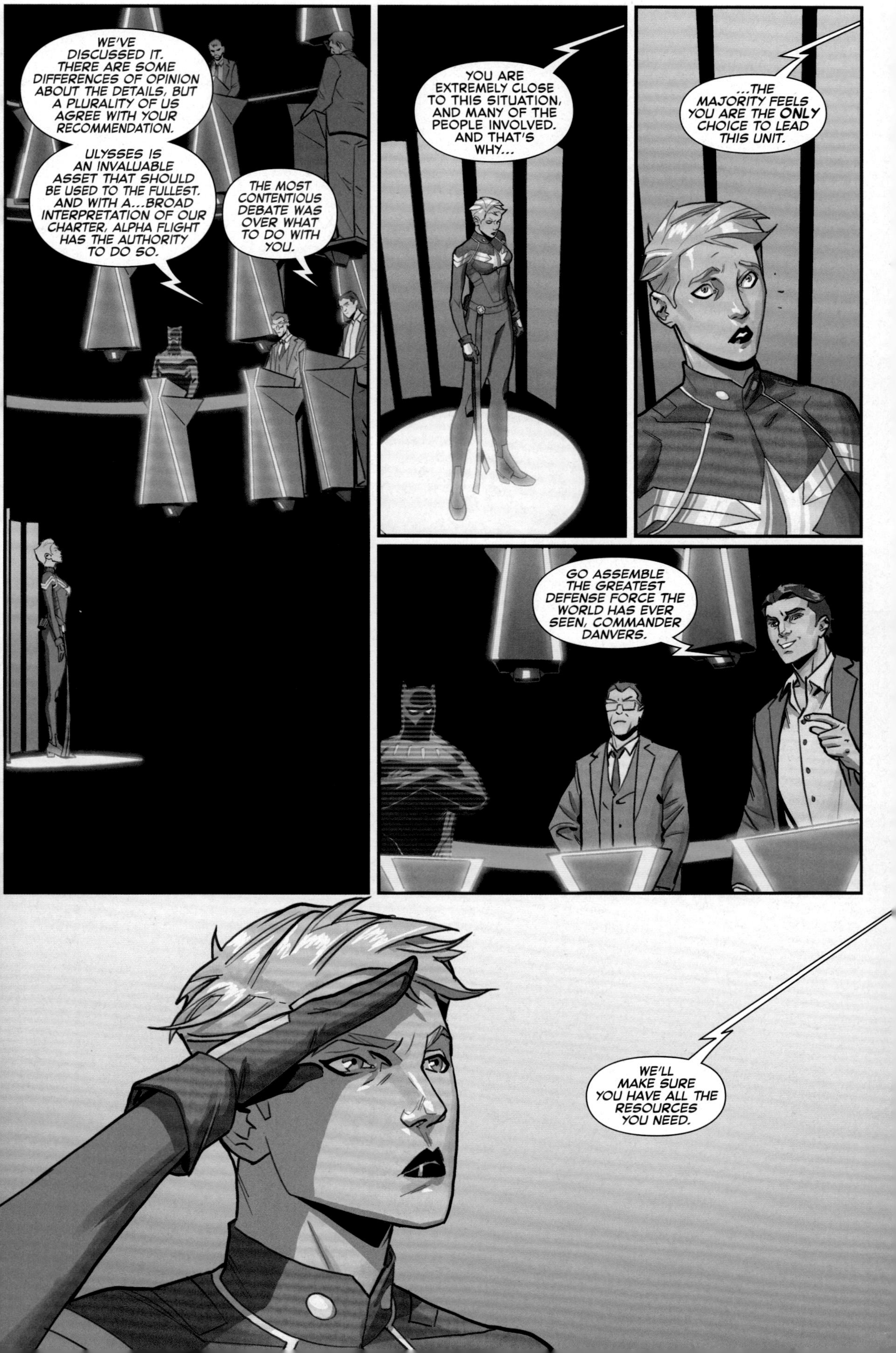
WE'VE DISCUSSED IT. THERE ARE SOME DIFFERENCES OF OPINION ABOUT THE DETAILS, BUT A PLURALITY OF US AGREE WITH YOUR RECOMMENDATION.
ULYSSES IS AN INVALUABLE ASSET THAT SHOULD BE USED TO THE FULLEST. AND WITH A...BROAD INTERPRETATION OF OUR CHARTER, ALPHA FLIGHT HAS THE AUTHORITY TO DO SO.
THE MOST CONTENTIOUS DEBATE WAS OVER WHAT TO DO WITH YOU.
YOU ARE EXTREMELY CLOSE TO THIS SITUATION, AND MANY OF THE PEOPLE INVOLVED. AND THAT'S WHY...
...THE MAJORITY FEELS YOU ARE THE **ONLY** CHOICE TO LEAD THIS UNIT.
GO ASSEMBLE THE GREATEST DEFENSE FORCE THE WORLD HAS EVER SEEN, COMMANDER DANVERS.
WE'LL MAKE SURE YOU HAVE ALL THE RESOURCES YOU NEED.

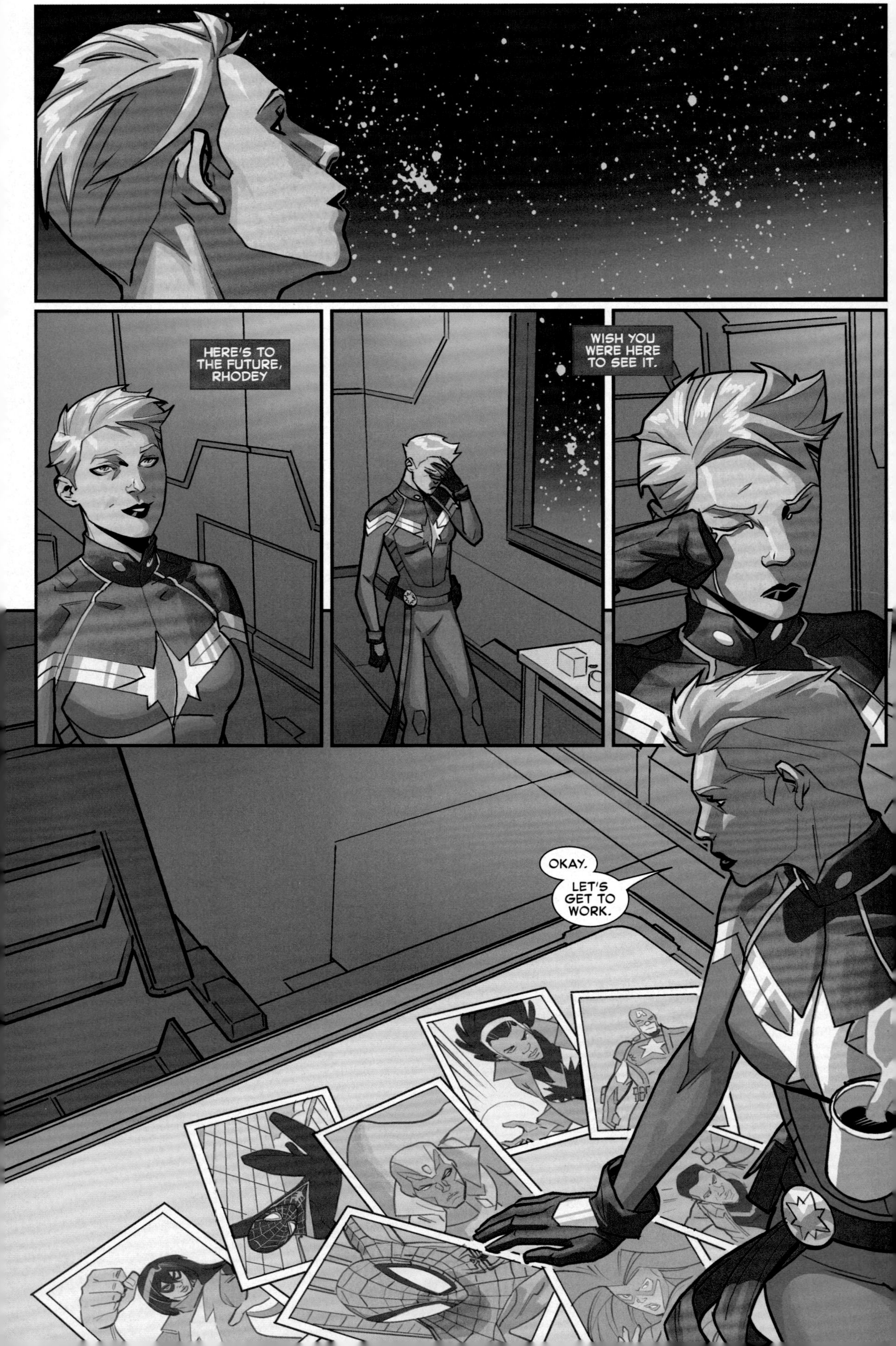
HERE'S TO THE FUTURE, RHODEY
WISH YOU WERE HERE TO SEE IT.
OKAY.
LET'S GET TO WORK.

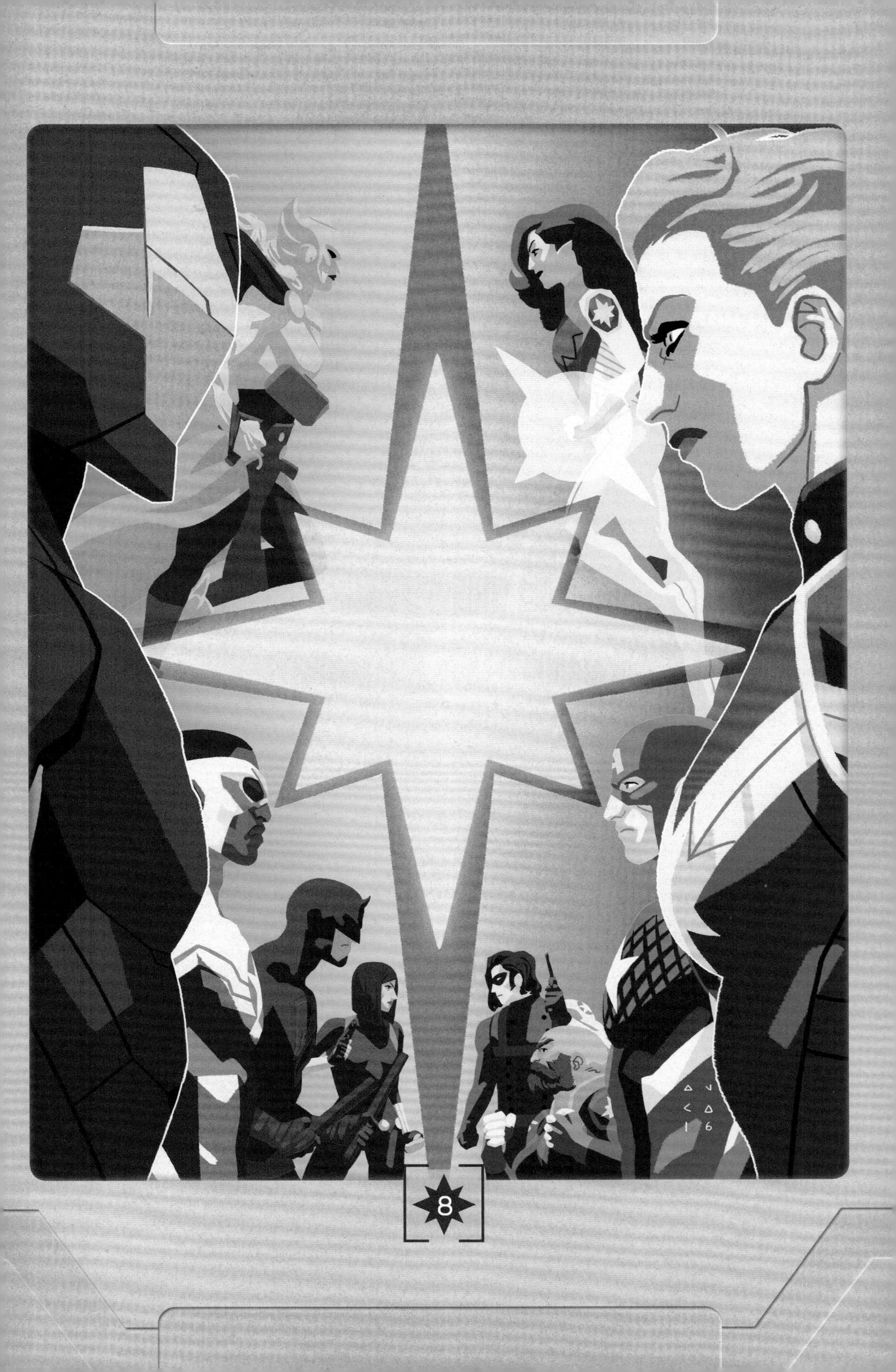

8

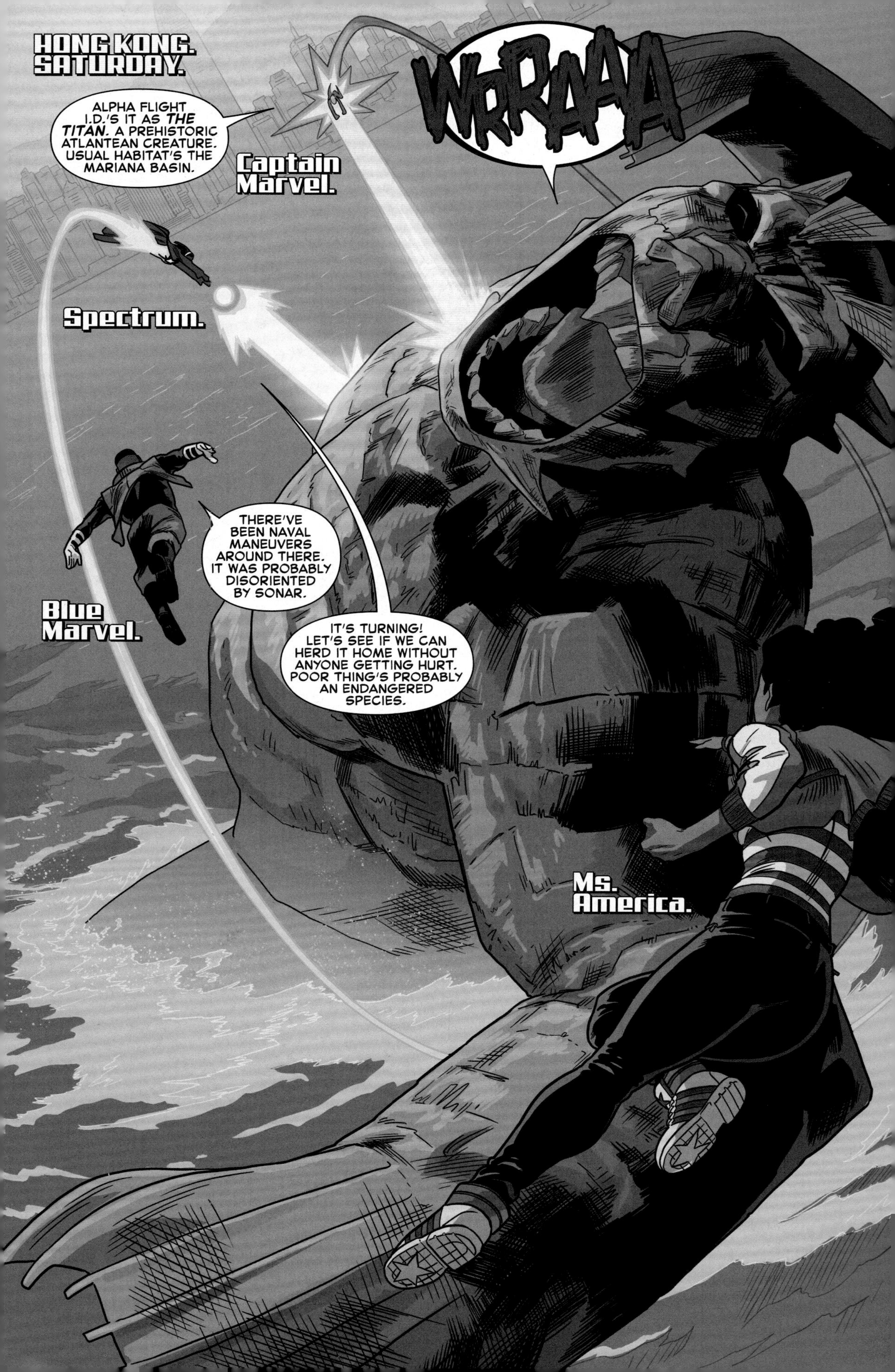
HONG KONG. SATURDAY.
ALPHA FLIGHT I.D.'S IT AS THE TITAN. A PREHISTORIC ATLANTEAN CREATURE. USUAL HABITAT'S THE MARIANA BASIN.
Captain Marvel.
WRRAAA
Spectrum.
Blue Marvel.
THERE'VE BEEN NAVAL MANEUVERS AROUND THERE. IT WAS PROBABLY DISORIENTED BY SONAR.
IT'S TURNING! LET'S SEE IF WE CAN HERD IT HOME WITHOUT ANYONE GETTING HURT. POOR THING'S PROBABLY AN ENDANGERED SPECIES.
Ms. America.

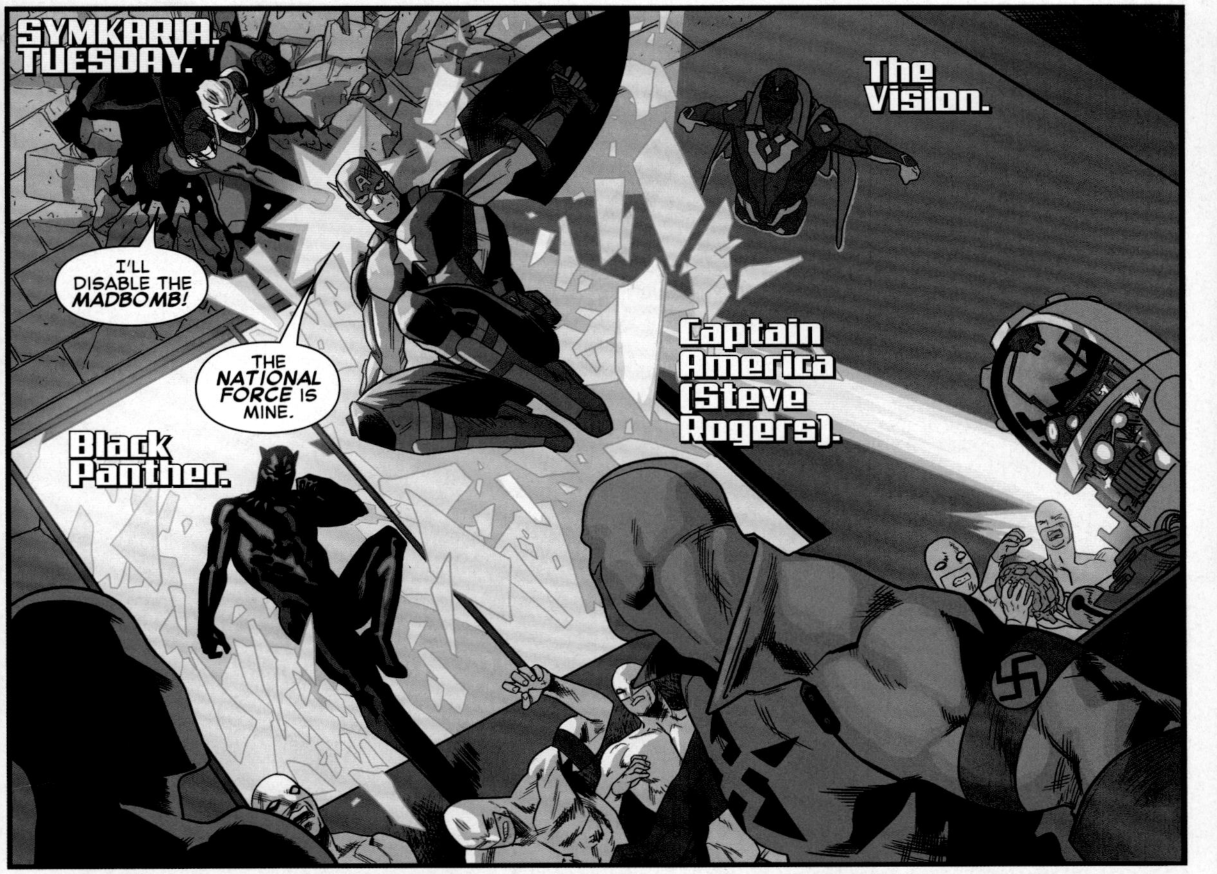
SYMKARIA. TUESDAY.
The Vision.
I'LL DISABLE THE MADBOMB!
THE NATIONAL FORCE IS MINE.
Captain America (Steve Rogers).
Black Panther.

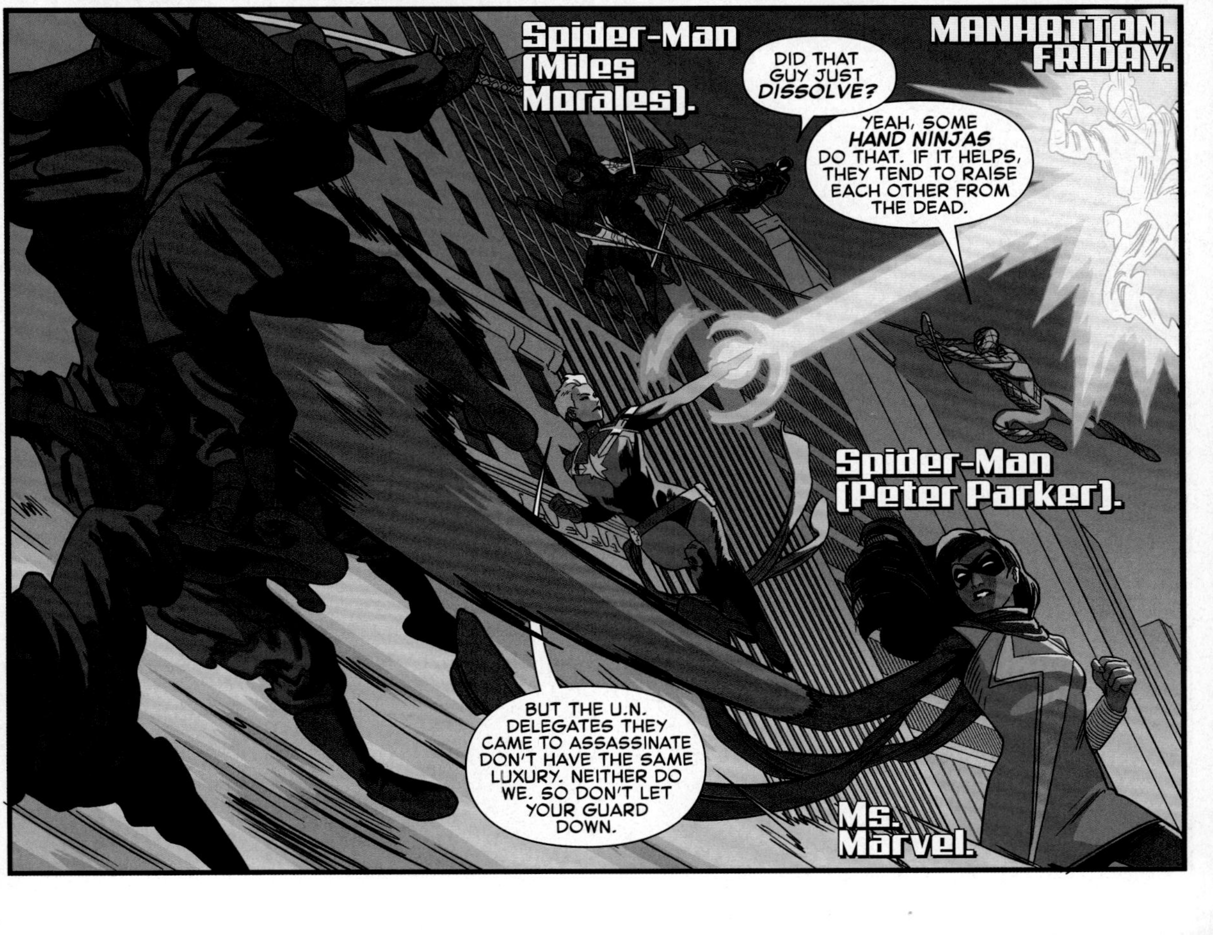
Spider-Man (Miles Morales).
MANHATTAN. FRIDAY.
DID THAT GUY JUST DISSOLVE?
YEAH, SOME HAND NINJAS DO THAT. IF IT HELPS, THEY TEND TO RAISE EACH OTHER FROM THE DEAD.
Spider-Man (Peter Parker).
BUT THE U.N. DELEGATES THEY CAME TO ASSASSINATE DON'T HAVE THE SAME LUXURY. NEITHER DO WE. SO DON'T LET YOUR GUARD DOWN.
Ms. Marvel.

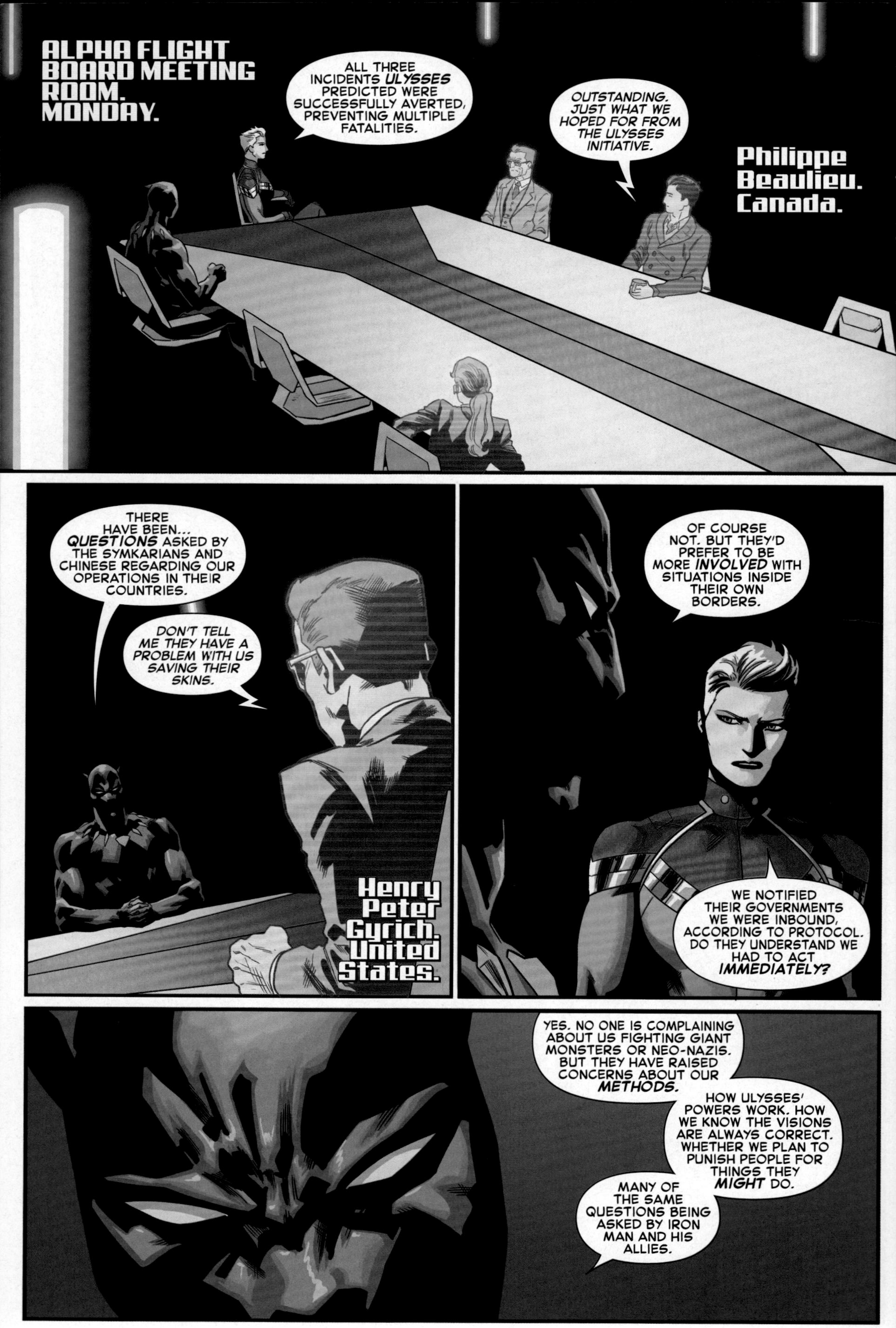
ALPHA FLIGHT BOARD MEETING ROOM. MONDAY.
ALL THREE INCIDENTS ULYSSES PREDICTED WERE SUCCESSFULLY AVERTED, PREVENTING MULTIPLE FATALITIES.
OUTSTANDING. JUST WHAT WE HOPED FOR FROM THE ULYSSES INITIATIVE.
Philippe Beaulieu. Canada.
THERE HAVE BEEN... QUESTIONS ASKED BY THE SYMKARIANS AND CHINESE REGARDING OUR OPERATIONS IN THEIR COUNTRIES.
DON'T TELL ME THEY HAVE A PROBLEM WITH US SAVING THEIR SKINS.
Henry Peter Gyrich. United States.
OF COURSE NOT. BUT THEY'D PREFER TO BE MORE INVOLVED WITH SITUATIONS INSIDE THEIR OWN BORDERS.
WE NOTIFIED THEIR GOVERNMENTS WE WERE INBOUND, ACCORDING TO PROTOCOL. DO THEY UNDERSTAND WE HAD TO ACT IMMEDIATELY?
YES. NO ONE IS COMPLAINING ABOUT US FIGHTING GIANT MONSTERS OR NEO-NAZIS. BUT THEY HAVE RAISED CONCERNS ABOUT OUR METHODS.
HOW ULYSSES' POWERS WORK. HOW WE KNOW THE VISIONS ARE ALWAYS CORRECT. WHETHER WE PLAN TO PUNISH PEOPLE FOR THINGS THEY MIGHT DO.
MANY OF THE SAME QUESTIONS BEING ASKED BY IRON MAN AND HIS ALLIES.

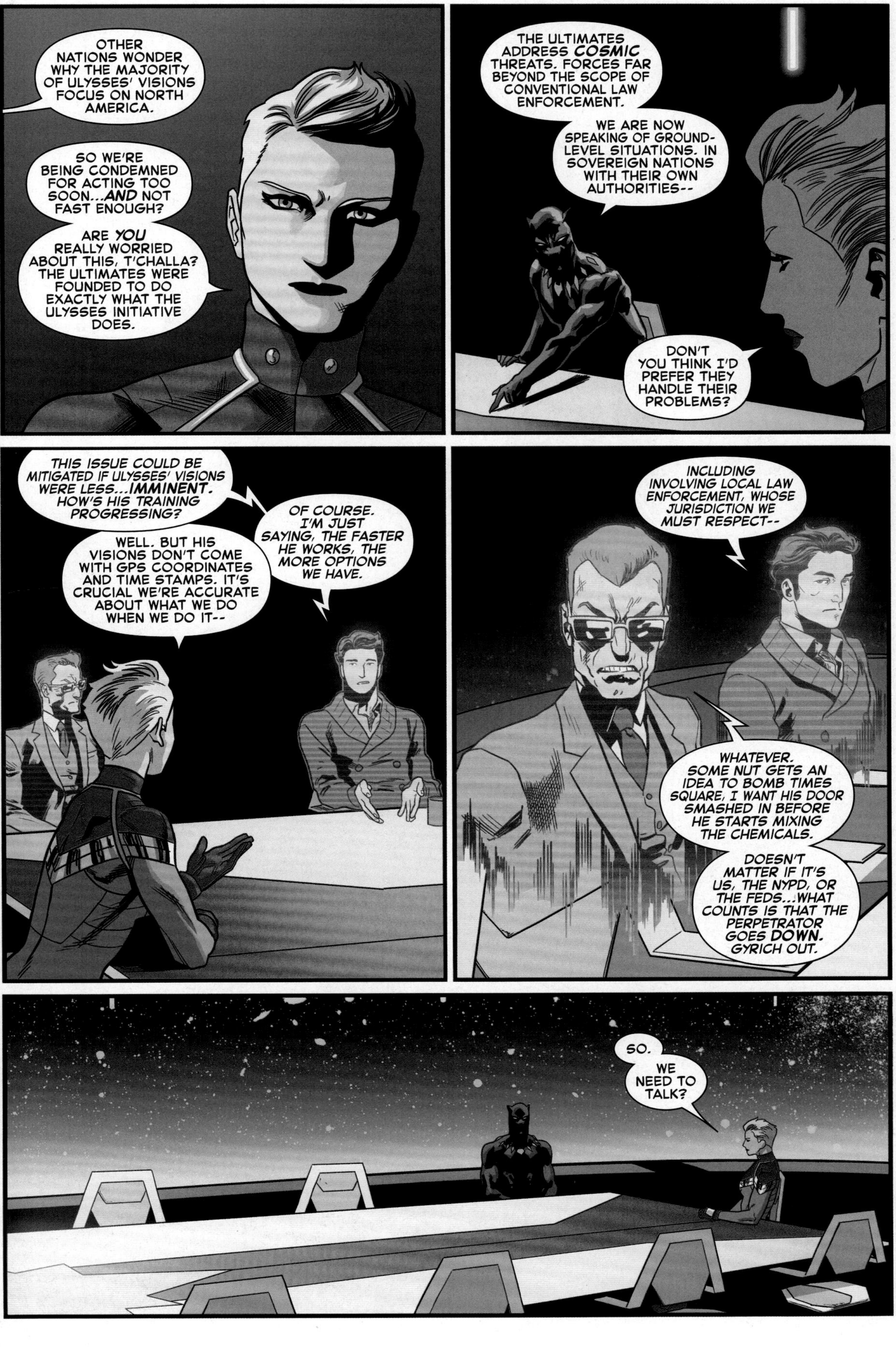
OTHER NATIONS WONDER WHY THE MAJORITY OF ULYSSES' VISIONS FOCUS ON NORTH AMERICA.
SO WE'RE BEING CONDEMNED FOR ACTING TOO SOON...AND NOT FAST ENOUGH?
ARE YOU REALLY WORRIED ABOUT THIS, T'CHALLA? THE ULTIMATES WERE FOUNDED TO DO EXACTLY WHAT THE ULYSSES INITIATIVE DOES.
THE ULTIMATES ADDRESS COSMIC THREATS. FORCES FAR BEYOND THE SCOPE OF CONVENTIONAL LAW ENFORCEMENT.
WE ARE NOW SPEAKING OF GROUND-LEVEL SITUATIONS. IN SOVEREIGN NATIONS WITH THEIR OWN AUTHORITIES--
DON'T YOU THINK I'D PREFER THEY HANDLE THEIR PROBLEMS?
THIS ISSUE COULD BE MITIGATED IF ULYSSES' VISIONS WERE LESS...IMMINENT. HOW'S HIS TRAINING PROGRESSING?
WELL. BUT HIS VISIONS DON'T COME WITH GPS COORDINATES AND TIME STAMPS. IT'S CRUCIAL WE'RE ACCURATE ABOUT WHAT WE DO WHEN WE DO IT--
OF COURSE. I'M JUST SAYING, THE FASTER HE WORKS, THE MORE OPTIONS WE HAVE.
INCLUDING INVOLVING LOCAL LAW ENFORCEMENT, WHOSE JURISDICTION WE MUST RESPECT--
WHATEVER. SOME NUT GETS AN IDEA TO BOMB TIMES SQUARE, I WANT HIS DOOR SMASHED IN BEFORE HE STARTS MIXING THE CHEMICALS.
DOESN'T MATTER IF IT'S US, THE NYPD, OR THE FEDS...WHAT COUNTS IS THAT THE PERPETRATOR GOES DOWN. GYRICH OUT.
SO.
WE NEED TO TALK?

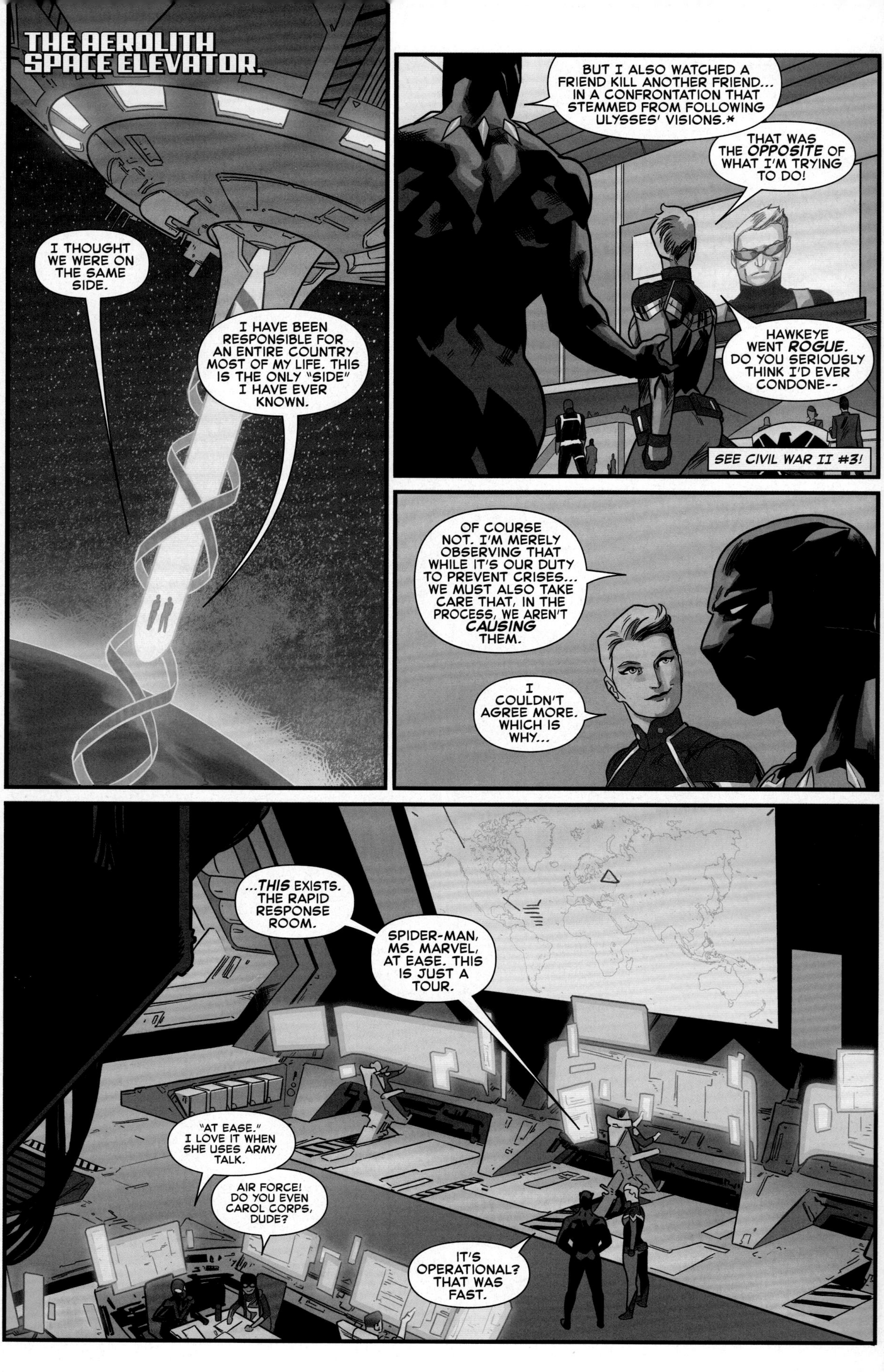
THE AEROLITH SPACE ELEVATOR.
I THOUGHT WE WERE ON THE SAME SIDE.
I HAVE BEEN RESPONSIBLE FOR AN ENTIRE COUNTRY MOST OF MY LIFE. THIS IS THE ONLY "SIDE" I HAVE EVER KNOWN.
BUT I ALSO WATCHED A FRIEND KILL ANOTHER FRIEND... IN A CONFRONTATION THAT STEMMED FROM FOLLOWING ULYSSES' VISIONS.*
THAT WAS THE OPPOSITE OF WHAT I'M TRYING TO DO!
HAWKEYE WENT ROGUE. DO YOU SERIOUSLY THINK I'D EVER CONDONE--
*SEE CIVIL WAR II #3!
OF COURSE NOT. I'M MERELY OBSERVING THAT WHILE IT'S OUR DUTY TO PREVENT CRISES... WE MUST ALSO TAKE CARE THAT, IN THE PROCESS, WE AREN'T CAUSING THEM.
I COULDN'T AGREE MORE. WHICH IS WHY...
...THIS EXISTS. THE RAPID RESPONSE ROOM.
SPIDER-MAN, MS. MARVEL, AT EASE. THIS IS JUST A TOUR.
"AT EASE." I LOVE IT WHEN SHE USES ARMY TALK.
AIR FORCE! DO YOU EVEN CAROL CORPS, DUDE?
IT'S OPERATIONAL? THAT WAS FAST.

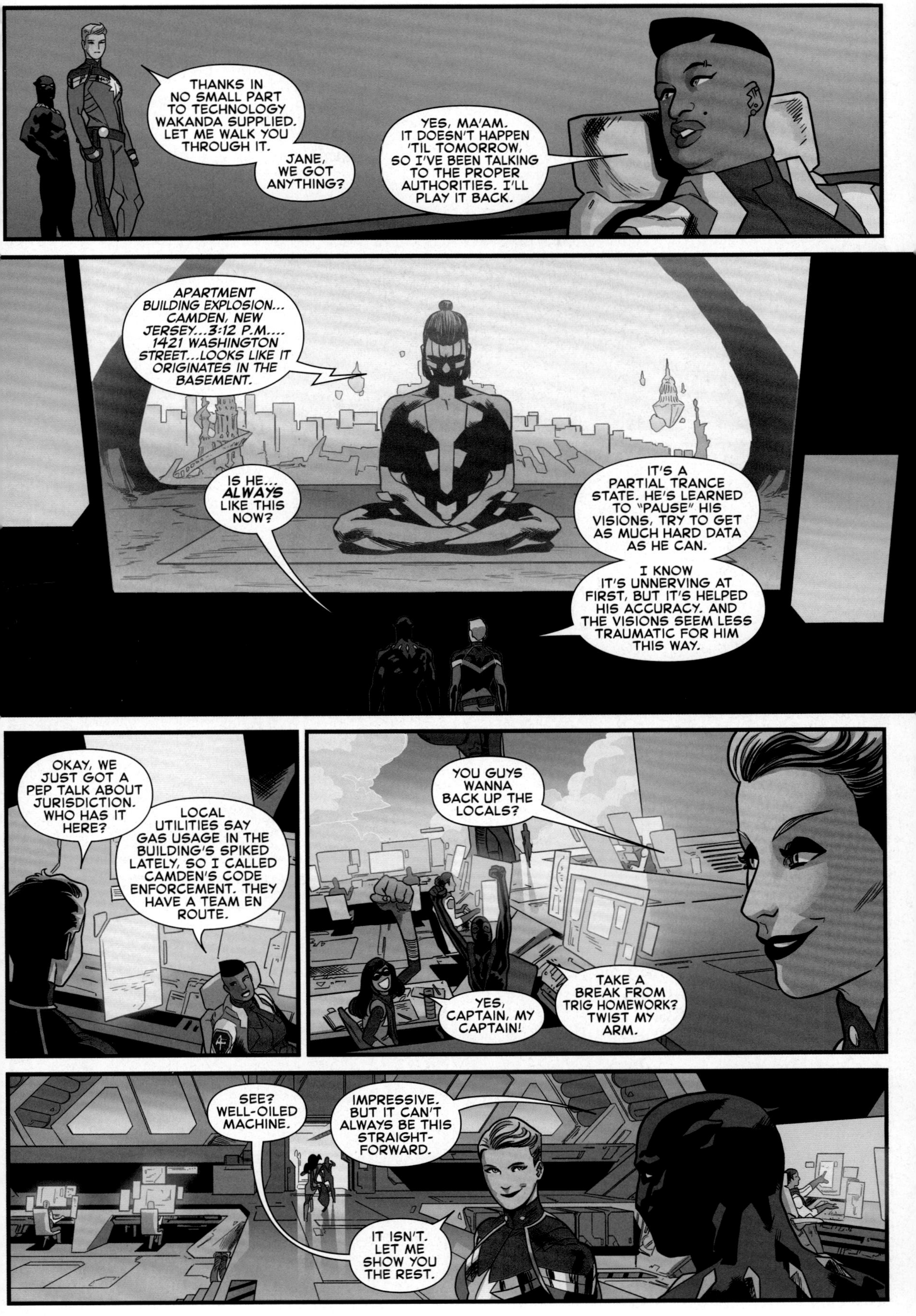
THANKS IN NO SMALL PART TO TECHNOLOGY WAKANDA SUPPLIED. LET ME WALK YOU THROUGH IT.
JANE, WE GOT ANYTHING?
YES, MA'AM. IT DOESN'T HAPPEN 'TIL TOMORROW, SO I'VE BEEN TALKING TO THE PROPER AUTHORITIES. I'LL PLAY IT BACK.
APARTMENT BUILDING EXPLOSION... CAMDEN, NEW JERSEY...3:12 P.M.... 1421 WASHINGTON STREET...LOOKS LIKE IT ORIGINATES IN THE BASEMENT.
IS HE... ALWAYS LIKE THIS NOW?
IT'S A PARTIAL TRANCE STATE. HE'S LEARNED TO "PAUSE" HIS VISIONS, TRY TO GET AS MUCH HARD DATA AS HE CAN.
I KNOW IT'S UNNERVING AT FIRST, BUT IT'S HELPED HIS ACCURACY. AND THE VISIONS SEEM LESS TRAUMATIC FOR HIM THIS WAY.
OKAY, WE JUST GOT A PEP TALK ABOUT JURISDICTION. WHO HAS IT HERE?
LOCAL UTILITIES SAY GAS USAGE IN THE BUILDING'S SPIKED LATELY, SO I CALLED CAMDEN'S CODE ENFORCEMENT. THEY HAVE A TEAM EN ROUTE.
YOU GUYS WANNA BACK UP THE LOCALS?
YES, CAPTAIN, MY CAPTAIN!
TAKE A BREAK FROM TRIG HOMEWORK? TWIST MY ARM.
SEE? WELL-OILED MACHINE.
IMPRESSIVE. BUT IT CAN'T ALWAYS BE THIS STRAIGHT-FORWARD.
IT ISN'T. LET ME SHOW YOU THE REST.

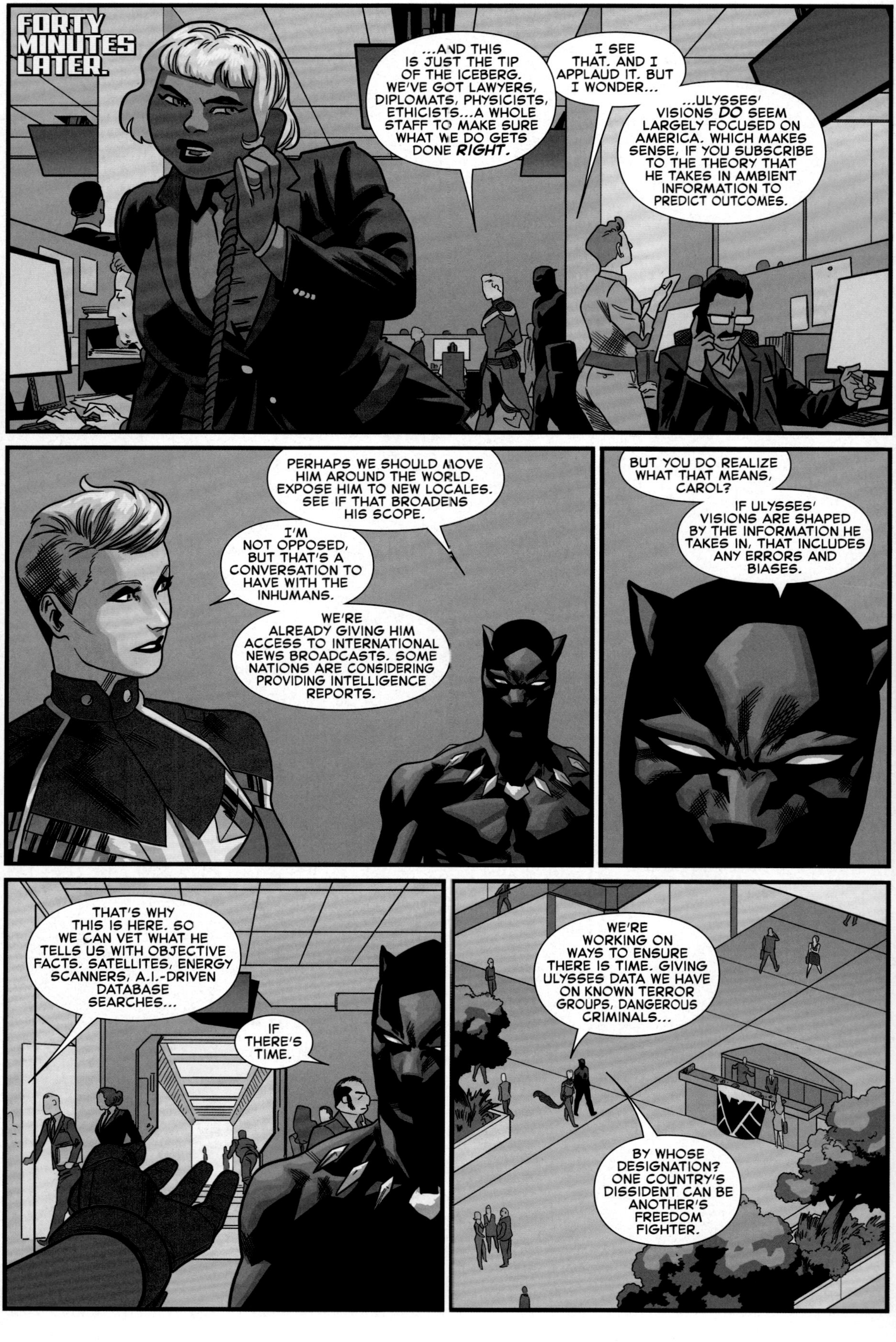
FORTY MINUTES LATER.
...AND THIS IS JUST THE TIP OF THE ICEBERG. WE'VE GOT LAWYERS, DIPLOMATS, PHYSICISTS, ETHICISTS...A WHOLE STAFF TO MAKE SURE WHAT WE DO GETS DONE RIGHT.
I SEE THAT. AND I APPLAUD IT. BUT I WONDER...
...ULYSSES' VISIONS DO SEEM LARGELY FOCUSED ON AMERICA. WHICH MAKES SENSE, IF YOU SUBSCRIBE TO THE THEORY THAT HE TAKES IN AMBIENT INFORMATION TO PREDICT OUTCOMES.
PERHAPS WE SHOULD MOVE HIM AROUND THE WORLD. EXPOSE HIM TO NEW LOCALES. SEE IF THAT BROADENS HIS SCOPE.
I'M NOT OPPOSED, BUT THAT'S A CONVERSATION TO HAVE WITH THE INHUMANS.
WE'RE ALREADY GIVING HIM ACCESS TO INTERNATIONAL NEWS BROADCASTS. SOME NATIONS ARE CONSIDERING PROVIDING INTELLIGENCE REPORTS.
BUT YOU DO REALIZE WHAT THAT MEANS, CAROL?
IF ULYSSES' VISIONS ARE SHAPED BY THE INFORMATION HE TAKES IN, THAT INCLUDES ANY ERRORS AND BIASES.
THAT'S WHY THIS IS HERE. SO WE CAN VET WHAT HE TELLS US WITH OBJECTIVE FACTS. SATELLITES, ENERGY SCANNERS, A.I.-DRIVEN DATABASE SEARCHES...
IF THERE'S TIME.
WE'RE WORKING ON WAYS TO ENSURE THERE IS TIME. GIVING ULYSSES DATA WE HAVE ON KNOWN TERROR GROUPS, DANGEROUS CRIMINALS...
BY WHOSE DESIGNATION? ONE COUNTRY'S DISSIDENT CAN BE ANOTHER'S FREEDOM FIGHTER.

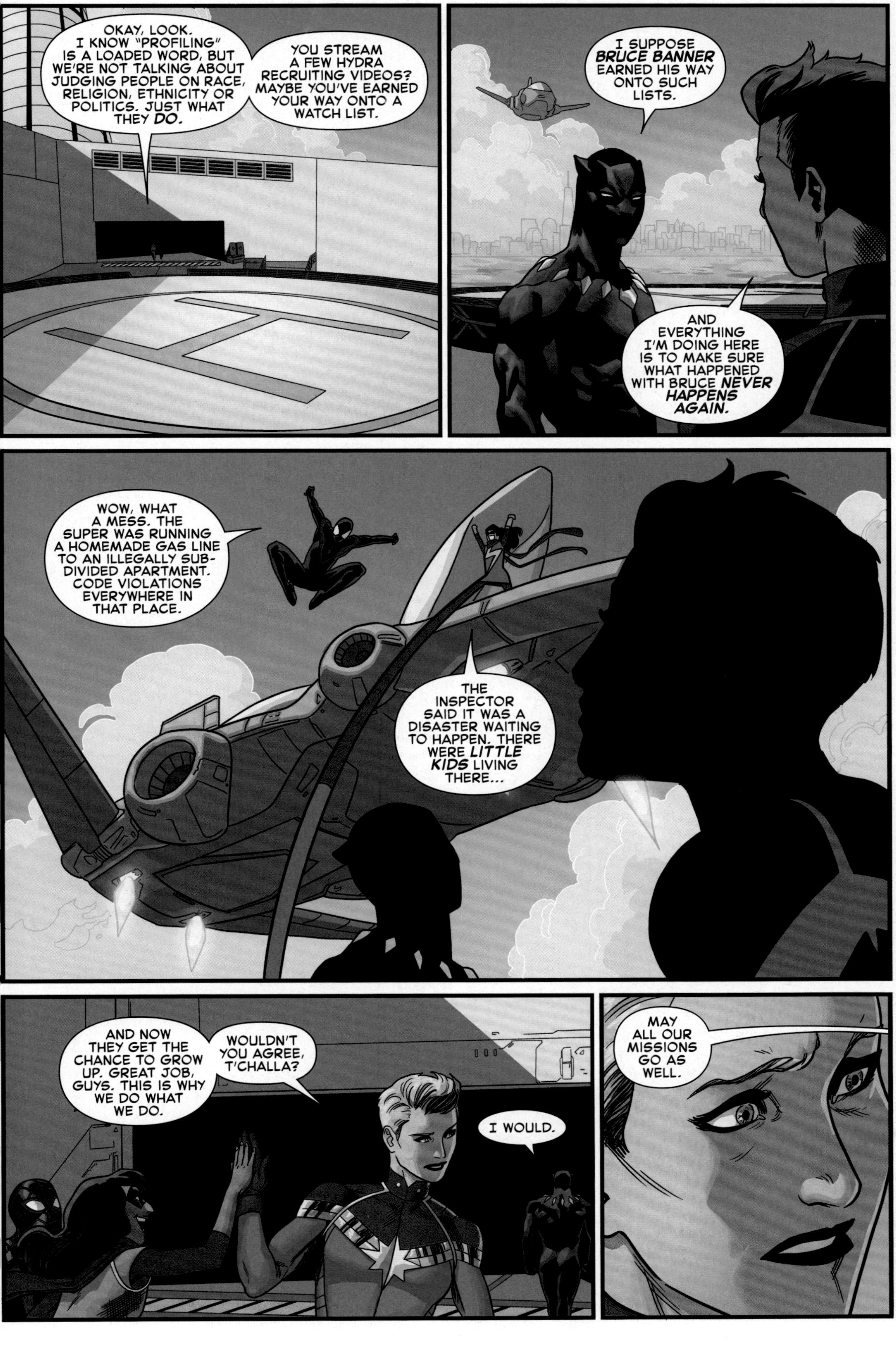

OKAY, LOOK. I KNOW "PROFILING" IS A LOADED WORD, BUT WE'RE NOT TALKING ABOUT JUDGING PEOPLE ON RACE, RELIGION, ETHNICITY OR POLITICS. JUST WHAT THEY DO.
YOU STREAM A FEW HYDRA RECRUITING VIDEOS? MAYBE YOU'VE EARNED YOUR WAY ONTO A WATCH LIST.
I SUPPOSE BRUCE BANNER EARNED HIS WAY ONTO SUCH LISTS.
AND EVERYTHING I'M DOING HERE IS TO MAKE SURE WHAT HAPPENED WITH BRUCE NEVER HAPPENS AGAIN.
WOW, WHAT A MESS. THE SUPER WAS RUNNING A HOMEMADE GAS LINE TO AN ILLEGALLY SUB-DIVIDED APARTMENT. CODE VIOLATIONS EVERYWHERE IN THAT PLACE.
THE INSPECTOR SAID IT WAS A DISASTER WAITING TO HAPPEN. THERE WERE LITTLE KIDS LIVING THERE...
AND NOW THEY GET THE CHANCE TO GROW UP. GREAT JOB, GUYS. THIS IS WHY WE DO WHAT WE DO.
WOULDN'T YOU AGREE, T'CHALLA?
I WOULD.
MAY ALL OUR MISSIONS GO AS WELL.

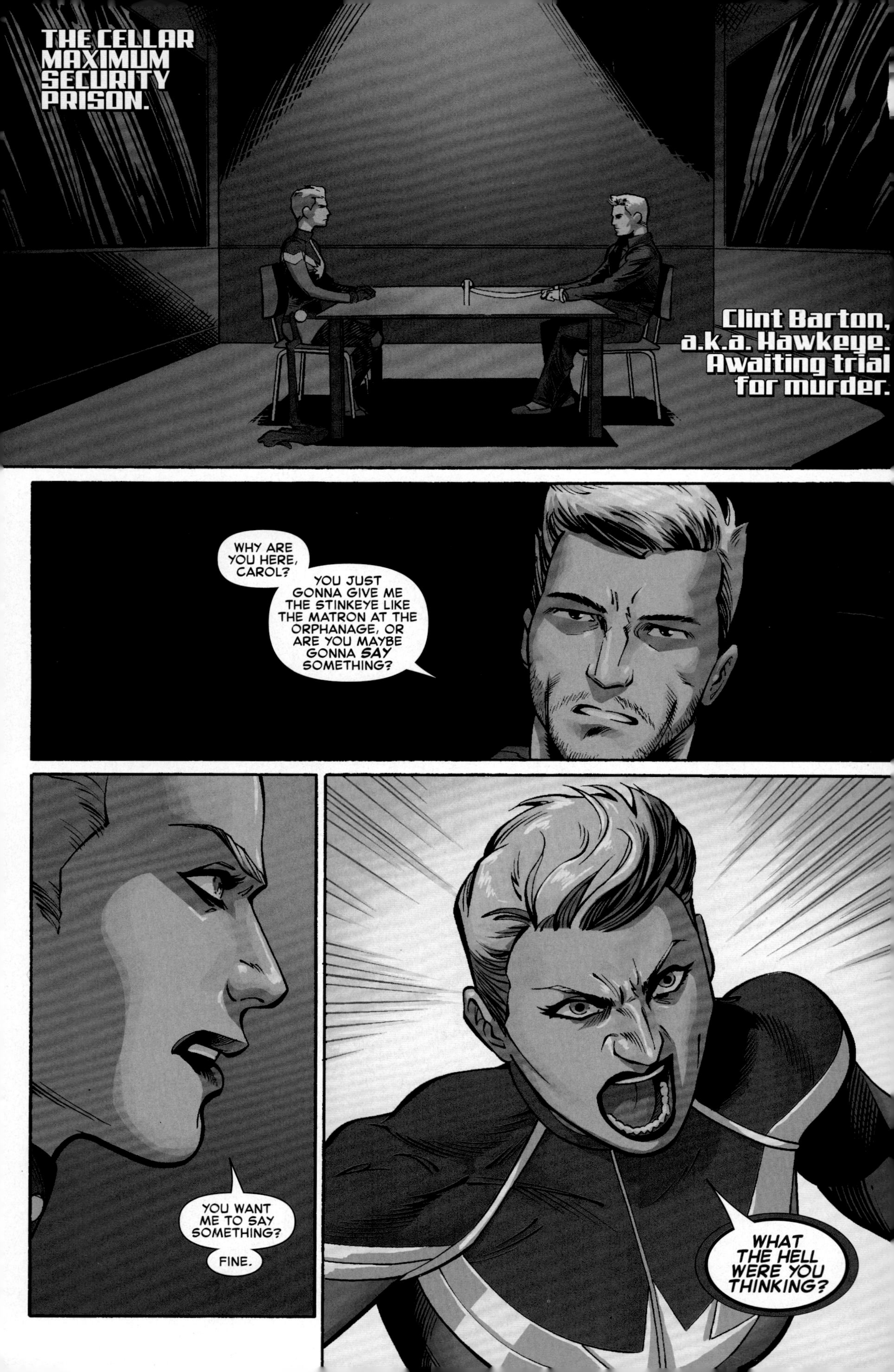
THE CELLAR MAXIMUM SECURITY PRISON.
Clint Barton, a.k.a. Hawkeye. Awaiting trial for murder.
WHY ARE YOU HERE, CAROL?
YOU JUST GONNA GIVE ME THE STINKEYE LIKE THE MATRON AT THE ORPHANAGE, OR ARE YOU MAYBE GONNA *SAY* SOMETHING?
YOU WANT ME TO SAY SOMETHING?
FINE.
WHAT THE HELL WERE YOU THINKING?

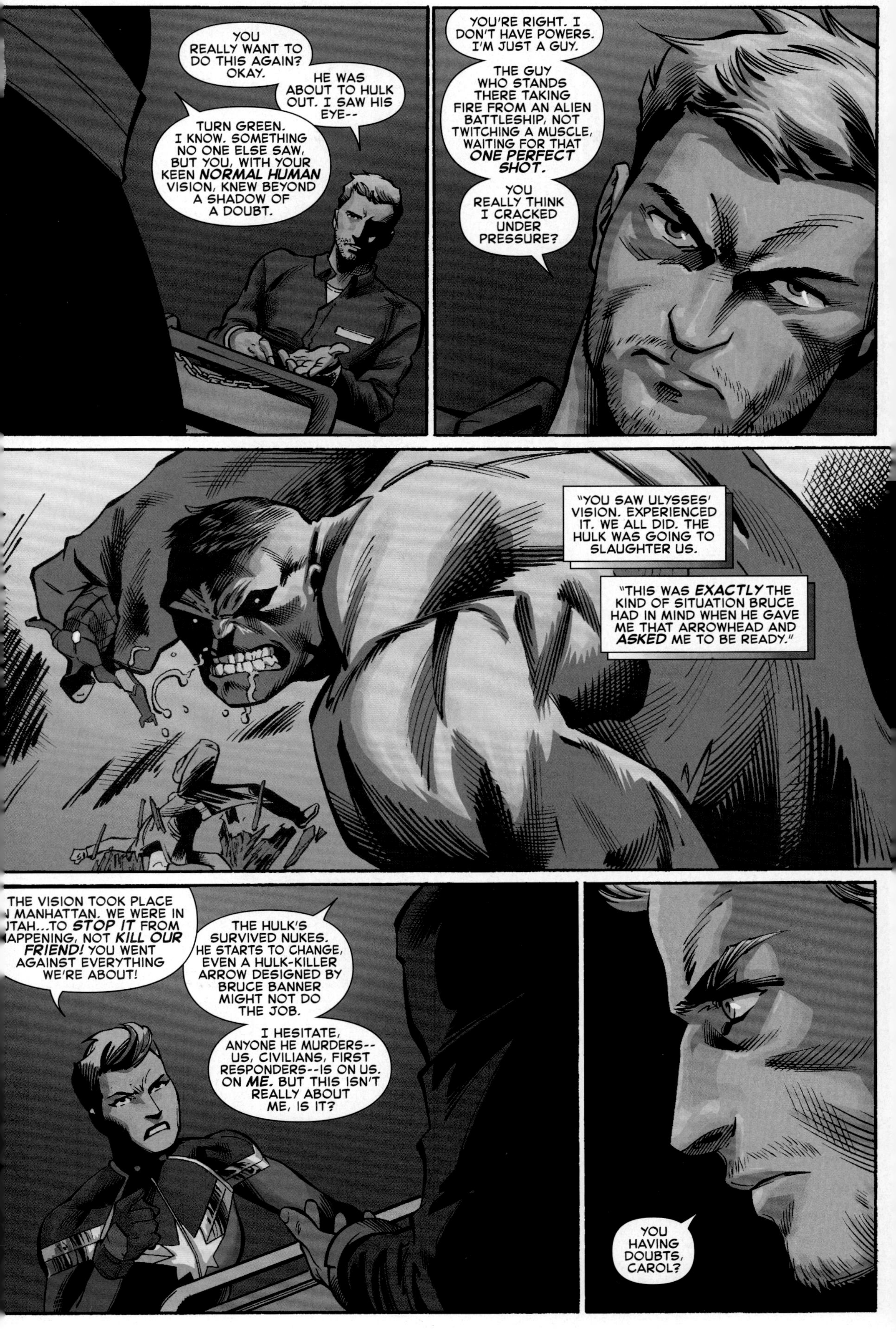
YOU REALLY WANT TO DO THIS AGAIN? OKAY.
HE WAS ABOUT TO HULK OUT. I SAW HIS EYE--
TURN GREEN. I KNOW. SOMETHING NO ONE ELSE SAW, BUT YOU, WITH YOUR KEEN NORMAL HUMAN VISION, KNEW BEYOND A SHADOW OF A DOUBT.
YOU'RE RIGHT. I DON'T HAVE POWERS. I'M JUST A GUY.
THE GUY WHO STANDS THERE TAKING FIRE FROM AN ALIEN BATTLESHIP, NOT TWITCHING A MUSCLE, WAITING FOR THAT ONE PERFECT SHOT.
YOU REALLY THINK I CRACKED UNDER PRESSURE?
"YOU SAW ULYSSES' VISION. EXPERIENCED IT. WE ALL DID. THE HULK WAS GOING TO SLAUGHTER US.
"THIS WAS EXACTLY THE KIND OF SITUATION BRUCE HAD IN MIND WHEN HE GAVE ME THAT ARROWHEAD AND ASKED ME TO BE READY."
THE VISION TOOK PLACE N MANHATTAN. WE WERE IN UTAH...TO STOP IT FROM APPENING, NOT KILL OUR FRIEND! YOU WENT AGAINST EVERYTHING WE'RE ABOUT!
THE HULK'S SURVIVED NUKES. HE STARTS TO CHANGE, EVEN A HULK-KILLER ARROW DESIGNED BY BRUCE BANNER MIGHT NOT DO THE JOB.
I HESITATE, ANYONE HE MURDERS-- US, CIVILIANS, FIRST RESPONDERS--IS ON US. ON ME. BUT THIS ISN'T REALLY ABOUT ME, IS IT?
YOU HAVING DOUBTS, CAROL?

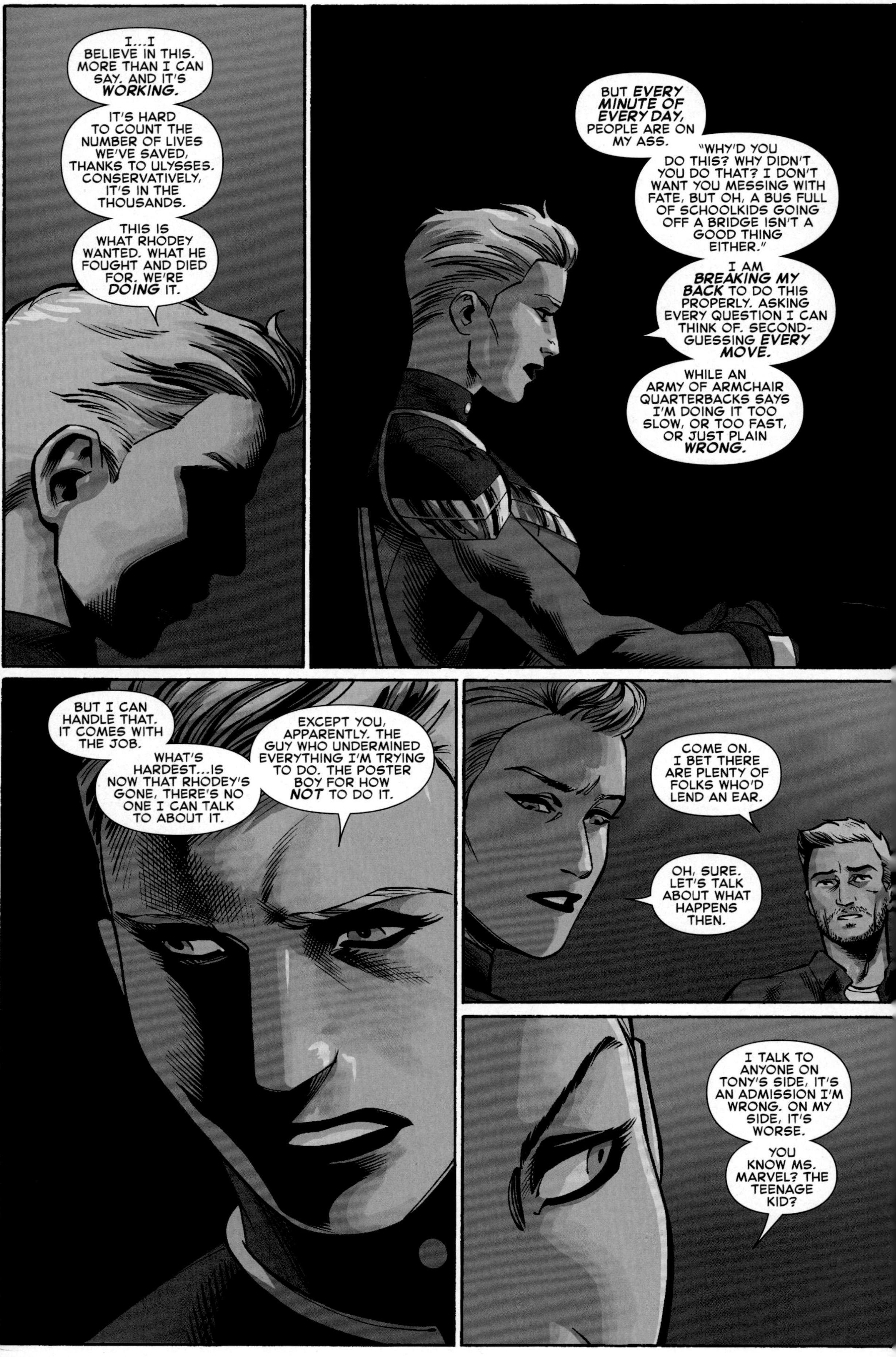
I...I BELIEVE IN THIS. MORE THAN I CAN SAY. AND IT'S WORKING.
IT'S HARD TO COUNT THE NUMBER OF LIVES WE'VE SAVED, THANKS TO ULYSSES. CONSERVATIVELY, IT'S IN THE THOUSANDS.
THIS IS WHAT RHODEY WANTED. WHAT HE FOUGHT AND DIED FOR. WE'RE DOING IT.
BUT EVERY MINUTE OF EVERY DAY, PEOPLE ARE ON MY ASS.
"WHY'D YOU DO THIS? WHY DIDN'T YOU DO THAT? I DON'T WANT YOU MESSING WITH FATE, BUT OH, A BUS FULL OF SCHOOLKIDS GOING OFF A BRIDGE ISN'T A GOOD THING EITHER."
I AM BREAKING MY BACK TO DO THIS PROPERLY. ASKING EVERY QUESTION I CAN THINK OF. SECOND-GUESSING EVERY MOVE.
WHILE AN ARMY OF ARMCHAIR QUARTERBACKS SAYS I'M DOING IT TOO SLOW, OR TOO FAST, OR JUST PLAIN WRONG.
BUT I CAN HANDLE THAT. IT COMES WITH THE JOB.
WHAT'S HARDEST...IS NOW THAT RHODEY'S GONE, THERE'S NO ONE I CAN TALK TO ABOUT IT.
EXCEPT YOU, APPARENTLY. THE GUY WHO UNDERMINED EVERYTHING I'M TRYING TO DO. THE POSTER BOY FOR HOW NOT TO DO IT.
COME ON. I BET THERE ARE PLENTY OF FOLKS WHO'D LEND AN EAR.
OH, SURE. LET'S TALK ABOUT WHAT HAPPENS THEN.
I TALK TO ANYONE ON TONY'S SIDE, IT'S AN ADMISSION I'M WRONG. ON MY SIDE, IT'S WORSE.
YOU KNOW MS. MARVEL? THE TEENAGE KID?

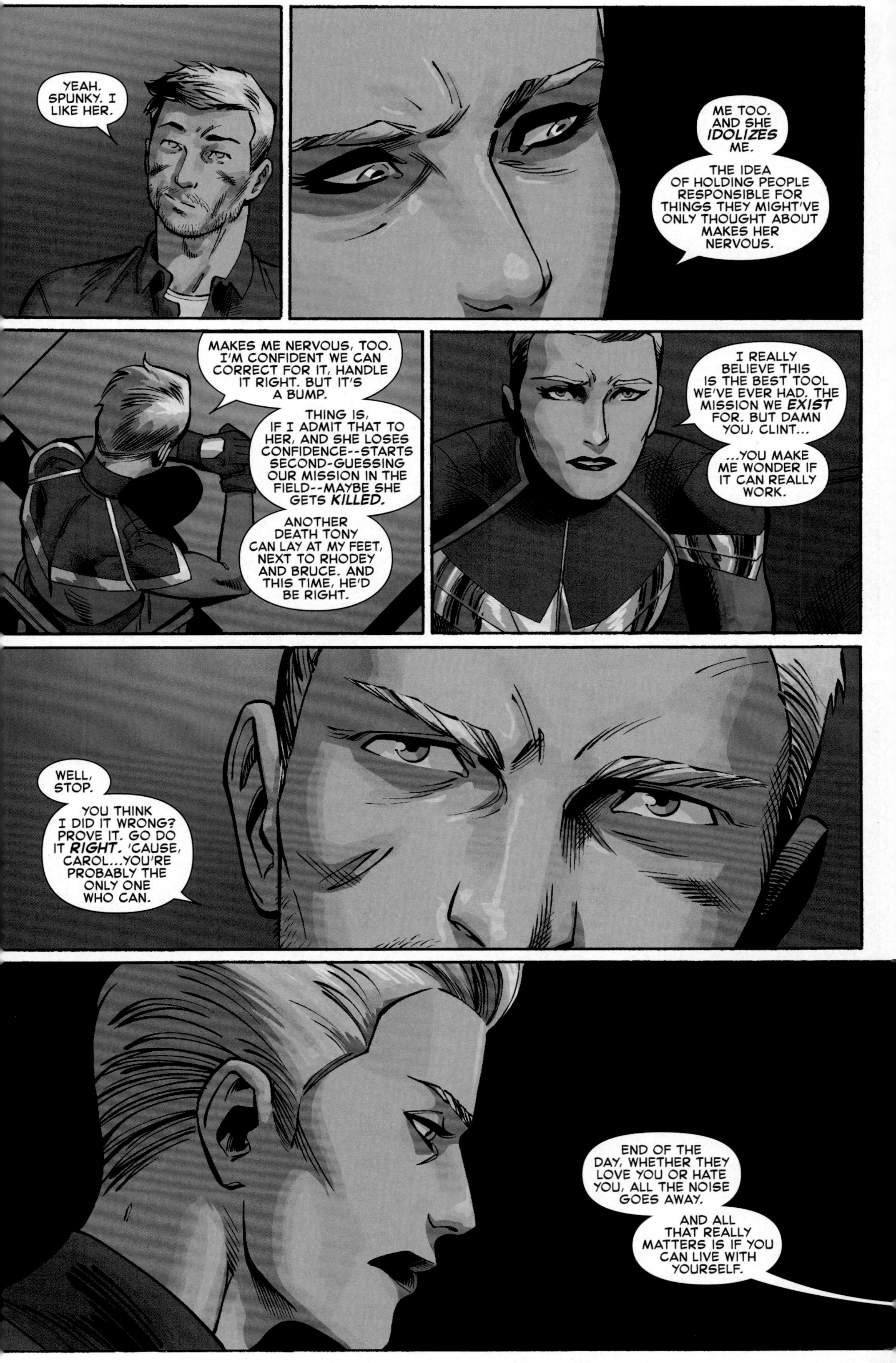
YEAH. SPUNKY. I LIKE HER.
ME TOO. AND SHE *IDOLIZES* ME.
THE IDEA OF HOLDING PEOPLE RESPONSIBLE FOR THINGS THEY MIGHT'VE ONLY THOUGHT ABOUT MAKES HER NERVOUS.
MAKES ME NERVOUS, TOO. I'M CONFIDENT WE CAN CORRECT FOR IT, HANDLE IT RIGHT. BUT IT'S A BUMP.
THING IS, IF I ADMIT THAT TO HER, AND SHE LOSES CONFIDENCE--STARTS SECOND-GUESSING OUR MISSION IN THE FIELD--MAYBE SHE GETS *KILLED.*
ANOTHER DEATH TONY CAN LAY AT MY FEET, NEXT TO RHODEY AND BRUCE. AND THIS TIME, HE'D BE RIGHT.
I REALLY BELIEVE THIS IS THE BEST TOOL WE'VE EVER HAD. THE MISSION WE *EXIST* FOR. BUT DAMN YOU, CLINT...
...YOU MAKE ME WONDER IF IT CAN REALLY WORK.
WELL, STOP.
YOU THINK I DID IT WRONG? PROVE IT. GO DO IT *RIGHT.* 'CAUSE, CAROL...YOU'RE PROBABLY THE ONLY ONE WHO CAN.
END OF THE DAY, WHETHER THEY LOVE YOU OR HATE YOU, ALL THE NOISE GOES AWAY.
AND ALL THAT REALLY MATTERS IS IF YOU CAN LIVE WITH YOURSELF.

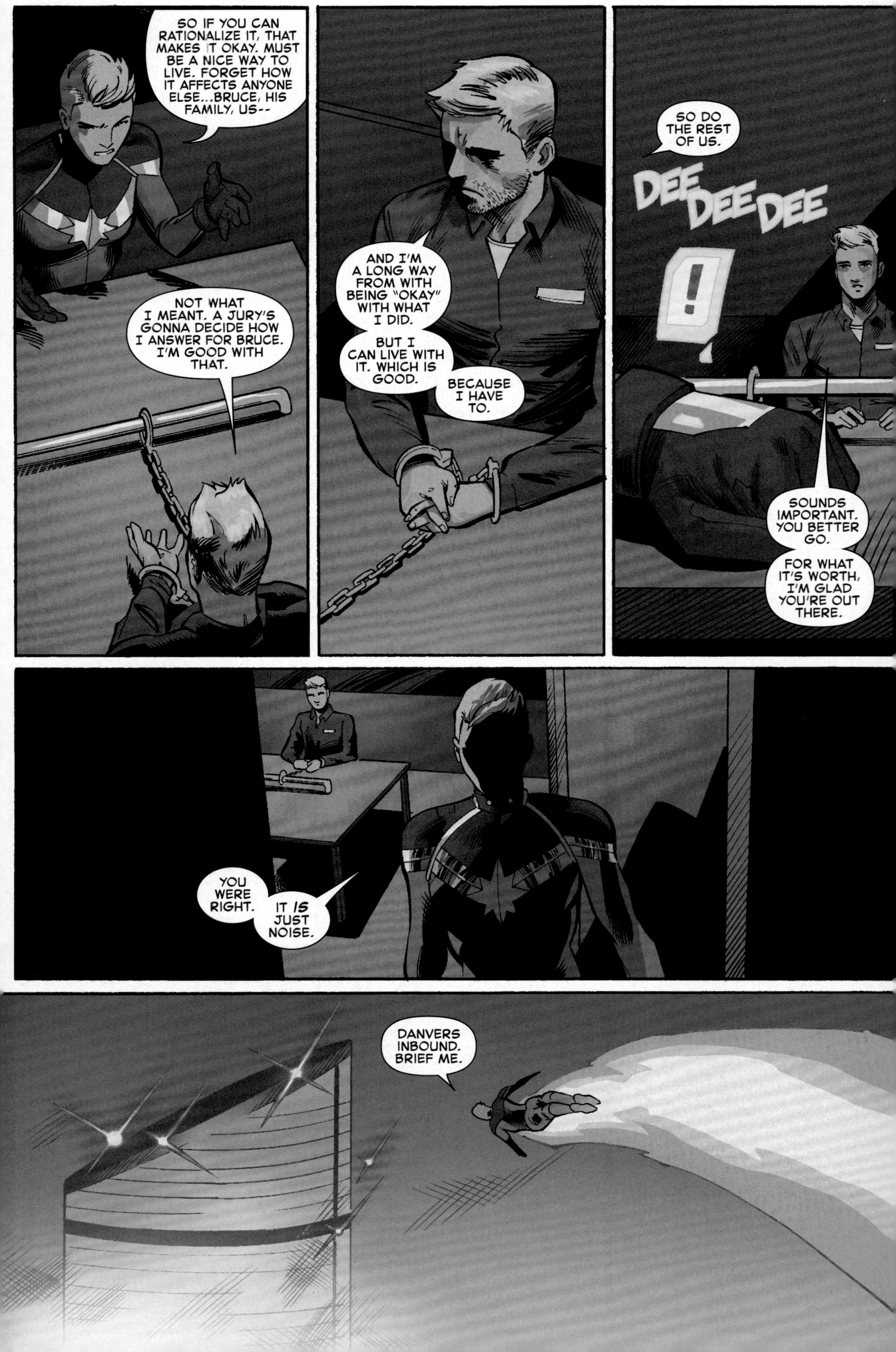
SO IF YOU CAN RATIONALIZE IT, THAT MAKES IT OKAY. MUST BE A NICE WAY TO LIVE. FORGET HOW IT AFFECTS ANYONE ELSE...BRUCE, HIS FAMILY, US--
NOT WHAT I MEANT. A JURY'S GONNA DECIDE HOW I ANSWER FOR BRUCE. I'M GOOD WITH THAT.
AND I'M A LONG WAY FROM WITH BEING "OKAY" WITH WHAT I DID.
BUT I CAN LIVE WITH IT. WHICH IS GOOD.
BECAUSE I HAVE TO.
SO DO THE REST OF US.
DEE DEE DEE
!
SOUNDS IMPORTANT. YOU BETTER GO.
FOR WHAT IT'S WORTH, I'M GLAD YOU'RE OUT THERE.
YOU WERE RIGHT.
IT *IS* JUST NOISE.
DANVERS INBOUND. BRIEF ME.

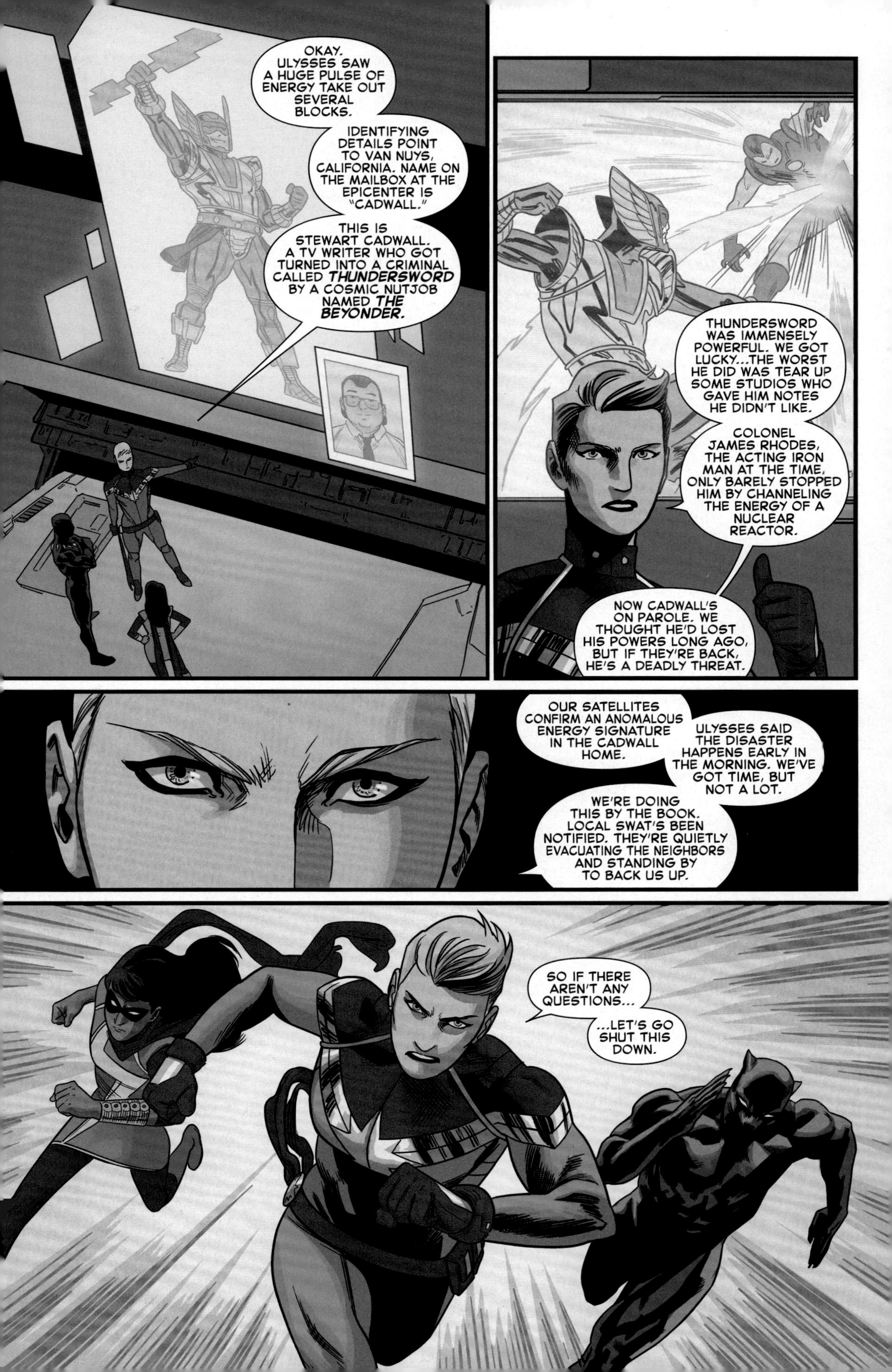
OKAY. ULYSSES SAW A HUGE PULSE OF ENERGY TAKE OUT SEVERAL BLOCKS.
IDENTIFYING DETAILS POINT TO VAN NUYS, CALIFORNIA. NAME ON THE MAILBOX AT THE EPICENTER IS "CADWALL."
THIS IS STEWART CADWALL. A TV WRITER WHO GOT TURNED INTO A CRIMINAL CALLED THUNDERSWORD BY A COSMIC NUTJOB NAMED THE BEYONDER.
THUNDERSWORD WAS IMMENSELY POWERFUL. WE GOT LUCKY...THE WORST HE DID WAS TEAR UP SOME STUDIOS WHO GAVE HIM NOTES HE DIDN'T LIKE.
COLONEL JAMES RHODES, THE ACTING IRON MAN AT THE TIME, ONLY BARELY STOPPED HIM BY CHANNELING THE ENERGY OF A NUCLEAR REACTOR.
NOW CADWALL'S ON PAROLE. WE THOUGHT HE'D LOST HIS POWERS LONG AGO, BUT IF THEY'RE BACK, HE'S A DEADLY THREAT.
OUR SATELLITES CONFIRM AN ANOMALOUS ENERGY SIGNATURE IN THE CADWALL HOME.
ULYSSES SAID THE DISASTER HAPPENS EARLY IN THE MORNING. WE'VE GOT TIME, BUT NOT A LOT.
WE'RE DOING THIS BY THE BOOK. LOCAL SWAT'S BEEN NOTIFIED. THEY'RE QUIETLY EVACUATING THE NEIGHBORS AND STANDING BY TO BACK US UP.
SO IF THERE AREN'T ANY QUESTIONS...
...LET'S GO SHUT THIS DOWN.

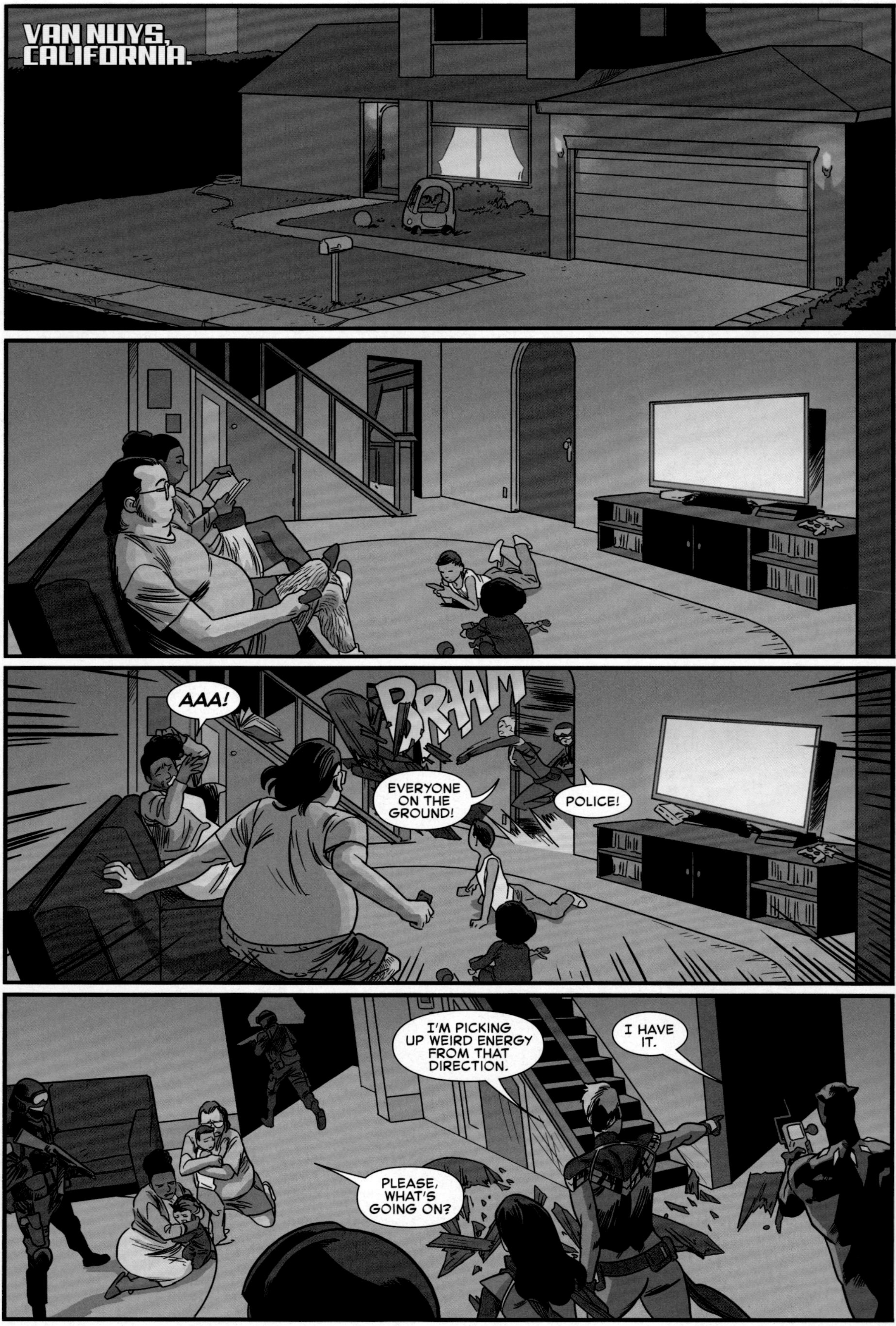

VAN NUYS, CALIFORNIA.
AAA!
BRAAM
EVERYONE ON THE GROUND!
POLICE!
I'M PICKING UP WEIRD ENERGY FROM THAT DIRECTION.
I HAVE IT.
PLEASE, WHAT'S GOING ON?

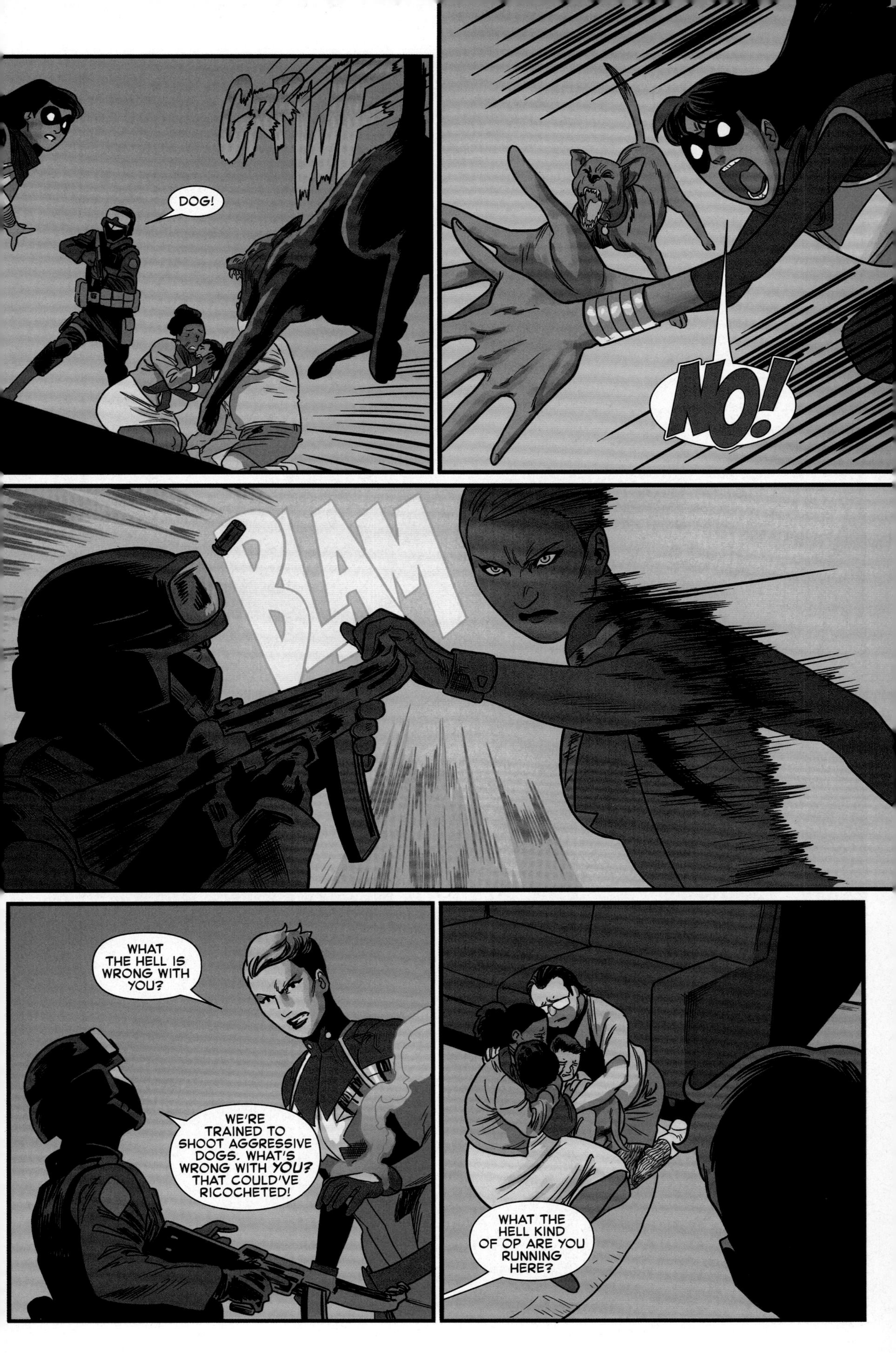
CRRWF
DOG!
NO!
BLAM
WHAT THE HELL IS WRONG WITH YOU?
WE'RE TRAINED TO SHOOT AGGRESSIVE DOGS. WHAT'S WRONG WITH *YOU?* THAT COULD'VE RICOCHETED!
WHAT THE HELL KIND OF OP ARE YOU RUNNING HERE?

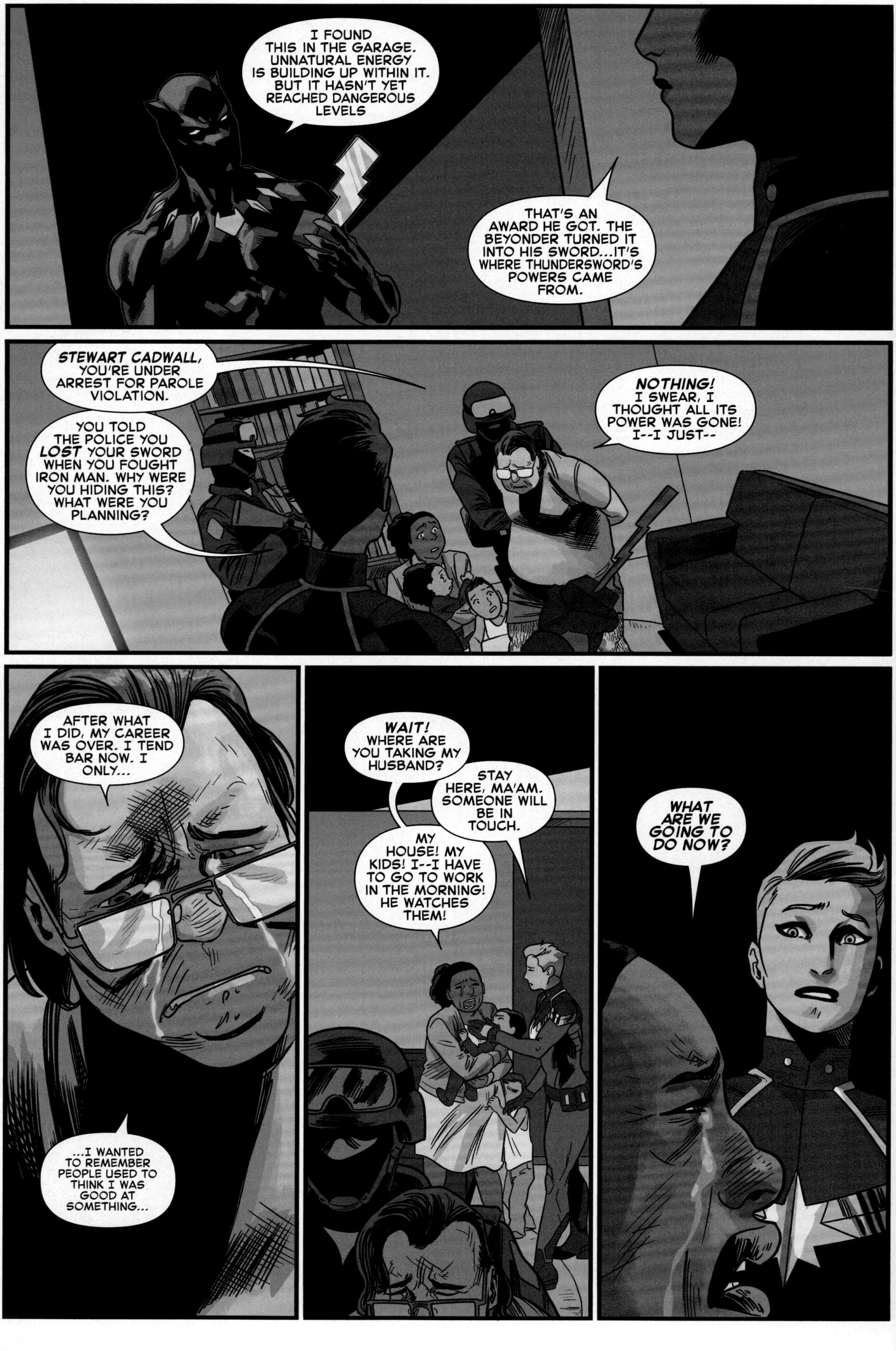
I FOUND THIS IN THE GARAGE. UNNATURAL ENERGY IS BUILDING UP WITHIN IT. BUT IT HASN'T YET REACHED DANGEROUS LEVELS
THAT'S AN AWARD HE GOT. THE BEYONDER TURNED IT INTO HIS SWORD...IT'S WHERE THUNDERSWORD'S POWERS CAME FROM.
STEWART CADWALL, YOU'RE UNDER ARREST FOR PAROLE VIOLATION.
YOU TOLD THE POLICE YOU LOST YOUR SWORD WHEN YOU FOUGHT IRON MAN. WHY WERE YOU HIDING THIS? WHAT WERE YOU PLANNING?
NOTHING! I SWEAR, I THOUGHT ALL ITS POWER WAS GONE! I--I JUST--
AFTER WHAT I DID, MY CAREER WAS OVER. I TEND BAR NOW. I ONLY...
...I WANTED TO REMEMBER PEOPLE USED TO THINK I WAS GOOD AT SOMETHING...
WAIT! WHERE ARE YOU TAKING MY HUSBAND?
STAY HERE, MA'AM. SOMEONE WILL BE IN TOUCH.
MY HOUSE! MY KIDS! I--I HAVE TO GO TO WORK IN THE MORNING! HE WATCHES THEM!
WHAT ARE WE GOING TO DO NOW?

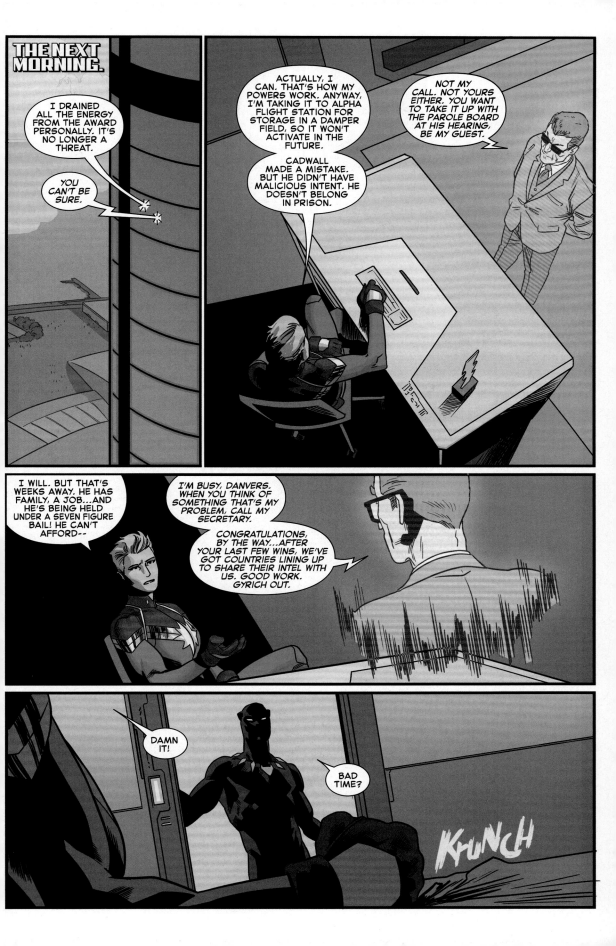

I DRAINED ALL THE ENERGY FROM THE AWARD PERSONALLY. IT'S NO LONGER A THREAT.

YOU CAN'T BE SURE.

ACTUALLY, I CAN. THAT'S HOW MY POWERS WORK. ANYWAY, I'M TAKING IT TO ALPHA FLIGHT STATION FOR STORAGE IN A DAMPER FIELD, SO IT WON'T ACTIVATE IN THE FUTURE.

CADWALL MADE A MISTAKE. BUT HE DIDN'T HAVE MALICIOUS INTENT. HE DOESN'T BELONG IN PRISON.

NOT MY CALL. NOT YOURS EITHER. YOU WANT TO TAKE IT UP WITH THE PAROLE BOARD AT HIS HEARING, BE MY GUEST.

I WILL. BUT THAT'S WEEKS AWAY. HE HAS FAMILY, A JOB...AND HE'S BEING HELD UNDER A SEVEN FIGURE BAIL! HE CAN'T AFFORD--

I'M BUSY, DANVERS. WHEN YOU THINK OF SOMETHING THAT'S MY PROBLEM, CALL MY SECRETARY.

CONGRATULATIONS, BY THE WAY...AFTER YOUR LAST FEW WINS, WE'VE GOT COUNTRIES LINING UP TO SHARE THEIR INTEL WITH US. GOOD WORK. GYRICH OUT.

DAMN IT!

BAD TIME?

KRUNCH

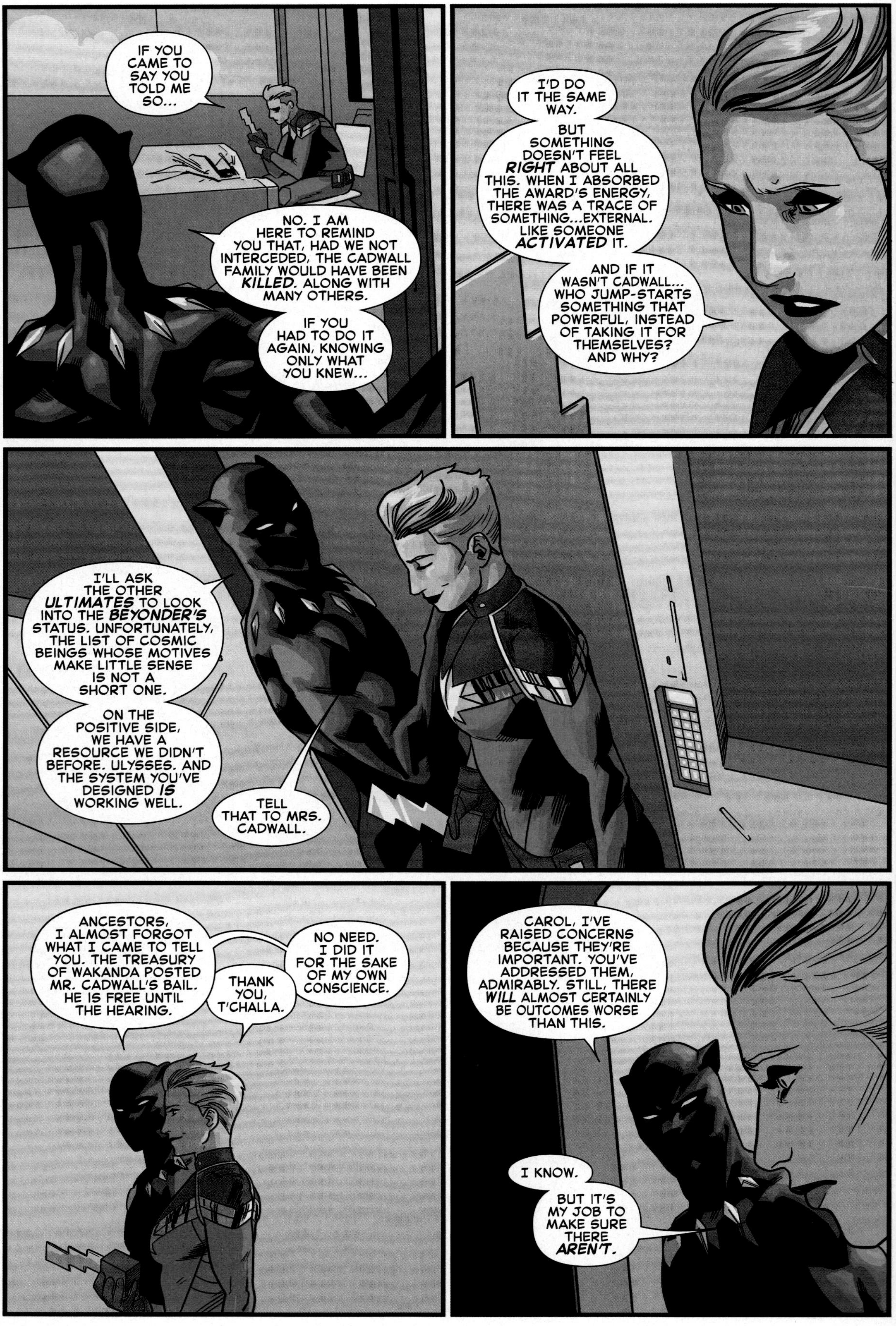
IF YOU CAME TO SAY YOU TOLD ME SO...
NO. I AM HERE TO REMIND YOU THAT, HAD WE NOT INTERCEDED, THE CADWALL FAMILY WOULD HAVE BEEN KILLED. ALONG WITH MANY OTHERS.
IF YOU HAD TO DO IT AGAIN, KNOWING ONLY WHAT YOU KNEW...
I'D DO IT THE SAME WAY.
BUT SOMETHING DOESN'T FEEL RIGHT ABOUT ALL THIS. WHEN I ABSORBED THE AWARD'S ENERGY, THERE WAS A TRACE OF SOMETHING...EXTERNAL. LIKE SOMEONE ACTIVATED IT.
AND IF IT WASN'T CADWALL... WHO JUMP-STARTS SOMETHING THAT POWERFUL, INSTEAD OF TAKING IT FOR THEMSELVES? AND WHY?
I'LL ASK THE OTHER ULTIMATES TO LOOK INTO THE BEYONDER'S STATUS. UNFORTUNATELY, THE LIST OF COSMIC BEINGS WHOSE MOTIVES MAKE LITTLE SENSE IS NOT A SHORT ONE.
ON THE POSITIVE SIDE, WE HAVE A RESOURCE WE DIDN'T BEFORE. ULYSSES. AND THE SYSTEM YOU'VE DESIGNED IS WORKING WELL.
TELL THAT TO MRS. CADWALL.
ANCESTORS, I ALMOST FORGOT WHAT I CAME TO TELL YOU. THE TREASURY OF WAKANDA POSTED MR. CADWALL'S BAIL. HE IS FREE UNTIL THE HEARING.
THANK YOU, T'CHALLA.
NO NEED. I DID IT FOR THE SAKE OF MY OWN CONSCIENCE.
CAROL, I'VE RAISED CONCERNS BECAUSE THEY'RE IMPORTANT. YOU'VE ADDRESSED THEM, ADMIRABLY. STILL, THERE WILL ALMOST CERTAINLY BE OUTCOMES WORSE THAN THIS.
I KNOW.
BUT IT'S MY JOB TO MAKE SURE THERE AREN'T.

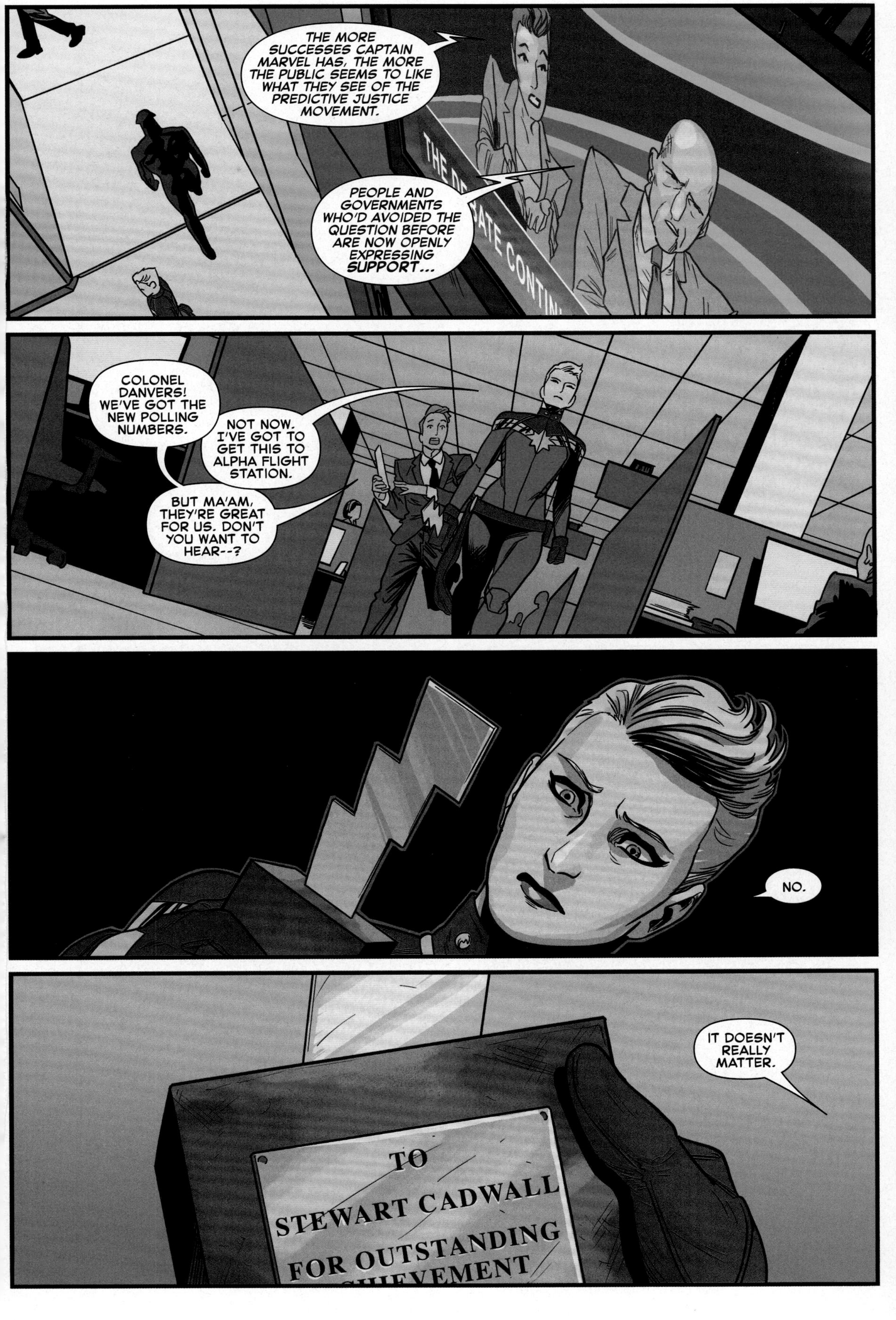
THE MORE SUCCESSES CAPTAIN MARVEL HAS, THE MORE THE PUBLIC SEEMS TO LIKE WHAT THEY SEE OF THE PREDICTIVE JUSTICE MOVEMENT.
PEOPLE AND GOVERNMENTS WHO'D AVOIDED THE QUESTION BEFORE ARE NOW OPENLY EXPRESSING **SUPPORT**...
COLONEL DANVERS! WE'VE GOT THE NEW POLLING NUMBERS.
NOT NOW. I'VE GOT TO GET THIS TO ALPHA FLIGHT STATION.
BUT MA'AM, THEY'RE GREAT FOR US. DON'T YOU WANT TO HEAR--?
NO.
IT DOESN'T REALLY MATTER.
TO
STEWART CADWALL
FOR OUTSTANDING

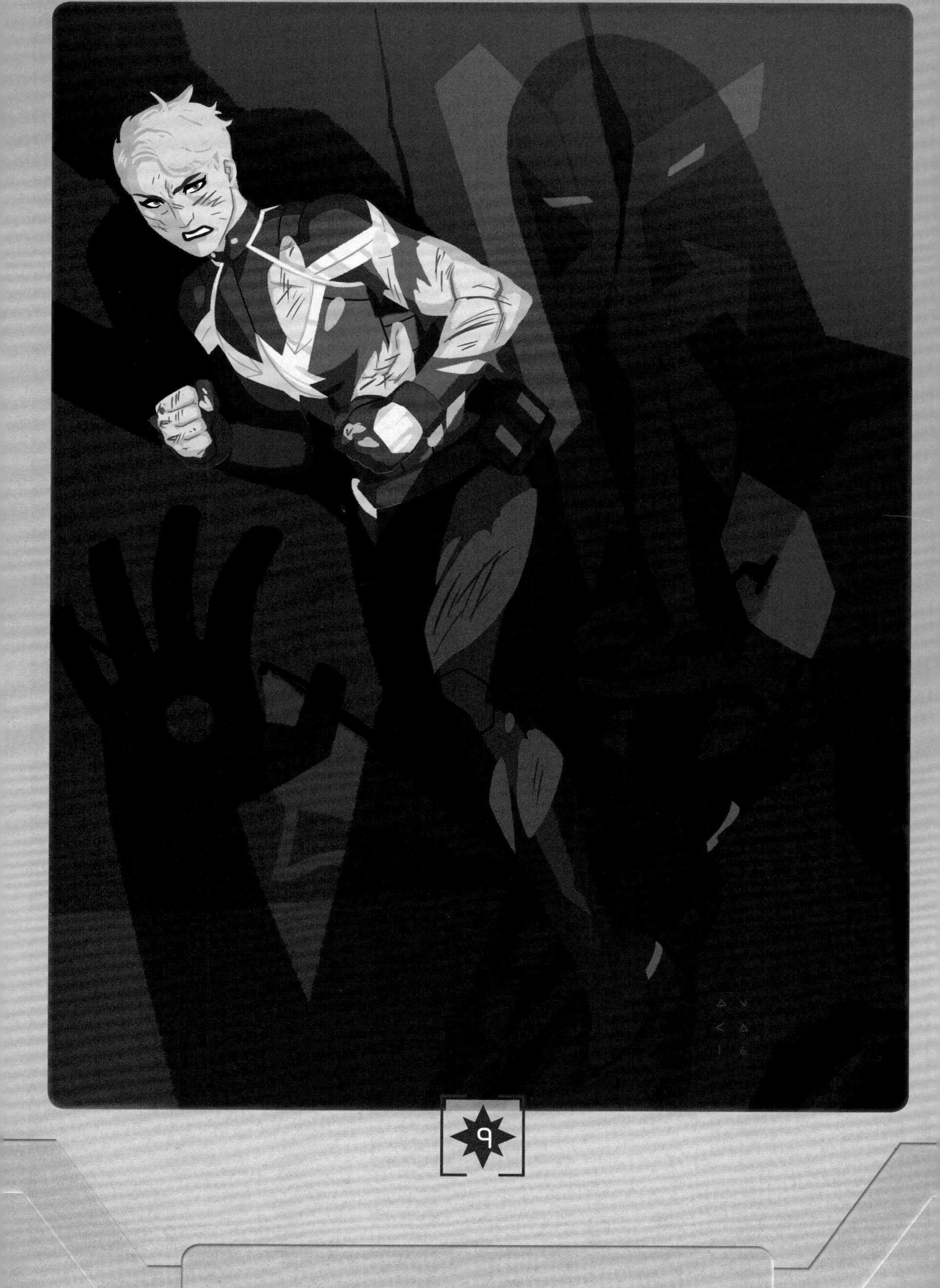

9

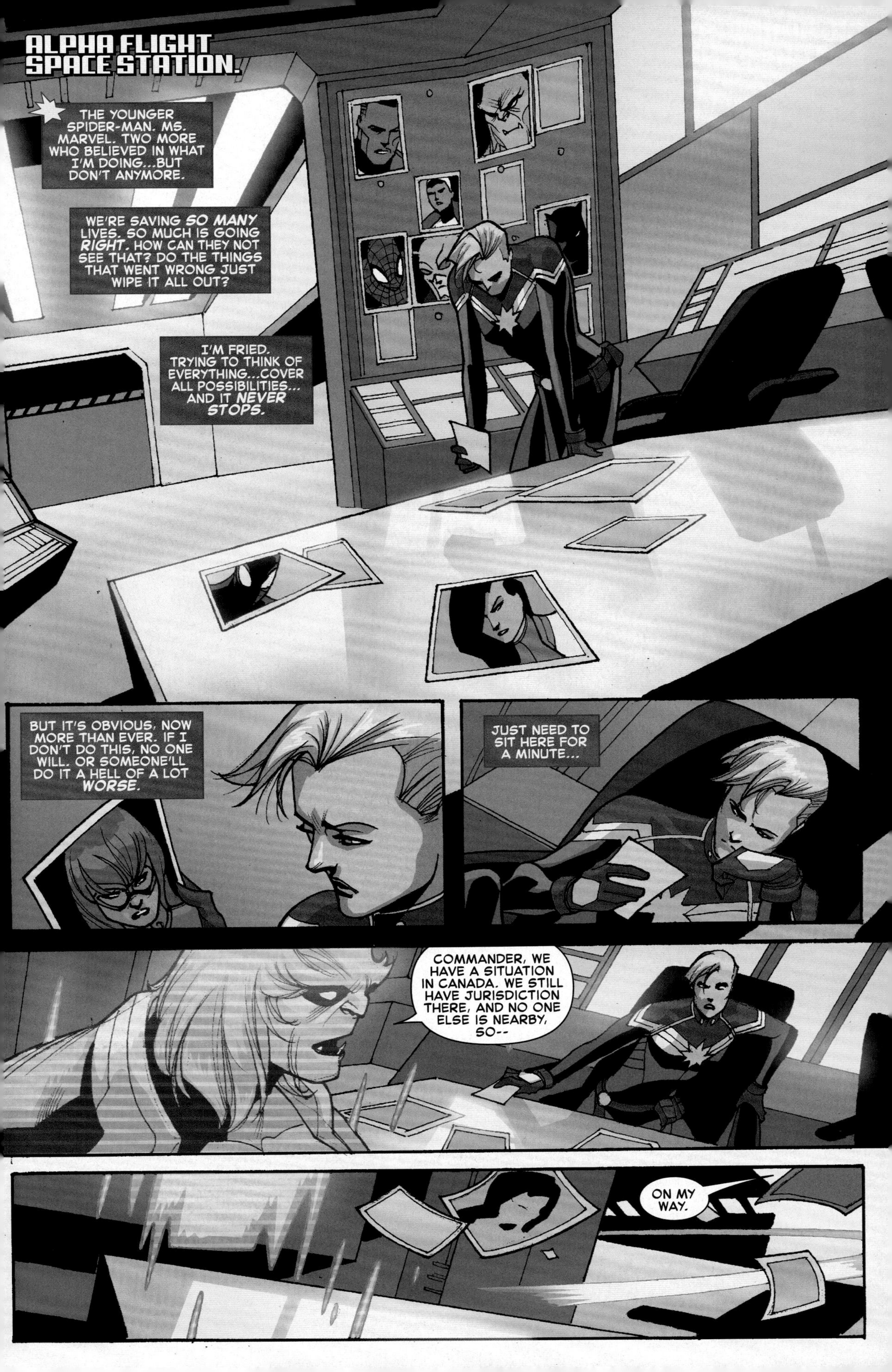
ALPHA FLIGHT SPACE STATION.
THE YOUNGER SPIDER-MAN. MS. MARVEL. TWO MORE WHO BELIEVED IN WHAT I'M DOING...BUT DON'T ANYMORE.
WE'RE SAVING SO MANY LIVES. SO MUCH IS GOING RIGHT. HOW CAN THEY NOT SEE THAT? DO THE THINGS THAT WENT WRONG JUST WIPE IT ALL OUT?
I'M FRIED. TRYING TO THINK OF EVERYTHING...COVER ALL POSSIBILITIES... AND IT NEVER STOPS.
BUT IT'S OBVIOUS, NOW MORE THAN EVER. IF I DON'T DO THIS, NO ONE WILL. OR SOMEONE'LL DO IT A HELL OF A LOT WORSE.
JUST NEED TO SIT HERE FOR A MINUTE...
COMMANDER, WE HAVE A SITUATION IN CANADA. WE STILL HAVE JURISDICTION THERE, AND NO ONE ELSE IS NEARBY, SO--
ON MY WAY.

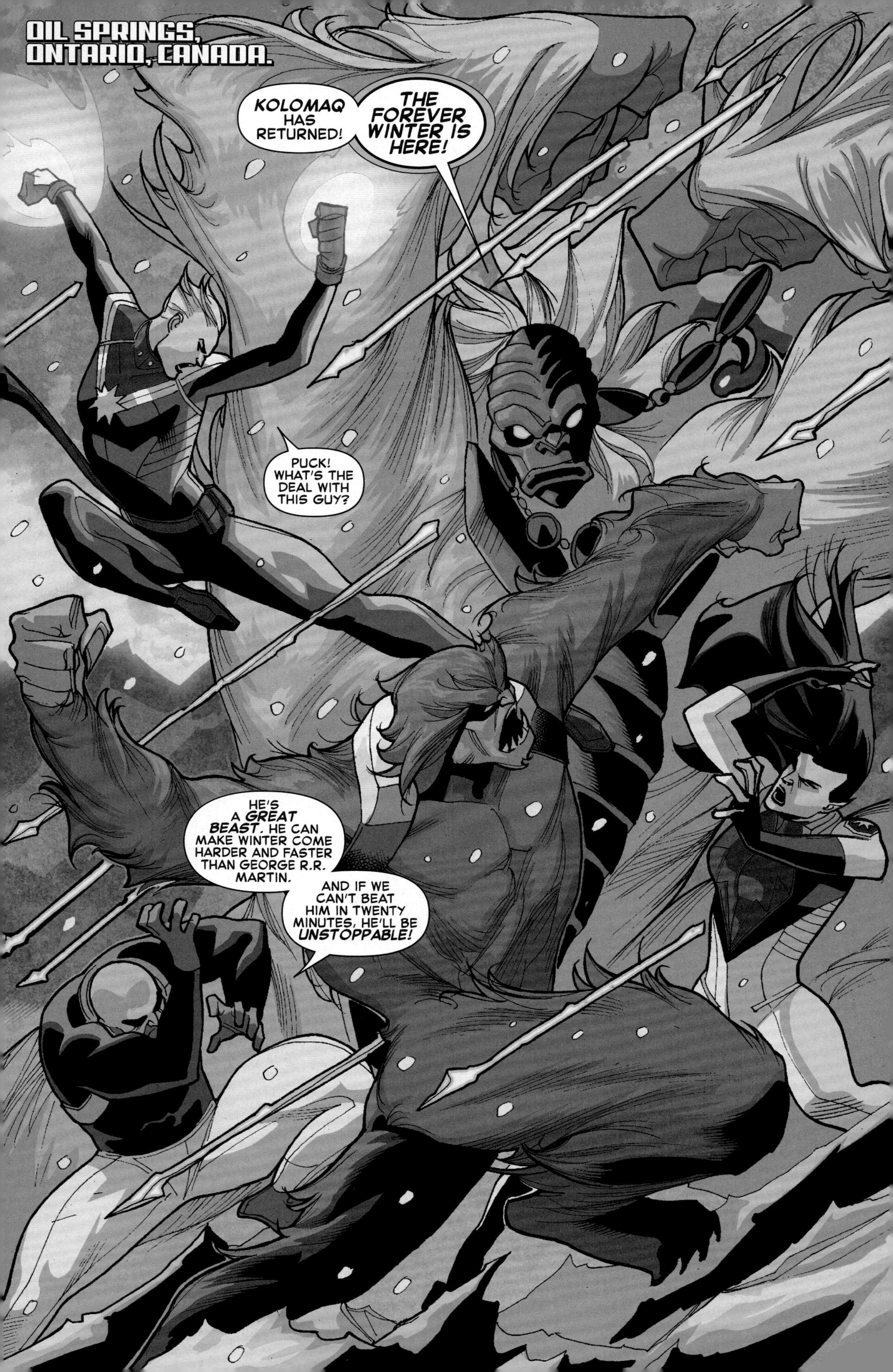
OIL SPRINGS, ONTARIO, CANADA.
KOLOMAQ HAS RETURNED!
THE FOREVER WINTER IS HERE!
PUCK! WHAT'S THE DEAL WITH THIS GUY?
HE'S A GREAT BEAST. HE CAN MAKE WINTER COME HARDER AND FASTER THAN GEORGE R.R. MARTIN.
AND IF WE CAN'T BEAT HIM IN TWENTY MINUTES, HE'LL BE UNSTOPPABLE!

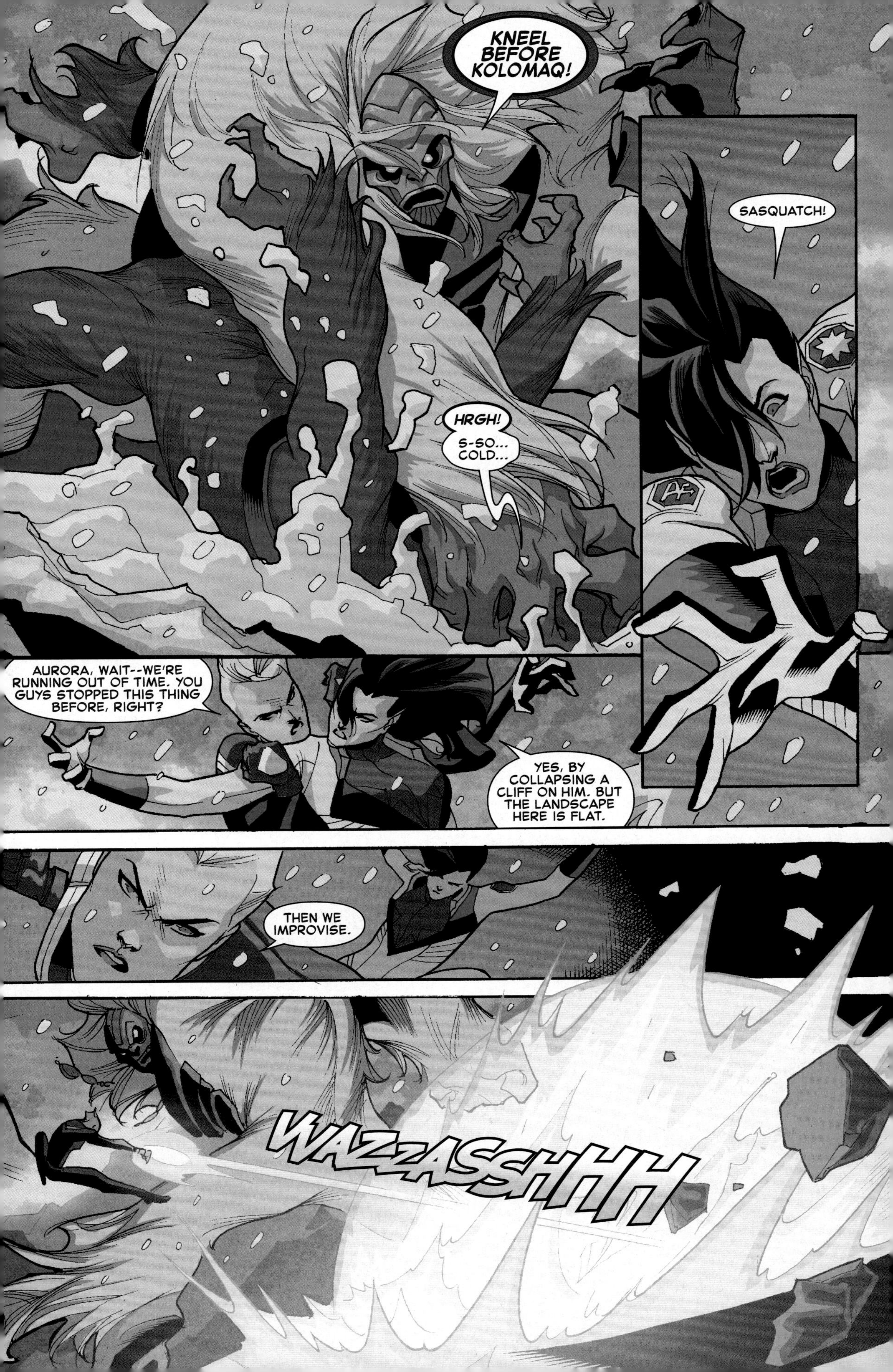
KNEEL BEFORE KOLOMAQ!
SASQUATCH!
HRGH!
S-SO... COLD...
AURORA, WAIT--WE'RE RUNNING OUT OF TIME. YOU GUYS STOPPED THIS THING BEFORE, RIGHT?
YES, BY COLLAPSING A CLIFF ON HIM. BUT THE LANDSCAPE HERE IS FLAT.
THEN WE IMPROVISE.
WAZZASSHHH

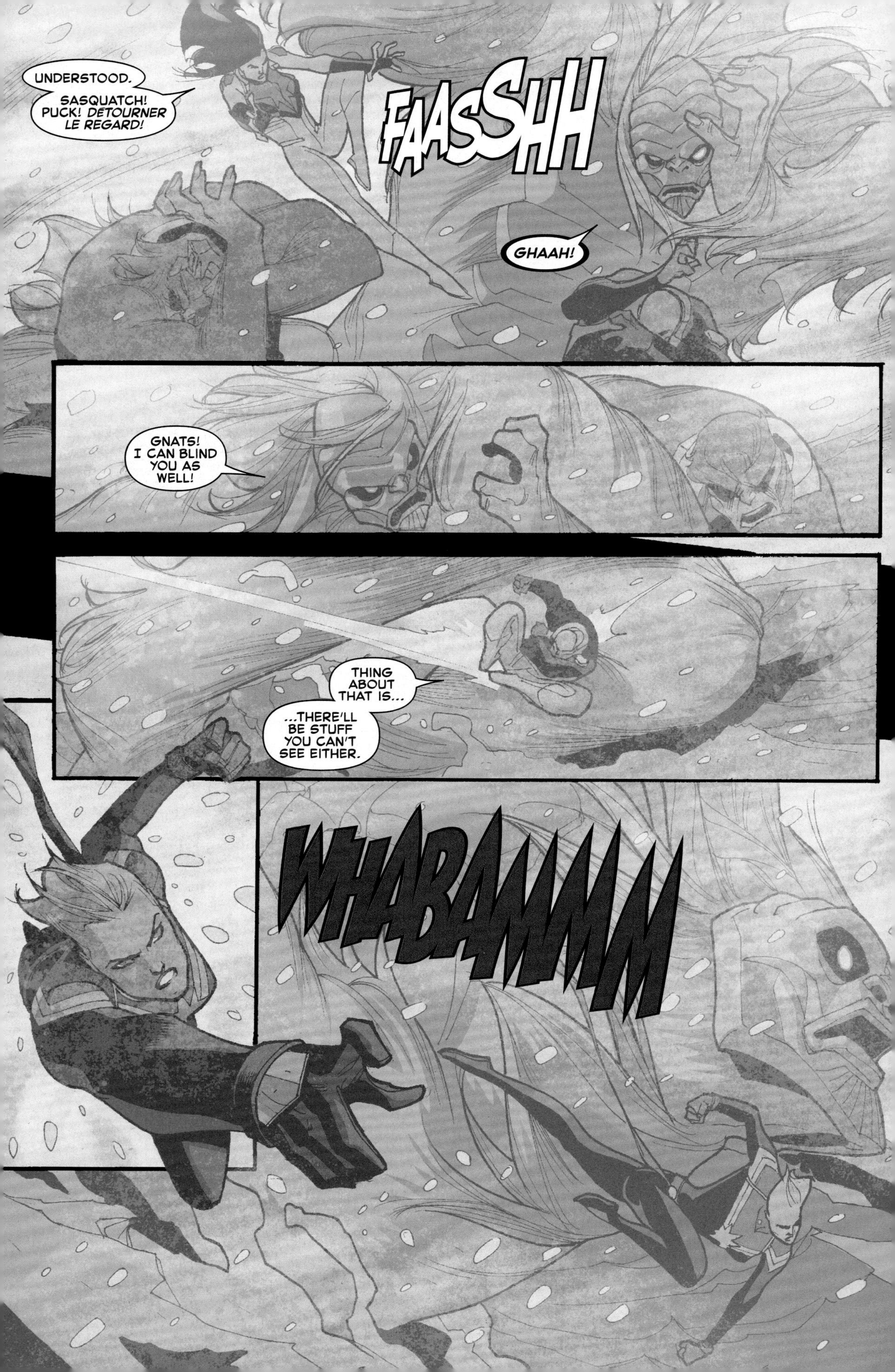
UNDERSTOOD.
SASQUATCH! PUCK! DÉTOURNER LE REGARD!
FAASSHH
GHAAH!
GNATS! I CAN BLIND YOU AS WELL!
THING ABOUT THAT IS...
...THERE'LL BE STUFF YOU CAN'T SEE EITHER.
WHABAMMM

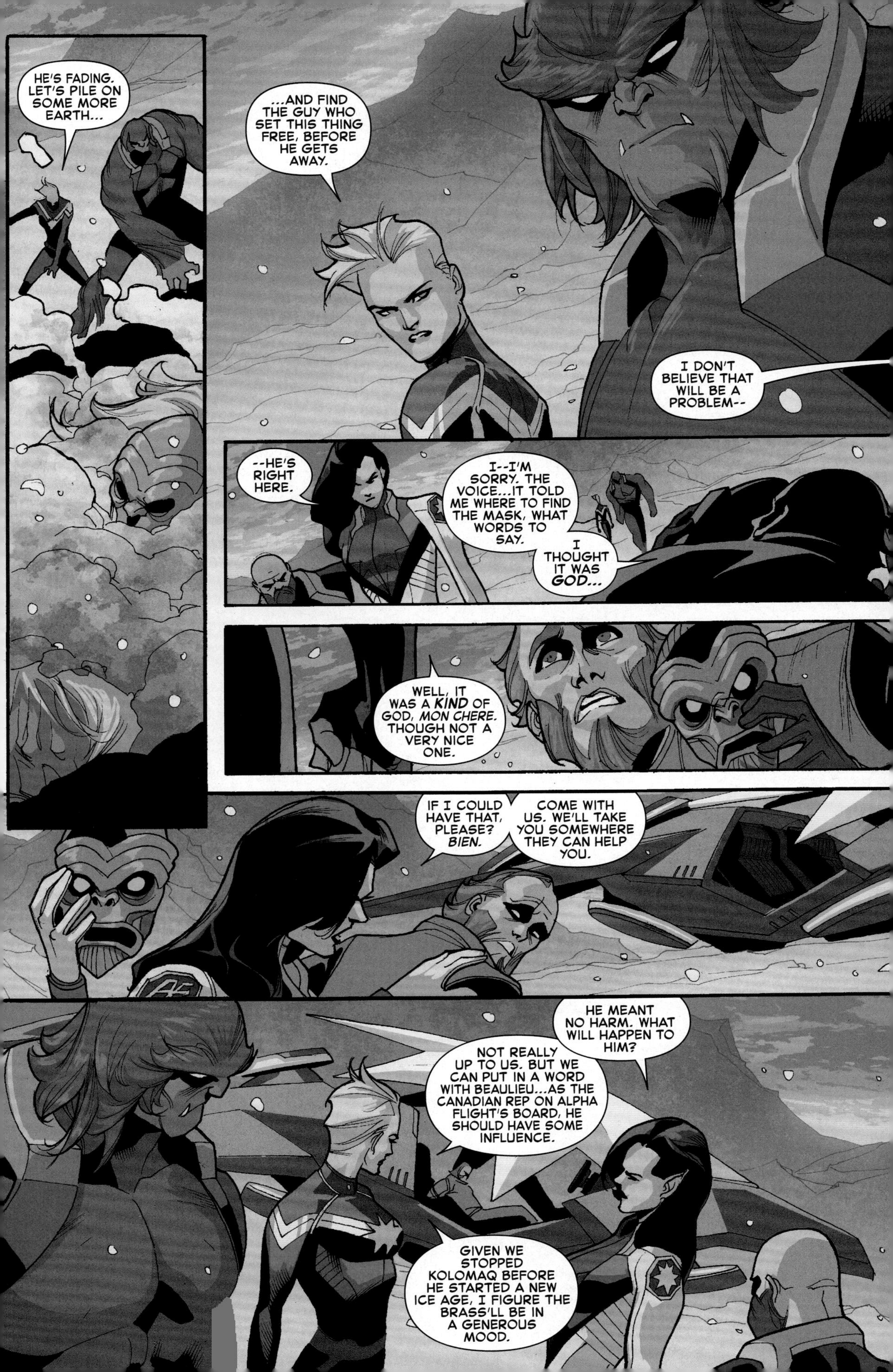
HE'S FADING. LET'S PILE ON SOME MORE EARTH...
...AND FIND THE GUY WHO SET THIS THING FREE, BEFORE HE GETS AWAY.
I DON'T BELIEVE THAT WILL BE A PROBLEM--
--HE'S RIGHT HERE.
I--I'M SORRY. THE VOICE...IT TOLD ME WHERE TO FIND THE MASK, WHAT WORDS TO SAY.
I THOUGHT IT WAS GOD...
WELL, IT WAS A KIND OF GOD, MON CHERE. THOUGH NOT A VERY NICE ONE.
IF I COULD HAVE THAT, PLEASE? BIEN.
COME WITH US. WE'LL TAKE YOU SOMEWHERE THEY CAN HELP YOU.
HE MEANT NO HARM. WHAT WILL HAPPEN TO HIM?
NOT REALLY UP TO US. BUT WE CAN PUT IN A WORD WITH BEAULIEU...AS THE CANADIAN REP ON ALPHA FLIGHT'S BOARD, HE SHOULD HAVE SOME INFLUENCE.
GIVEN WE STOPPED KOLOMAQ BEFORE HE STARTED A NEW ICE AGE, I FIGURE THE BRASS'LL BE IN A GENEROUS MOOD.

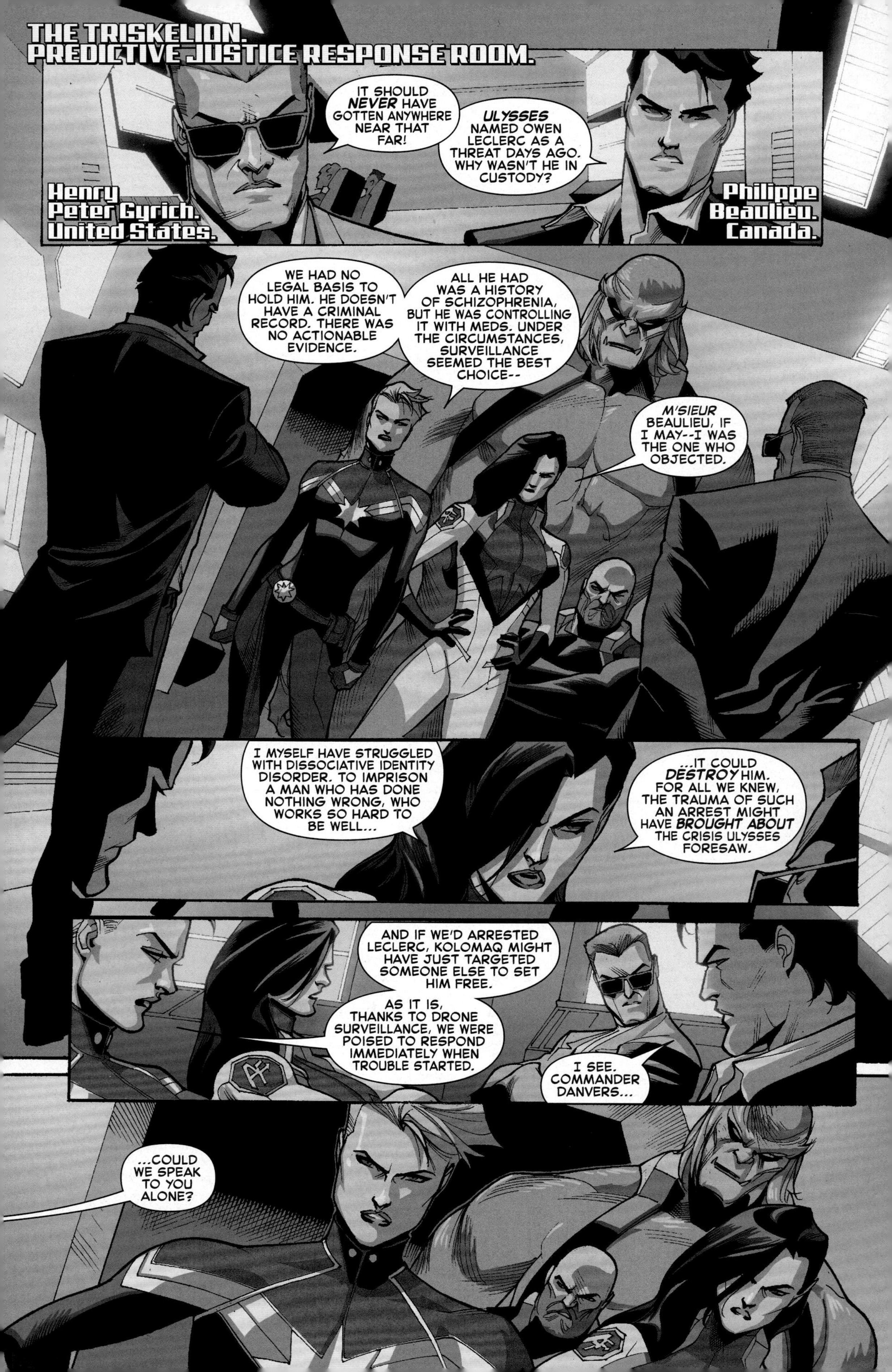
THE TRISKELION.
PREDICTIVE JUSTICE RESPONSE ROOM.
IT SHOULD NEVER HAVE GOTTEN ANYWHERE NEAR THAT FAR!
ULYSSES NAMED OWEN LECLERC AS A THREAT DAYS AGO. WHY WASN'T HE IN CUSTODY?
Henry Peter Gyrich. United States.
Philippe Beaulieu. Canada.
WE HAD NO LEGAL BASIS TO HOLD HIM. HE DOESN'T HAVE A CRIMINAL RECORD. THERE WAS NO ACTIONABLE EVIDENCE.
ALL HE HAD WAS A HISTORY OF SCHIZOPHRENIA, BUT HE WAS CONTROLLING IT WITH MEDS. UNDER THE CIRCUMSTANCES, SURVEILLANCE SEEMED THE BEST CHOICE--
M'SIEUR BEAULIEU, IF I MAY--I WAS THE ONE WHO OBJECTED.
I MYSELF HAVE STRUGGLED WITH DISSOCIATIVE IDENTITY DISORDER. TO IMPRISON A MAN WHO HAS DONE NOTHING WRONG, WHO WORKS SO HARD TO BE WELL...
...IT COULD DESTROY HIM. FOR ALL WE KNEW, THE TRAUMA OF SUCH AN ARREST MIGHT HAVE BROUGHT ABOUT THE CRISIS ULYSSES FORESAW.
AND IF WE'D ARRESTED LECLERC, KOLOMAQ MIGHT HAVE JUST TARGETED SOMEONE ELSE TO SET HIM FREE.
AS IT IS, THANKS TO DRONE SURVEILLANCE, WE WERE POISED TO RESPOND IMMEDIATELY WHEN TROUBLE STARTED.
I SEE. COMMANDER DANVERS...
...COULD WE SPEAK TO YOU ALONE?

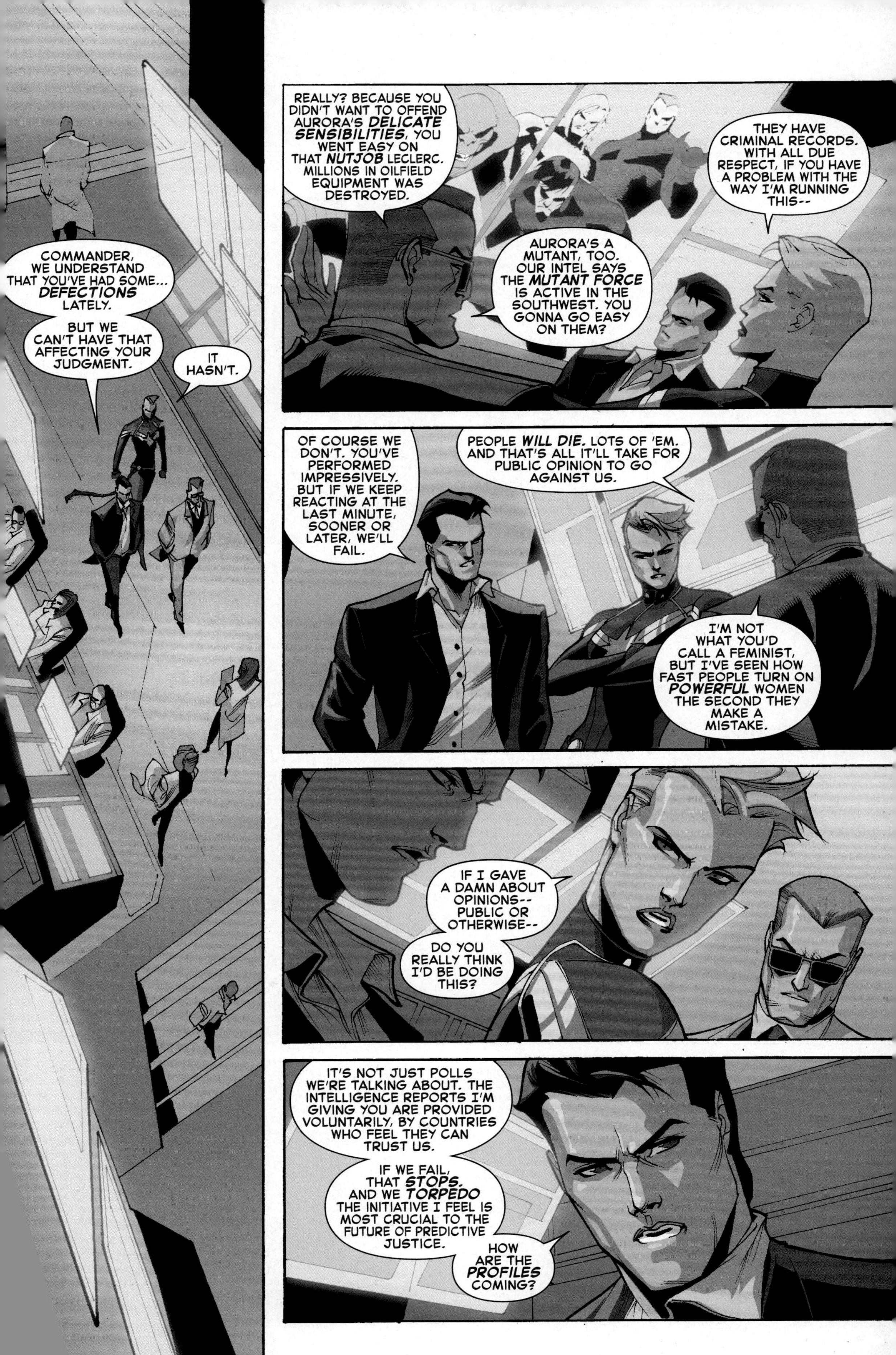

COMMANDER, WE UNDERSTAND THAT YOU'VE HAD SOME... DEFECTIONS LATELY.
BUT WE CAN'T HAVE THAT AFFECTING YOUR JUDGMENT.
IT HASN'T.
REALLY? BECAUSE YOU DIDN'T WANT TO OFFEND AURORA'S DELICATE SENSIBILITIES, YOU WENT EASY ON THAT NUTJOB LECLERC. MILLIONS IN OILFIELD EQUIPMENT WAS DESTROYED.
THEY HAVE CRIMINAL RECORDS. WITH ALL DUE RESPECT, IF YOU HAVE A PROBLEM WITH THE WAY I'M RUNNING THIS--
AURORA'S A MUTANT, TOO. OUR INTEL SAYS THE MUTANT FORCE IS ACTIVE IN THE SOUTHWEST. YOU GONNA GO EASY ON THEM?
OF COURSE WE DON'T. YOU'VE PERFORMED IMPRESSIVELY. BUT IF WE KEEP REACTING AT THE LAST MINUTE, SOONER OR LATER, WE'LL FAIL.
PEOPLE WILL DIE. LOTS OF 'EM. AND THAT'S ALL IT'LL TAKE FOR PUBLIC OPINION TO GO AGAINST US.
I'M NOT WHAT YOU'D CALL A FEMINIST, BUT I'VE SEEN HOW FAST PEOPLE TURN ON POWERFUL WOMEN THE SECOND THEY MAKE A MISTAKE.
IF I GAVE A DAMN ABOUT OPINIONS-- PUBLIC OR OTHERWISE--
DO YOU REALLY THINK I'D BE DOING THIS?
IT'S NOT JUST POLLS WE'RE TALKING ABOUT. THE INTELLIGENCE REPORTS I'M GIVING YOU ARE PROVIDED VOLUNTARILY, BY COUNTRIES WHO FEEL THEY CAN TRUST US.
IF WE FAIL, THAT STOPS. AND WE TORPEDO THE INITIATIVE I FEEL IS MOST CRUCIAL TO THE FUTURE OF PREDICTIVE JUSTICE.
HOW ARE THE PROFILES COMING?

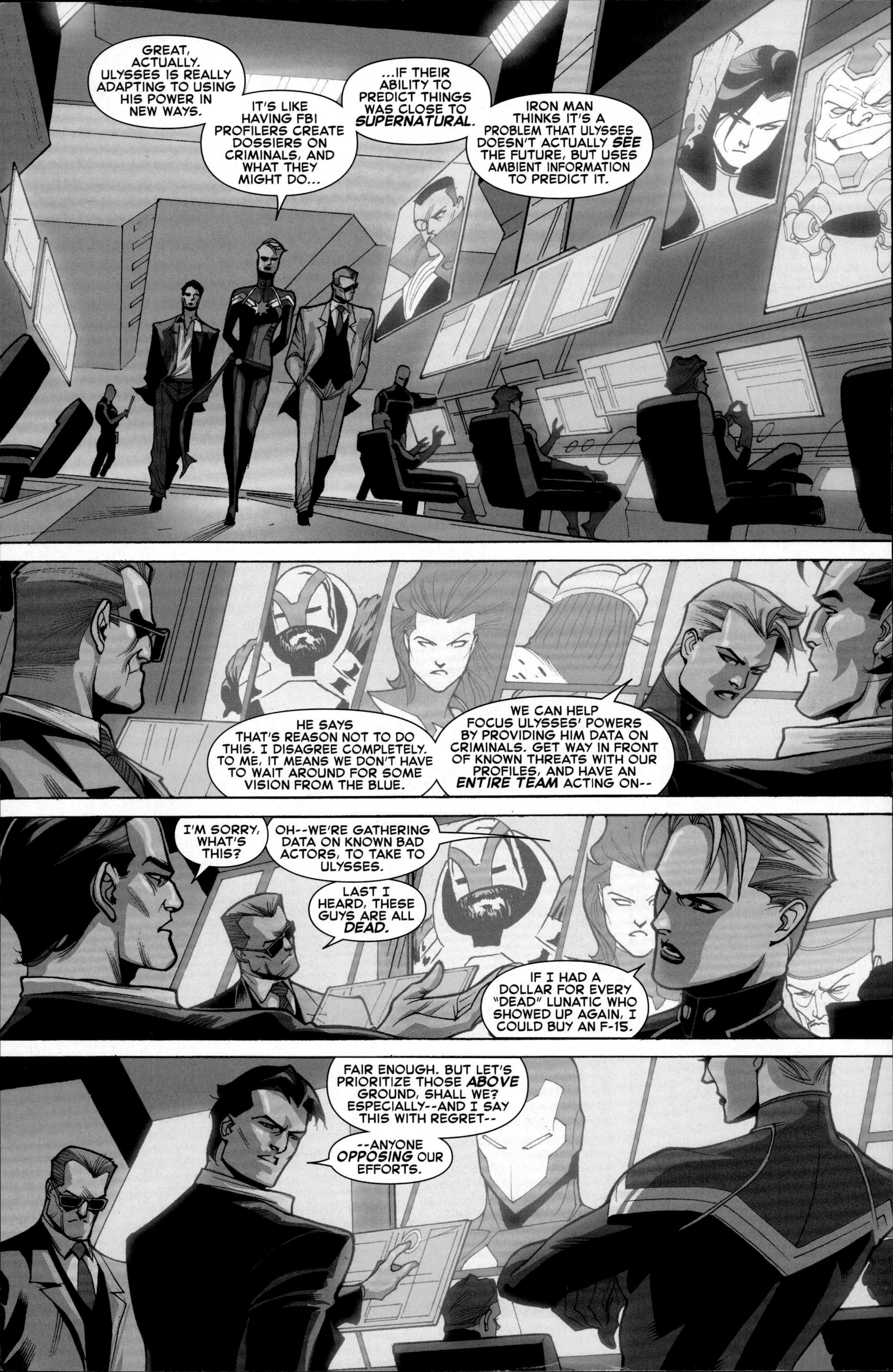
GREAT, ACTUALLY. ULYSSES IS REALLY ADAPTING TO USING HIS POWER IN NEW WAYS.
IT'S LIKE HAVING FBI PROFILERS CREATE DOSSIERS ON CRIMINALS, AND WHAT THEY MIGHT DO...
...IF THEIR ABILITY TO PREDICT THINGS WAS CLOSE TO SUPERNATURAL.
IRON MAN THINKS IT'S A PROBLEM THAT ULYSSES DOESN'T ACTUALLY SEE THE FUTURE, BUT USES AMBIENT INFORMATION TO PREDICT IT.
HE SAYS THAT'S REASON NOT TO DO THIS. I DISAGREE COMPLETELY. TO ME, IT MEANS WE DON'T HAVE TO WAIT AROUND FOR SOME VISION FROM THE BLUE.
WE CAN HELP FOCUS ULYSSES' POWERS BY PROVIDING HIM DATA ON CRIMINALS. GET WAY IN FRONT OF KNOWN THREATS WITH OUR PROFILES, AND HAVE AN ENTIRE TEAM ACTING ON--
I'M SORRY, WHAT'S THIS?
OH--WE'RE GATHERING DATA ON KNOWN BAD ACTORS, TO TAKE TO ULYSSES.
LAST I HEARD, THESE GUYS ARE ALL DEAD.
IF I HAD A DOLLAR FOR EVERY "DEAD" LUNATIC WHO SHOWED UP AGAIN, I COULD BUY AN F-15.
FAIR ENOUGH. BUT LET'S PRIORITIZE THOSE ABOVE GROUND, SHALL WE? ESPECIALLY--AND I SAY THIS WITH REGRET--
--ANYONE OPPOSING OUR EFFORTS.

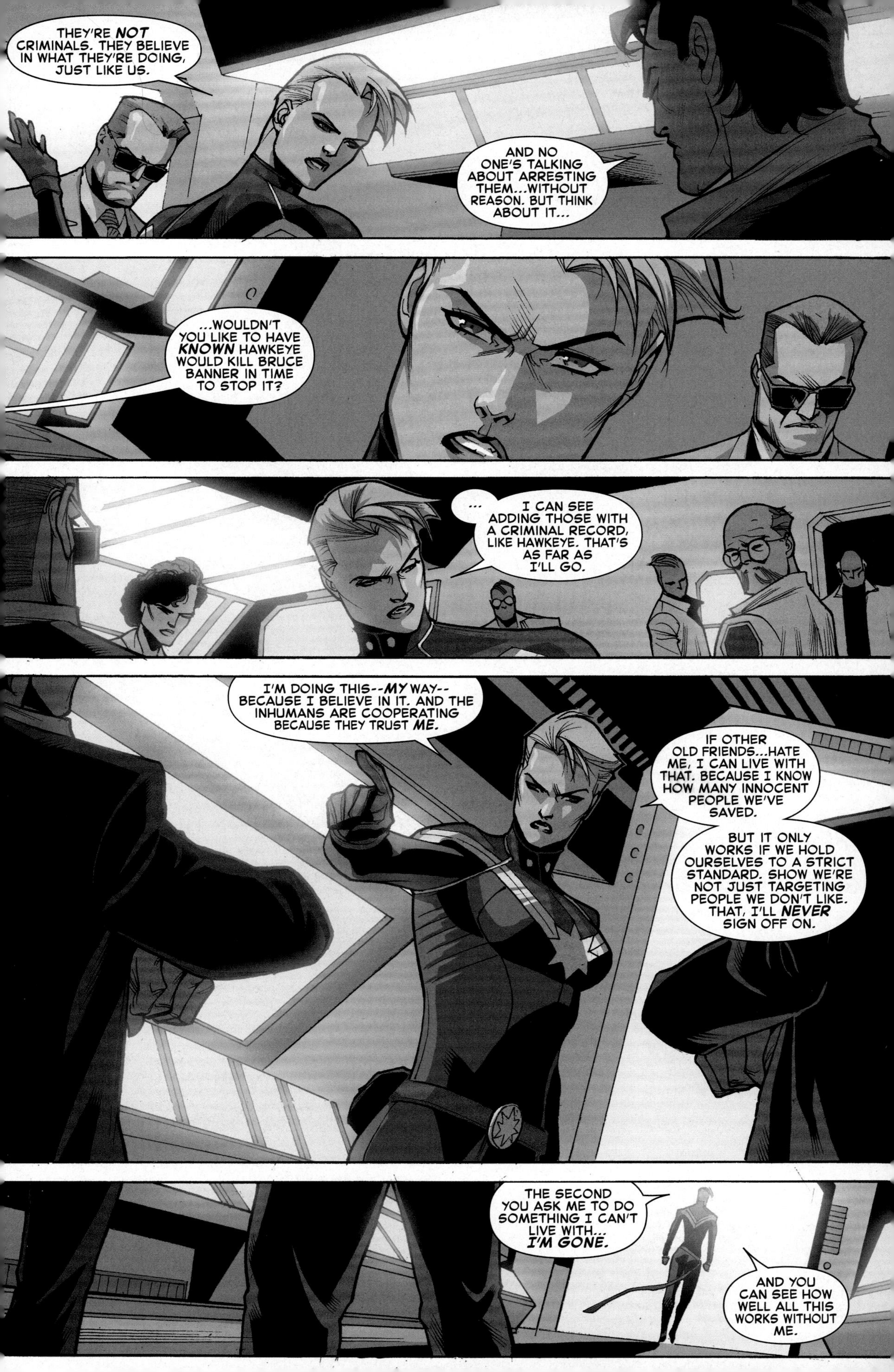
THEY'RE NOT CRIMINALS. THEY BELIEVE IN WHAT THEY'RE DOING, JUST LIKE US.
AND NO ONE'S TALKING ABOUT ARRESTING THEM...WITHOUT REASON. BUT THINK ABOUT IT...
...WOULDN'T YOU LIKE TO HAVE KNOWN HAWKEYE WOULD KILL BRUCE BANNER IN TIME TO STOP IT?
... I CAN SEE ADDING THOSE WITH A CRIMINAL RECORD, LIKE HAWKEYE. THAT'S AS FAR AS I'LL GO.
I'M DOING THIS--MY WAY--BECAUSE I BELIEVE IN IT. AND THE INHUMANS ARE COOPERATING BECAUSE THEY TRUST ME.
IF OTHER OLD FRIENDS...HATE ME, I CAN LIVE WITH THAT. BECAUSE I KNOW HOW MANY INNOCENT PEOPLE WE'VE SAVED.
BUT IT ONLY WORKS IF WE HOLD OURSELVES TO A STRICT STANDARD. SHOW WE'RE NOT JUST TARGETING PEOPLE WE DON'T LIKE. THAT, I'LL NEVER SIGN OFF ON.
THE SECOND YOU ASK ME TO DO SOMETHING I CAN'T LIVE WITH... I'M GONE.
AND YOU CAN SEE HOW WELL ALL THIS WORKS WITHOUT ME.

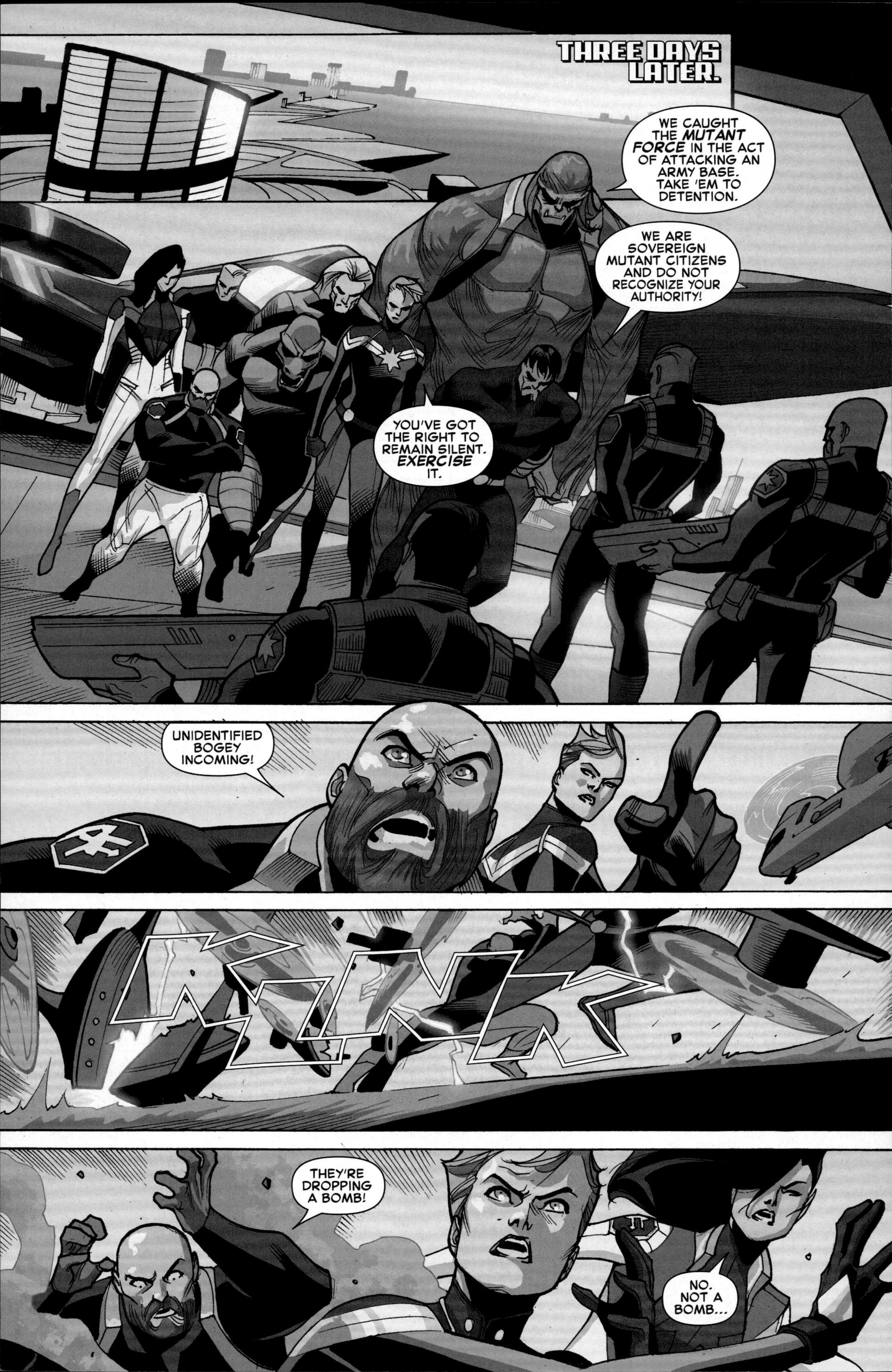

THREE DAYS LATER.
WE CAUGHT THE MUTANT FORCE IN THE ACT OF ATTACKING AN ARMY BASE. TAKE 'EM TO DETENTION.
WE ARE SOVEREIGN MUTANT CITIZENS AND DO NOT RECOGNIZE YOUR AUTHORITY!
YOU'VE GOT THE RIGHT TO REMAIN SILENT. EXERCISE IT.
UNIDENTIFIED BOGEY INCOMING!
KRAK
THEY'RE DROPPING A BOMB!
NO. NOT A BOMB...

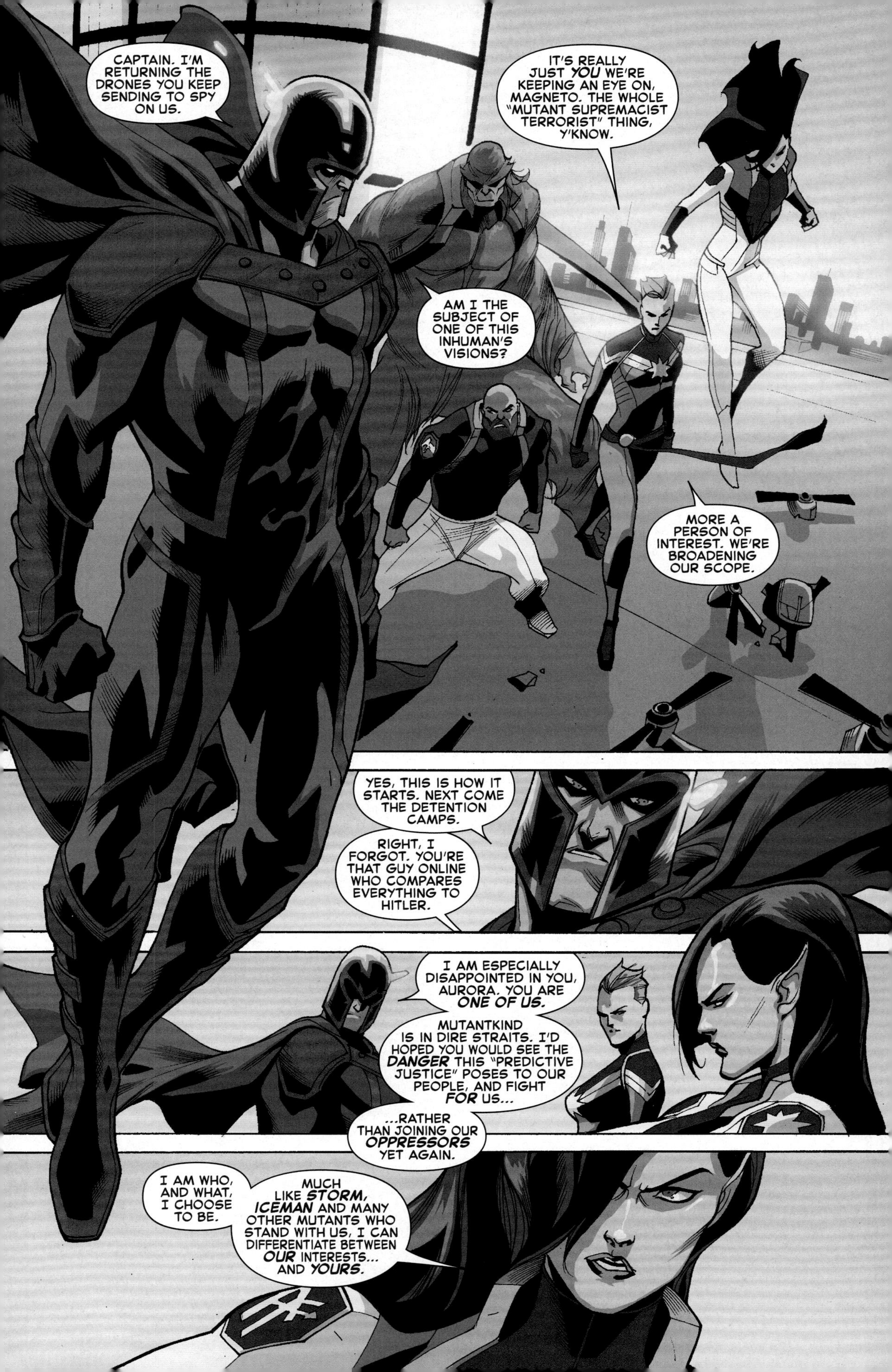
CAPTAIN. I'M RETURNING THE DRONES YOU KEEP SENDING TO SPY ON US.
IT'S REALLY JUST YOU WE'RE KEEPING AN EYE ON, MAGNETO. THE WHOLE "MUTANT SUPREMACIST TERRORIST" THING, Y'KNOW.
AM I THE SUBJECT OF ONE OF THIS INHUMAN'S VISIONS?
MORE A PERSON OF INTEREST. WE'RE BROADENING OUR SCOPE.
YES, THIS IS HOW IT STARTS. NEXT COME THE DETENTION CAMPS.
RIGHT, I FORGOT. YOU'RE THAT GUY ONLINE WHO COMPARES EVERYTHING TO HITLER.
I AM ESPECIALLY DISAPPOINTED IN YOU, AURORA. YOU ARE ONE OF US.
MUTANTKIND IS IN DIRE STRAITS. I'D HOPED YOU WOULD SEE THE DANGER THIS "PREDICTIVE JUSTICE" POSES TO OUR PEOPLE, AND FIGHT FOR US...
...RATHER THAN JOINING OUR OPPRESSORS YET AGAIN.
I AM WHO, AND WHAT, I CHOOSE TO BE.
MUCH LIKE STORM, ICEMAN AND MANY OTHER MUTANTS WHO STAND WITH US, I CAN DIFFERENTIATE BETWEEN OUR INTERESTS... AND YOURS.

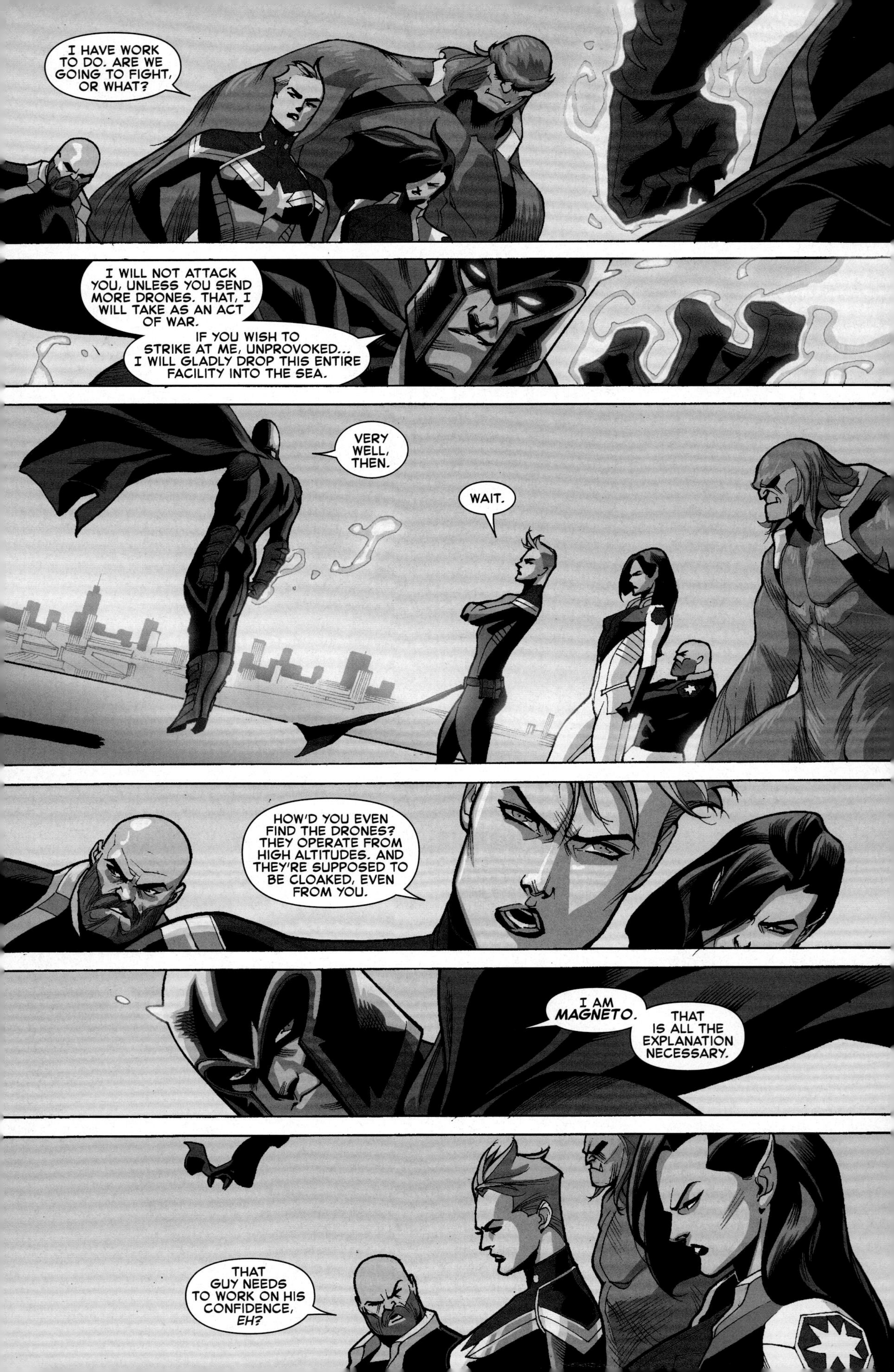

I HAVE WORK TO DO. ARE WE GOING TO FIGHT, OR WHAT?
I WILL NOT ATTACK YOU, UNLESS YOU SEND MORE DRONES. THAT, I WILL TAKE AS AN ACT OF WAR.
IF YOU WISH TO STRIKE AT ME, UNPROVOKED... I WILL GLADLY DROP THIS ENTIRE FACILITY INTO THE SEA.
VERY WELL, THEN.
WAIT.
HOW'D YOU EVEN FIND THE DRONES? THEY OPERATE FROM HIGH ALTITUDES. AND THEY'RE SUPPOSED TO BE CLOAKED, EVEN FROM YOU.
I AM MAGNETO.
THAT IS ALL THE EXPLANATION NECESSARY.
THAT GUY NEEDS TO WORK ON HIS CONFIDENCE, EH?

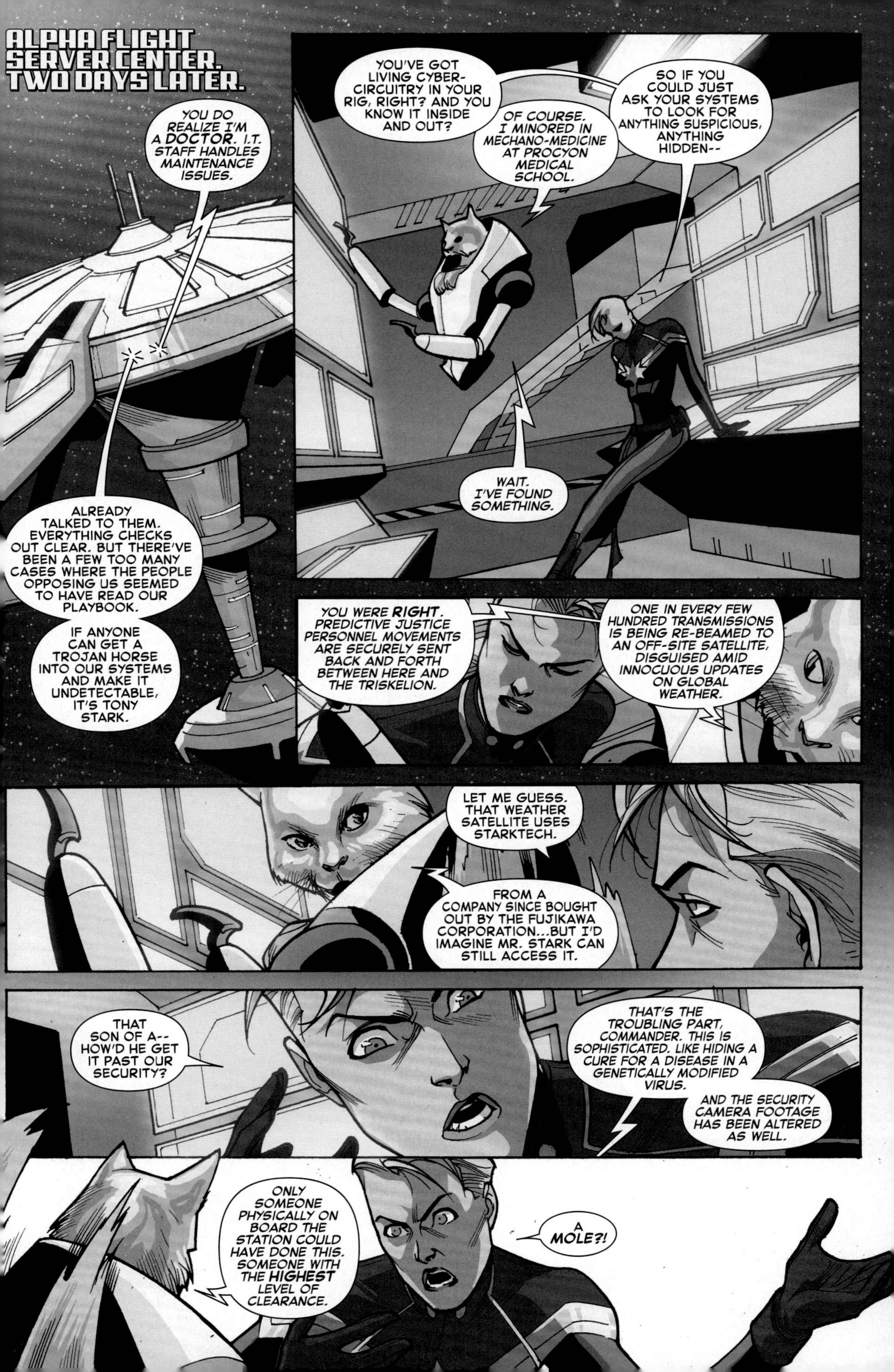
ALPHA FLIGHT SERVER CENTER. TWO DAYS LATER.
YOU DO REALIZE I'M A DOCTOR. I.T. STAFF HANDLES MAINTENANCE ISSUES.
ALREADY TALKED TO THEM. EVERYTHING CHECKS OUT CLEAR. BUT THERE'VE BEEN A FEW TOO MANY CASES WHERE THE PEOPLE OPPOSING US SEEMED TO HAVE READ OUR PLAYBOOK.
IF ANYONE CAN GET A TROJAN HORSE INTO OUR SYSTEMS AND MAKE IT UNDETECTABLE, IT'S TONY STARK.
YOU'VE GOT LIVING CYBER-CIRCUITRY IN YOUR RIG, RIGHT? AND YOU KNOW IT INSIDE AND OUT?
OF COURSE. I MINORED IN MECHANO-MEDICINE AT PROCYON MEDICAL SCHOOL.
SO IF YOU COULD JUST ASK YOUR SYSTEMS TO LOOK FOR ANYTHING SUSPICIOUS, ANYTHING HIDDEN--
WAIT. I'VE FOUND SOMETHING.
YOU WERE RIGHT. PREDICTIVE JUSTICE PERSONNEL MOVEMENTS ARE SECURELY SENT BACK AND FORTH BETWEEN HERE AND THE TRISKELION.
ONE IN EVERY FEW HUNDRED TRANSMISSIONS IS BEING RE-BEAMED TO AN OFF-SITE SATELLITE, DISGUISED AMID INNOCUOUS UPDATES ON GLOBAL WEATHER.
LET ME GUESS. THAT WEATHER SATELLITE USES STARKTECH.
FROM A COMPANY SINCE BOUGHT OUT BY THE FUJIKAWA CORPORATION...BUT I'D IMAGINE MR. STARK CAN STILL ACCESS IT.
THAT SON OF A--HOW'D HE GET IT PAST OUR SECURITY?
THAT'S THE TROUBLING PART, COMMANDER. THIS IS SOPHISTICATED. LIKE HIDING A CURE FOR A DISEASE IN A GENETICALLY MODIFIED VIRUS.
AND THE SECURITY CAMERA FOOTAGE HAS BEEN ALTERED AS WELL.
ONLY SOMEONE PHYSICALLY ON BOARD THE STATION COULD HAVE DONE THIS. SOMEONE WITH THE HIGHEST LEVEL OF CLEARANCE.
A MOLE?!

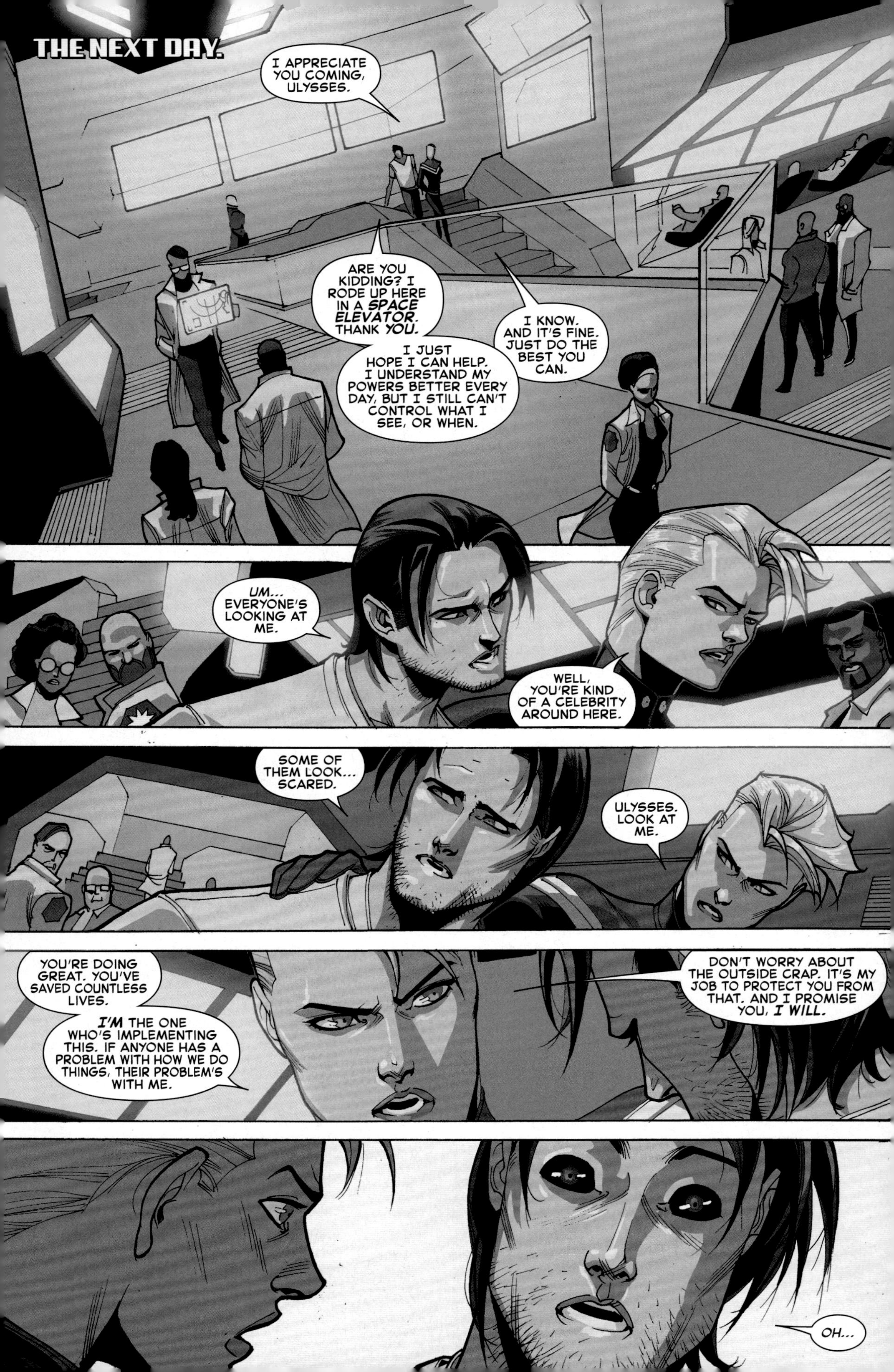
THE NEXT DAY.
I APPRECIATE YOU COMING, ULYSSES.
ARE YOU KIDDING? I RODE UP HERE IN A SPACE ELEVATOR. THANK YOU.
I JUST HOPE I CAN HELP. I UNDERSTAND MY POWERS BETTER EVERY DAY, BUT I STILL CAN'T CONTROL WHAT I SEE, OR WHEN.
I KNOW. AND IT'S FINE. JUST DO THE BEST YOU CAN.
UM... EVERYONE'S LOOKING AT ME.
WELL, YOU'RE KIND OF A CELEBRITY AROUND HERE.
SOME OF THEM LOOK... SCARED.
ULYSSES. LOOK AT ME.
YOU'RE DOING GREAT. YOU'VE SAVED COUNTLESS LIVES.
I'M THE ONE WHO'S IMPLEMENTING THIS. IF ANYONE HAS A PROBLEM WITH HOW WE DO THINGS, THEIR PROBLEM'S WITH ME.
DON'T WORRY ABOUT THE OUTSIDE CRAP. IT'S MY JOB TO PROTECT YOU FROM THAT. AND I PROMISE YOU, I WILL.
OH...

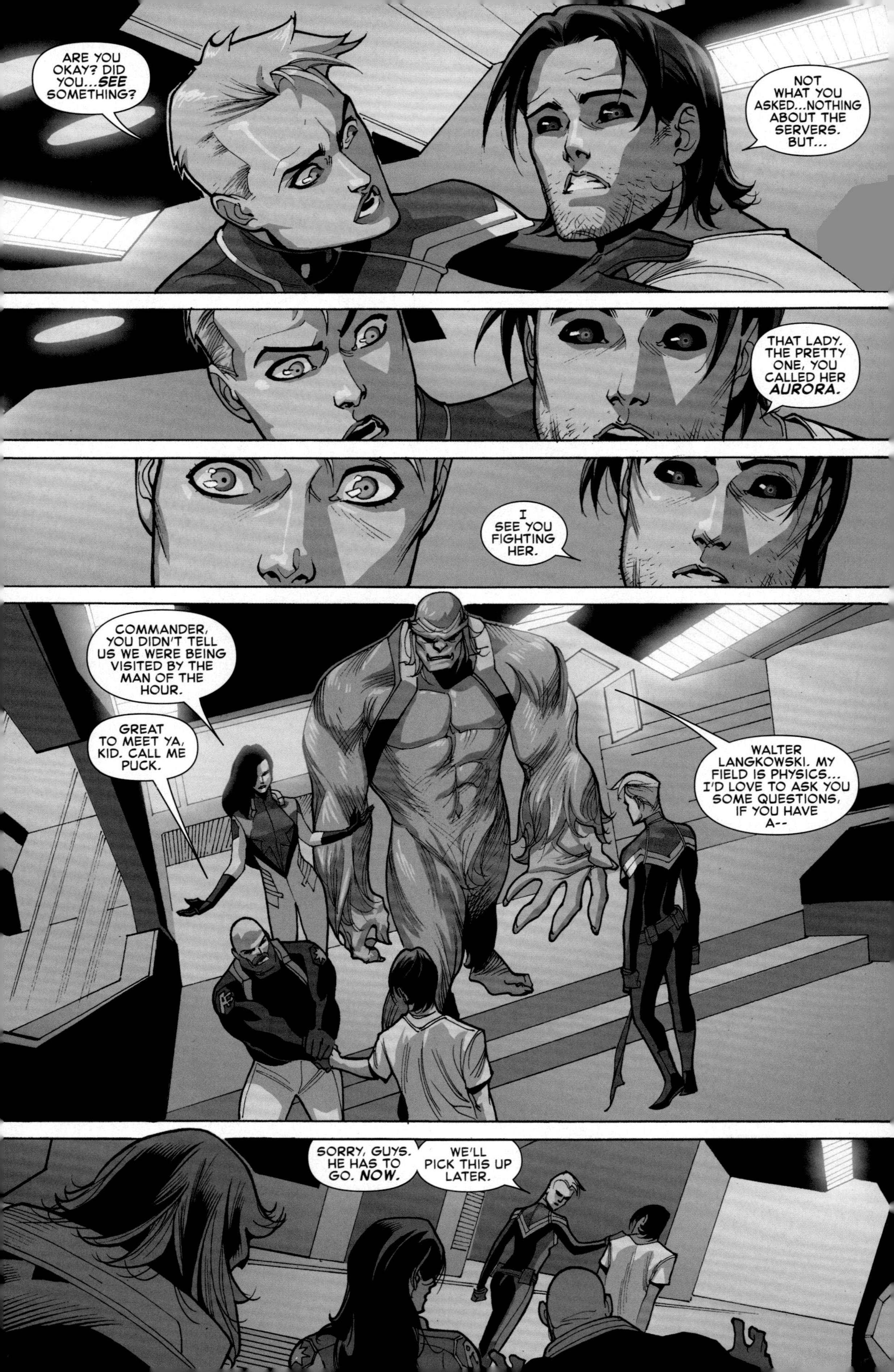
ARE YOU OKAY? DID YOU...SEE SOMETHING?
NOT WHAT YOU ASKED...NOTHING ABOUT THE SERVERS. BUT...
THAT LADY. THE PRETTY ONE, YOU CALLED HER AURORA.
I SEE YOU FIGHTING HER.
COMMANDER, YOU DIDN'T TELL US WE WERE BEING VISITED BY THE MAN OF THE HOUR.
GREAT TO MEET YA, KID. CALL ME PUCK.
WALTER LANGKOWSKI. MY FIELD IS PHYSICS... I'D LOVE TO ASK YOU SOME QUESTIONS, IF YOU HAVE A--
SORRY, GUYS. HE HAS TO GO. NOW.
WE'LL PICK THIS UP LATER.

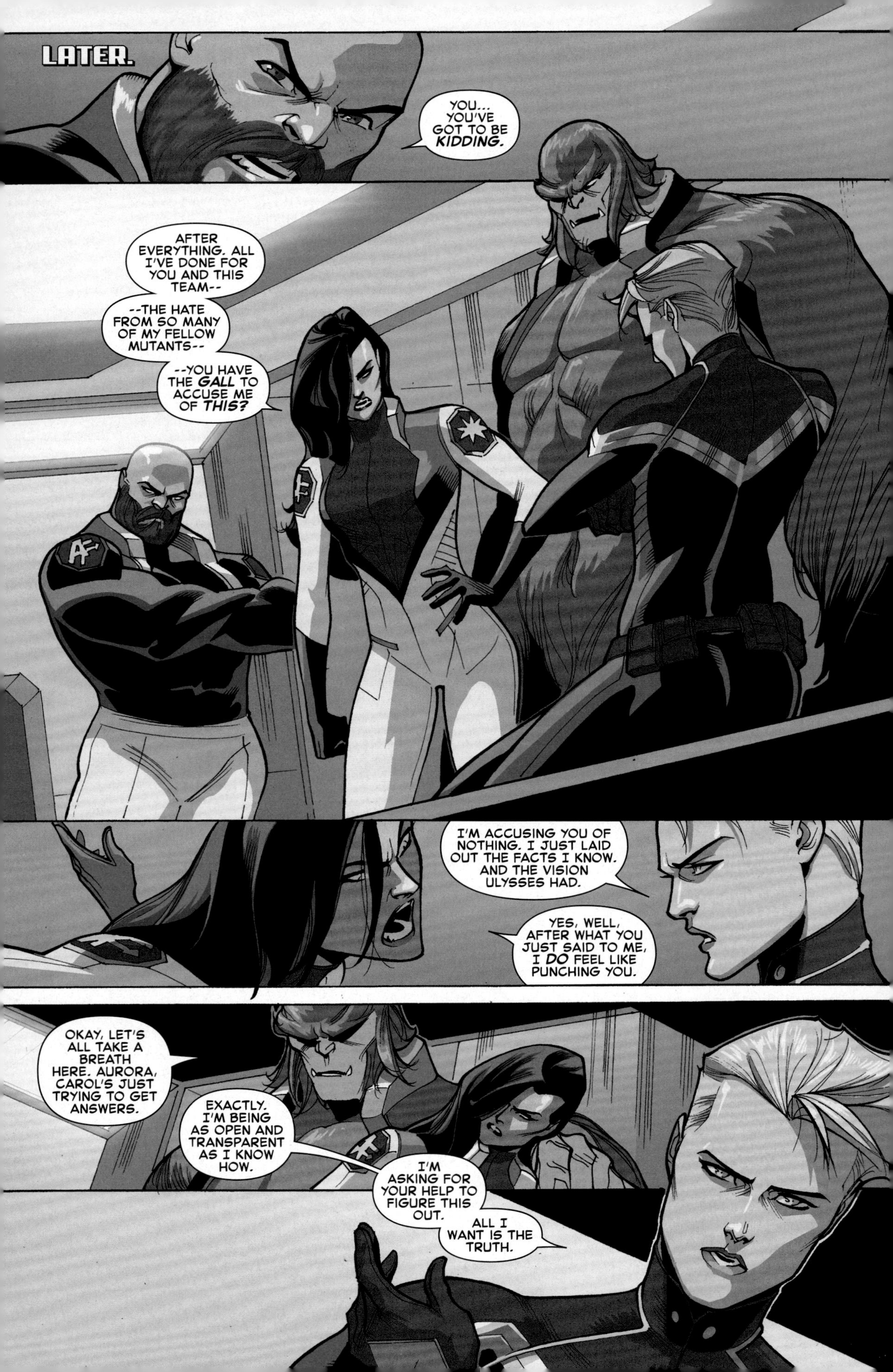
LATER.
YOU... YOU'VE GOT TO BE KIDDING.
AFTER EVERYTHING. ALL I'VE DONE FOR YOU AND THIS TEAM--
--THE HATE FROM SO MANY OF MY FELLOW MUTANTS--
--YOU HAVE THE GALL TO ACCUSE ME OF THIS?
I'M ACCUSING YOU OF NOTHING. I JUST LAID OUT THE FACTS I KNOW. AND THE VISION ULYSSES HAD.
YES, WELL, AFTER WHAT YOU JUST SAID TO ME, I DO FEEL LIKE PUNCHING YOU.
OKAY, LET'S ALL TAKE A BREATH HERE. AURORA, CAROL'S JUST TRYING TO GET ANSWERS.
EXACTLY. I'M BEING AS OPEN AND TRANSPARENT AS I KNOW HOW.
I'M ASKING FOR YOUR HELP TO FIGURE THIS OUT.
ALL I WANT IS THE TRUTH.

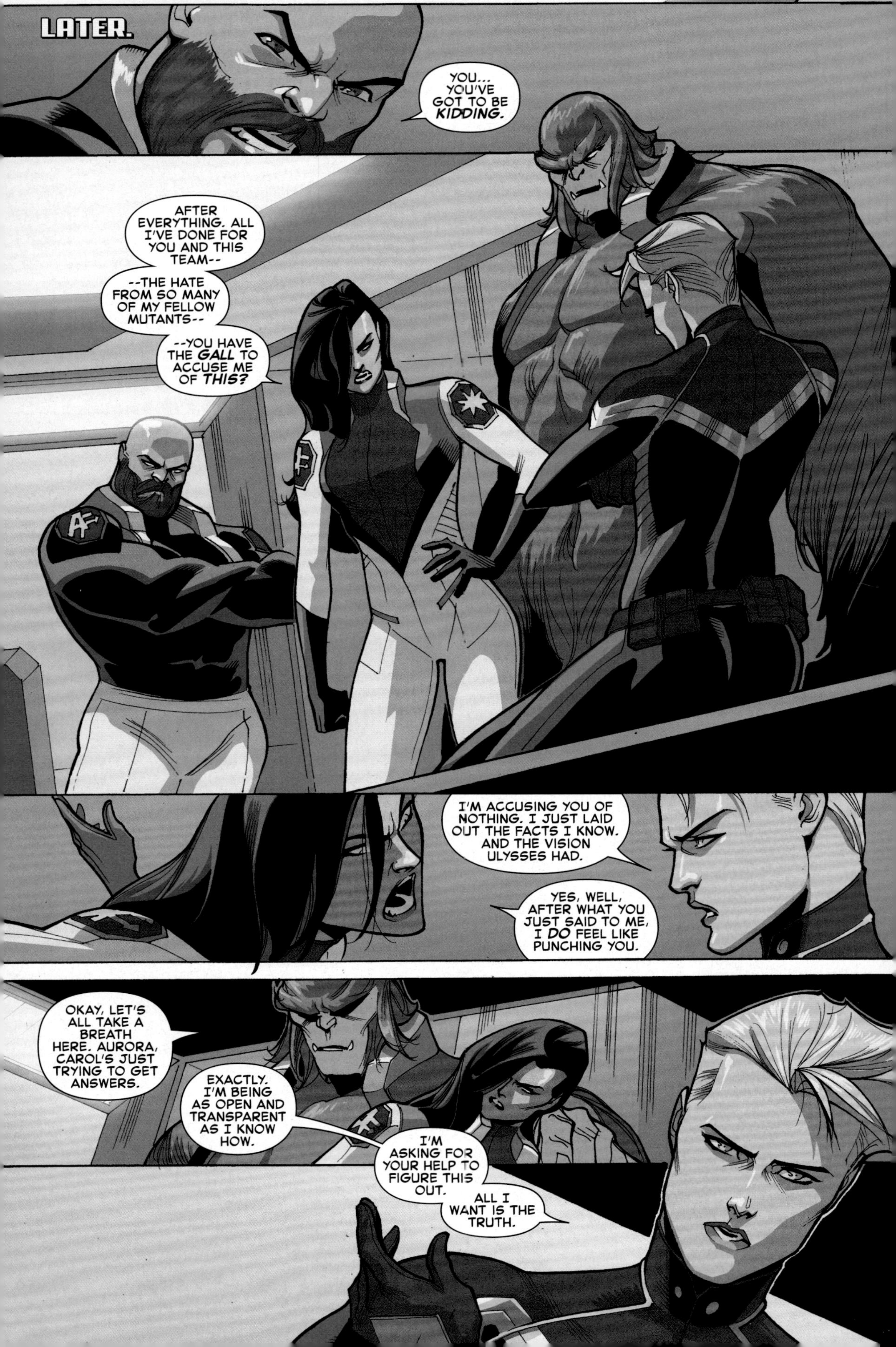
LATER.
YOU... YOU'VE GOT TO BE KIDDING.
AFTER EVERYTHING. ALL I'VE DONE FOR YOU AND THIS TEAM--
--THE HATE FROM SO MANY OF MY FELLOW MUTANTS--
--YOU HAVE THE GALL TO ACCUSE ME OF THIS?
I'M ACCUSING YOU OF NOTHING. I JUST LAID OUT THE FACTS I KNOW. AND THE VISION ULYSSES HAD.
YES, WELL, AFTER WHAT YOU JUST SAID TO ME, I DO FEEL LIKE PUNCHING YOU.
OKAY, LET'S ALL TAKE A BREATH HERE. AURORA, CAROL'S JUST TRYING TO GET ANSWERS.
EXACTLY. I'M BEING AS OPEN AND TRANSPARENT AS I KNOW HOW.
I'M ASKING FOR YOUR HELP TO FIGURE THIS OUT.
ALL I WANT IS THE TRUTH.

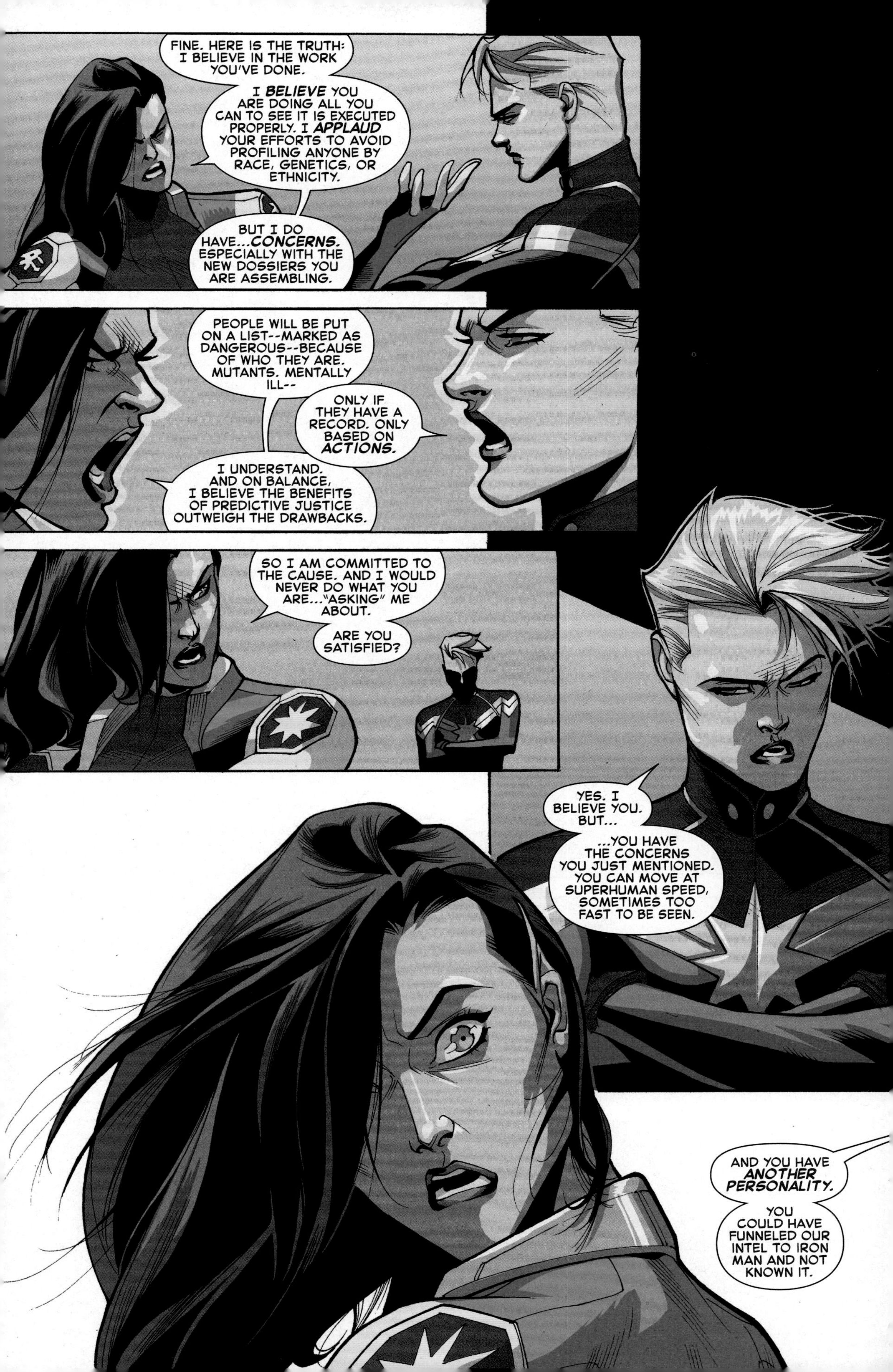
FINE. HERE IS THE TRUTH: I BELIEVE IN THE WORK YOU'VE DONE.
I BELIEVE YOU ARE DOING ALL YOU CAN TO SEE IT IS EXECUTED PROPERLY. I APPLAUD YOUR EFFORTS TO AVOID PROFILING ANYONE BY RACE, GENETICS, OR ETHNICITY.
BUT I DO HAVE...CONCERNS. ESPECIALLY WITH THE NEW DOSSIERS YOU ARE ASSEMBLING.
PEOPLE WILL BE PUT ON A LIST--MARKED AS DANGEROUS--BECAUSE OF WHO THEY ARE. MUTANTS. MENTALLY ILL--
ONLY IF THEY HAVE A RECORD. ONLY BASED ON ACTIONS.
I UNDERSTAND. AND ON BALANCE, I BELIEVE THE BENEFITS OF PREDICTIVE JUSTICE OUTWEIGH THE DRAWBACKS.
SO I AM COMMITTED TO THE CAUSE. AND I WOULD NEVER DO WHAT YOU ARE..."ASKING" ME ABOUT.
ARE YOU SATISFIED?
YES. I BELIEVE YOU. BUT...
...YOU HAVE THE CONCERNS YOU JUST MENTIONED. YOU CAN MOVE AT SUPERHUMAN SPEED, SOMETIMES TOO FAST TO BE SEEN.
AND YOU HAVE ANOTHER PERSONALITY.
YOU COULD HAVE FUNNELED OUR INTEL TO IRON MAN AND NOT KNOWN IT.

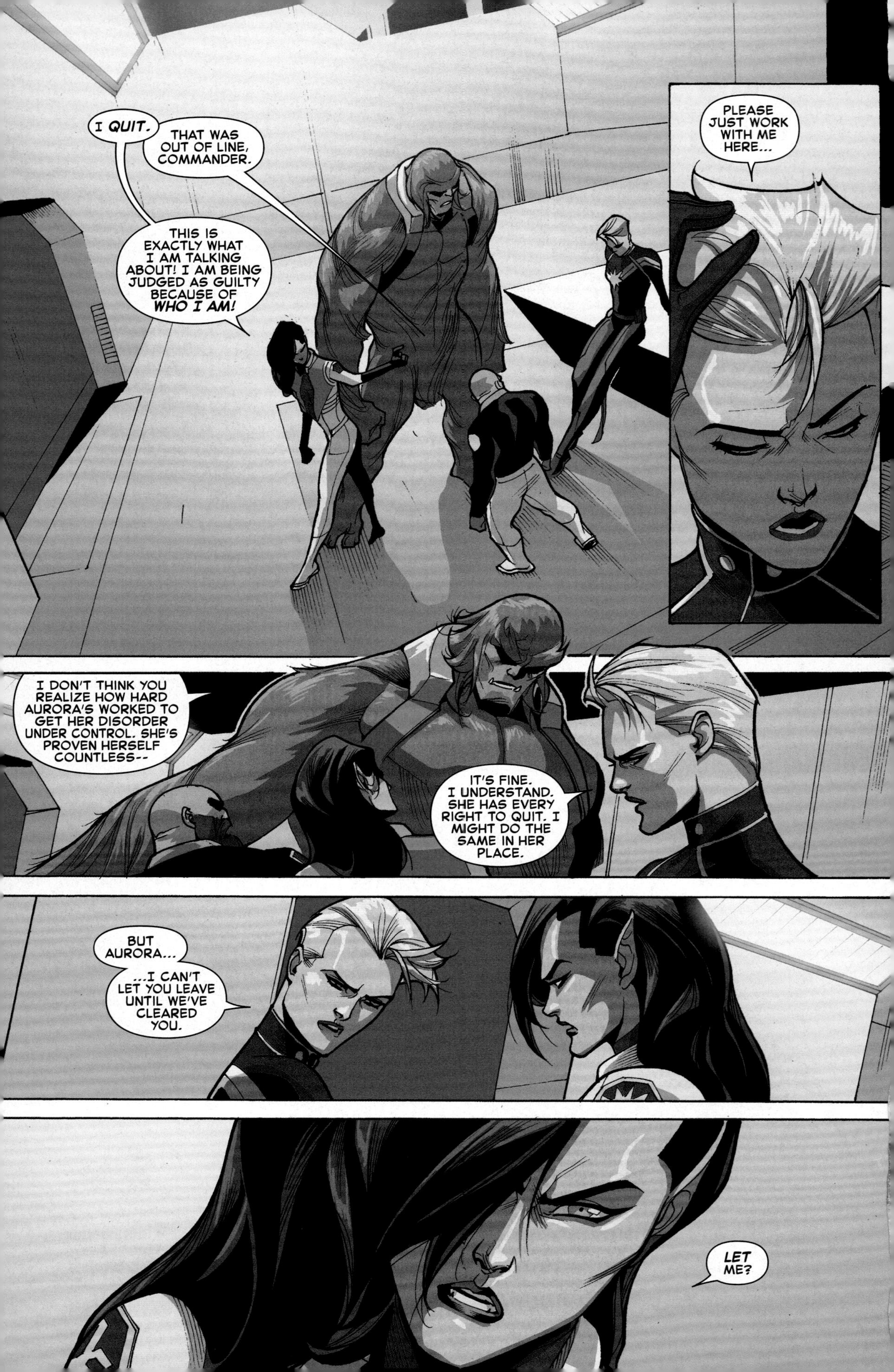
I QUIT.
THAT WAS OUT OF LINE, COMMANDER.
THIS IS EXACTLY WHAT I AM TALKING ABOUT! I AM BEING JUDGED AS GUILTY BECAUSE OF WHO I AM!
PLEASE JUST WORK WITH ME HERE...
I DON'T THINK YOU REALIZE HOW HARD AURORA'S WORKED TO GET HER DISORDER UNDER CONTROL. SHE'S PROVEN HERSELF COUNTLESS--
IT'S FINE. I UNDERSTAND. SHE HAS EVERY RIGHT TO QUIT. I MIGHT DO THE SAME IN HER PLACE.
BUT AURORA...
...I CAN'T LET YOU LEAVE UNTIL WE'VE CLEARED YOU.
LET ME?

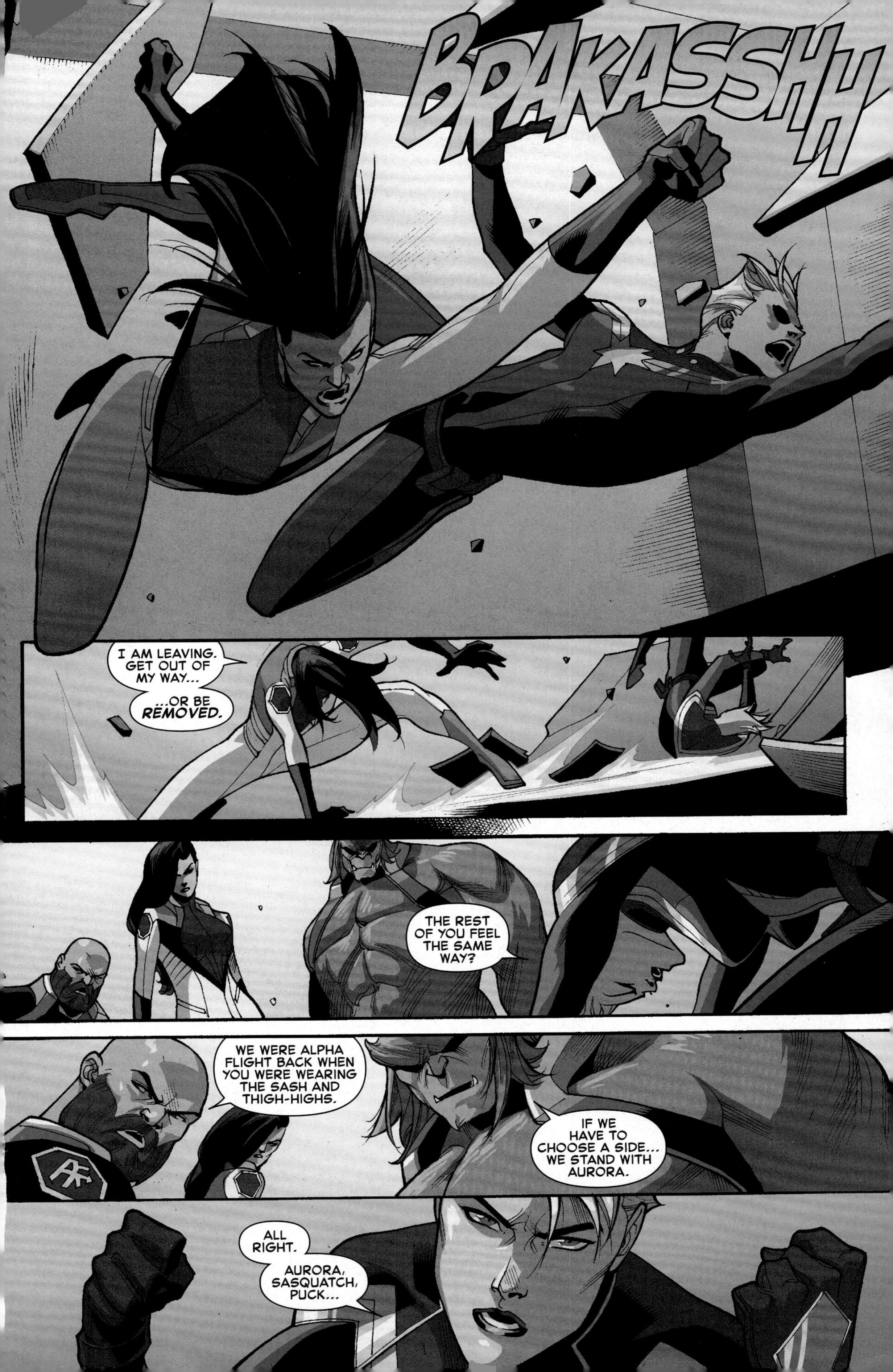
BRAKASSHH
I AM LEAVING. GET OUT OF MY WAY...
...OR BE *REMOVED.*
THE REST OF YOU FEEL THE SAME WAY?
WE WERE ALPHA FLIGHT BACK WHEN YOU WERE WEARING THE SASH AND THIGH-HIGHS.
IF WE HAVE TO CHOOSE A SIDE... WE STAND WITH AURORA.
ALL RIGHT.
AURORA, SASQUATCH, PUCK...

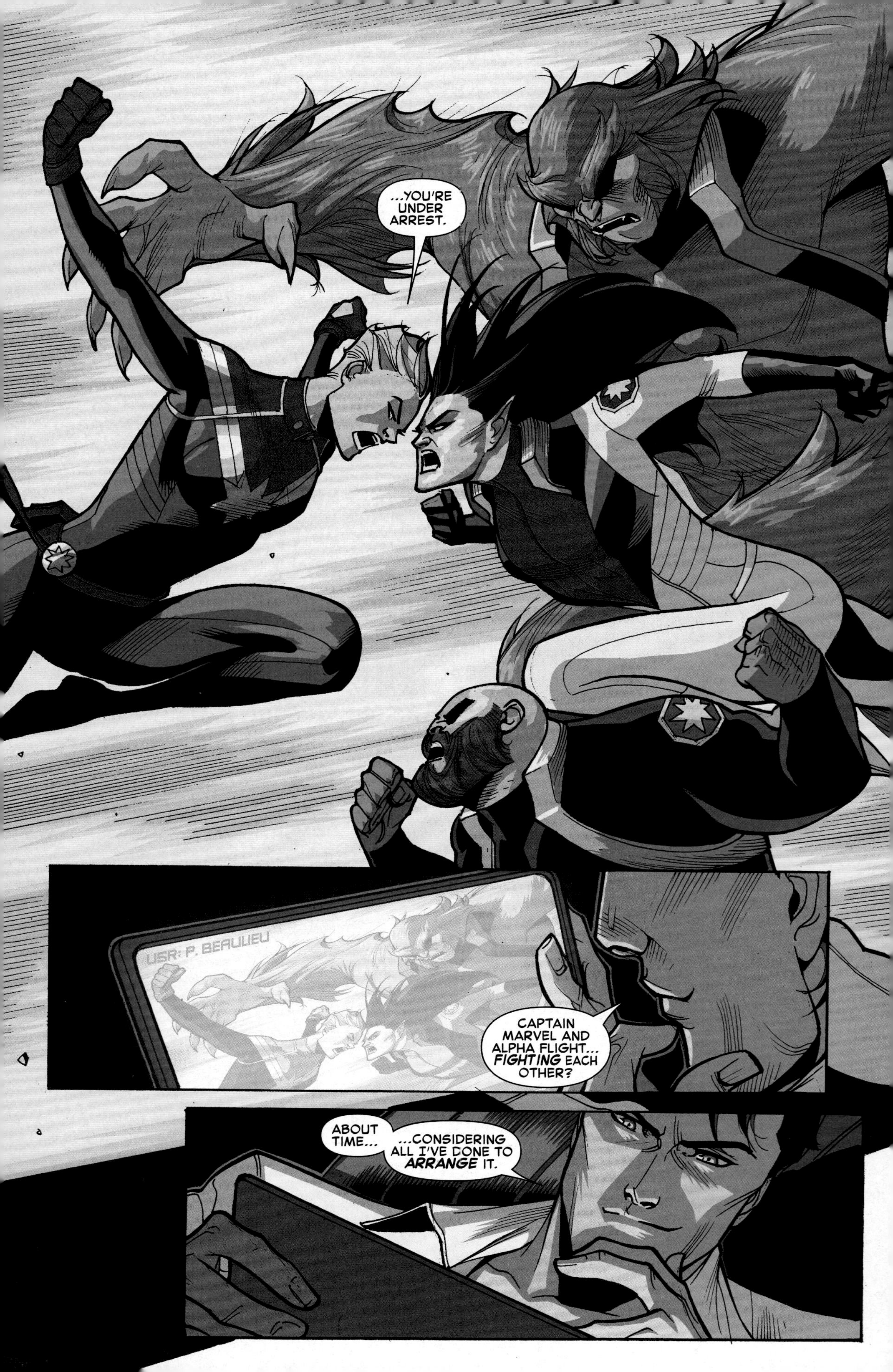
...YOU'RE UNDER ARREST.
USR: P. BEAULIEU
CAPTAIN MARVEL AND ALPHA FLIGHT... FIGHTING EACH OTHER?
ABOUT TIME...
...CONSIDERING ALL I'VE DONE TO ARRANGE IT.

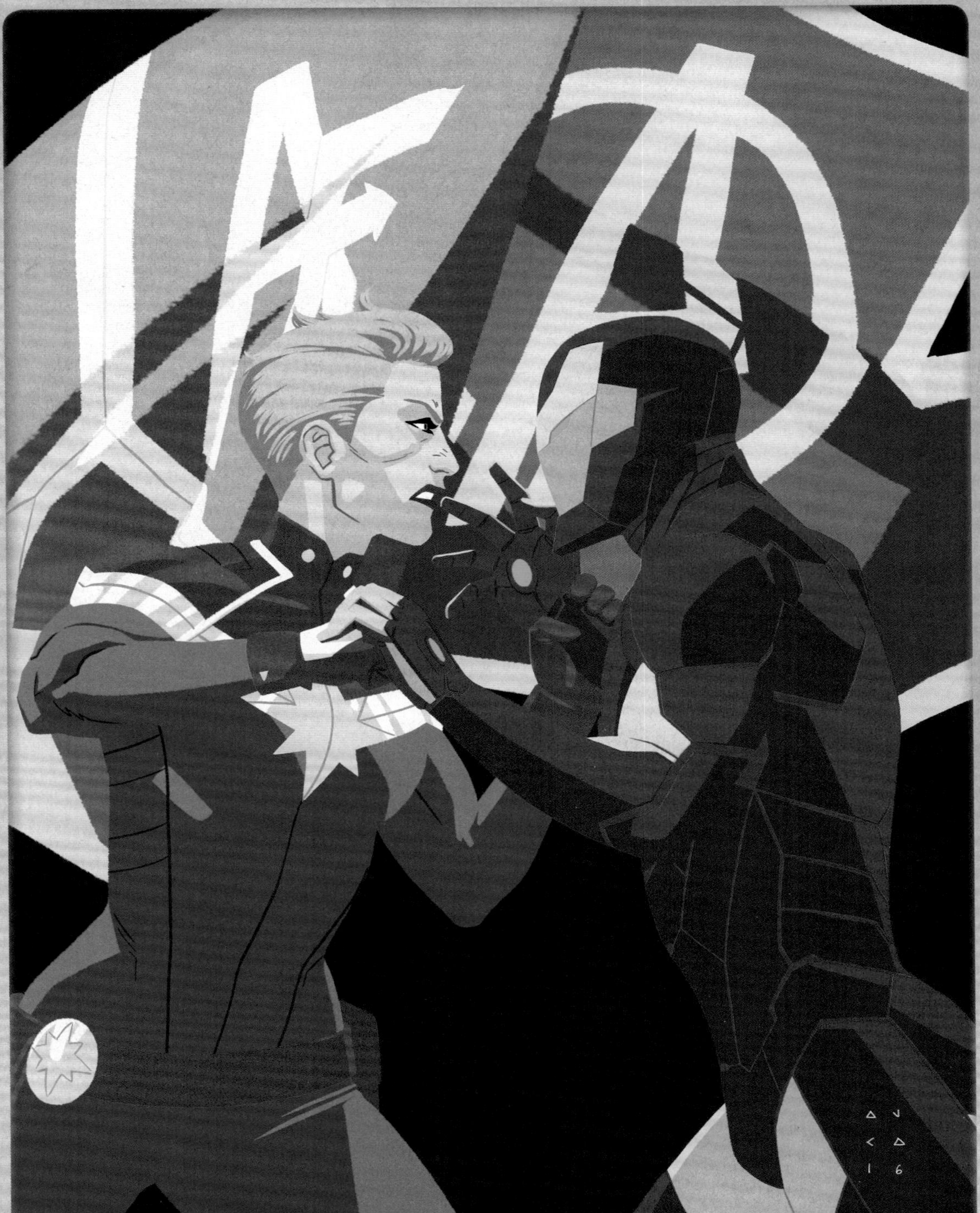

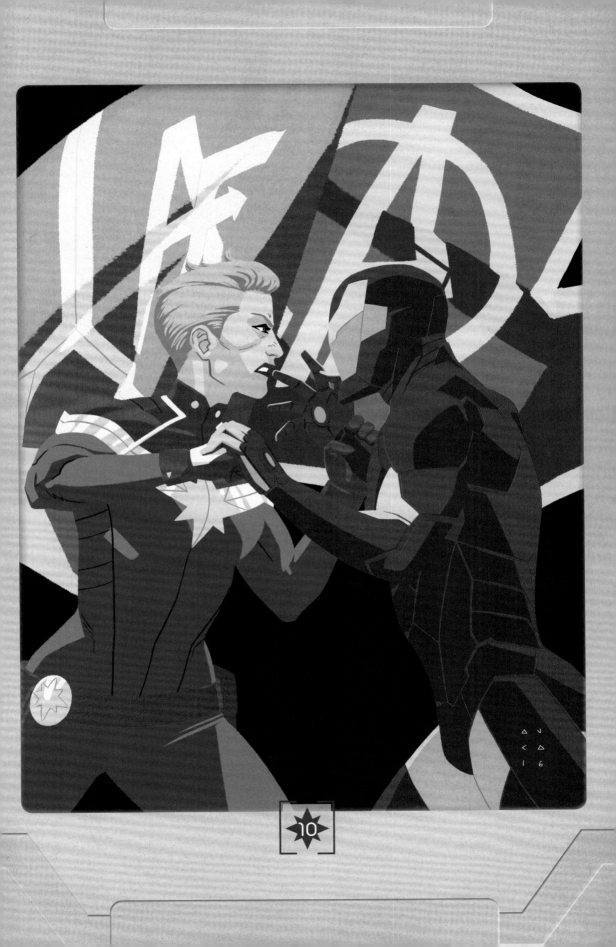

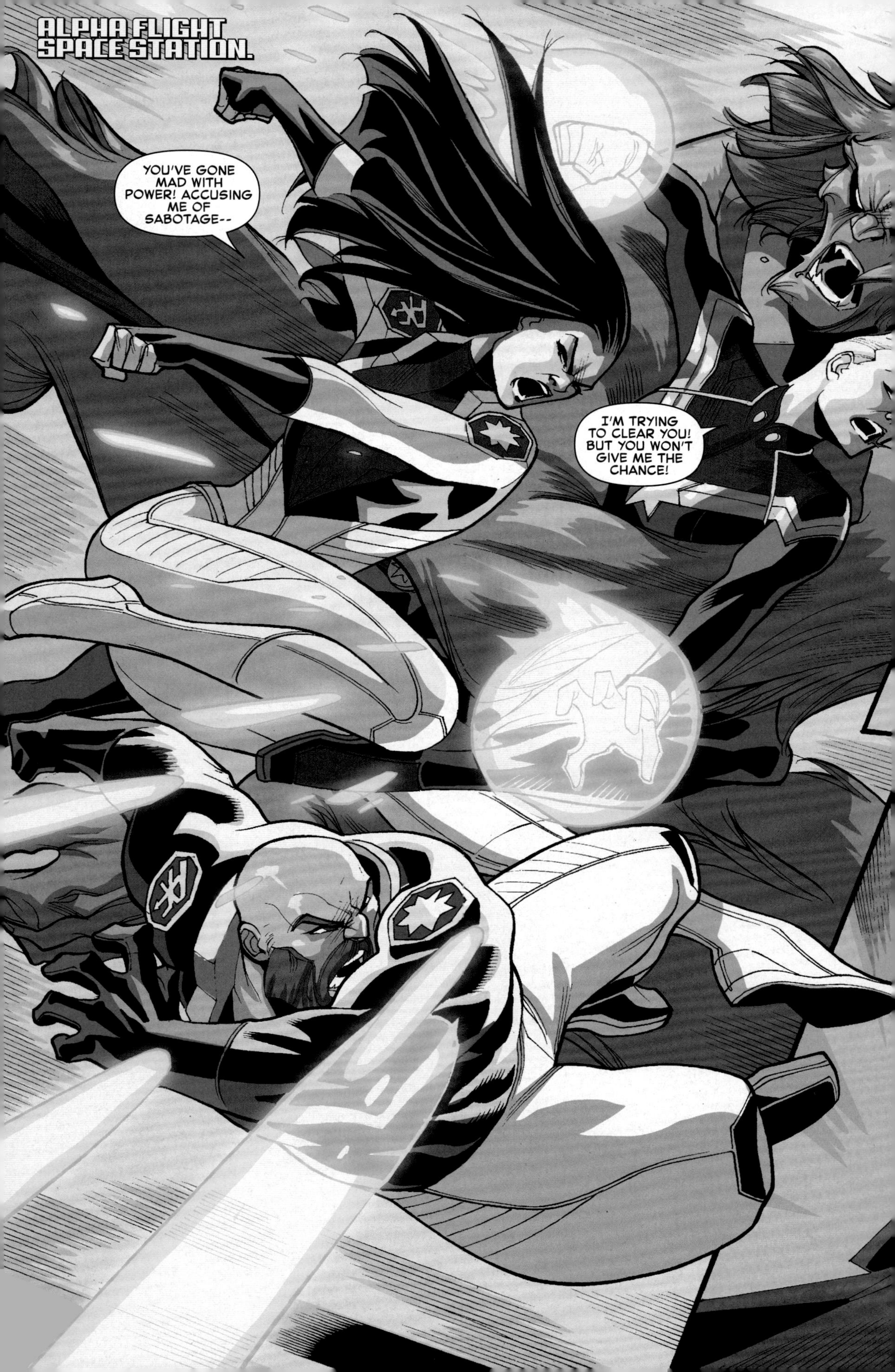
ALPHA FLIGHT SPACE STATION.
YOU'VE GONE MAD WITH POWER! ACCUSING ME OF SABOTAGE--
I'M TRYING TO CLEAR YOU! BUT YOU WON'T GIVE ME THE CHANCE!

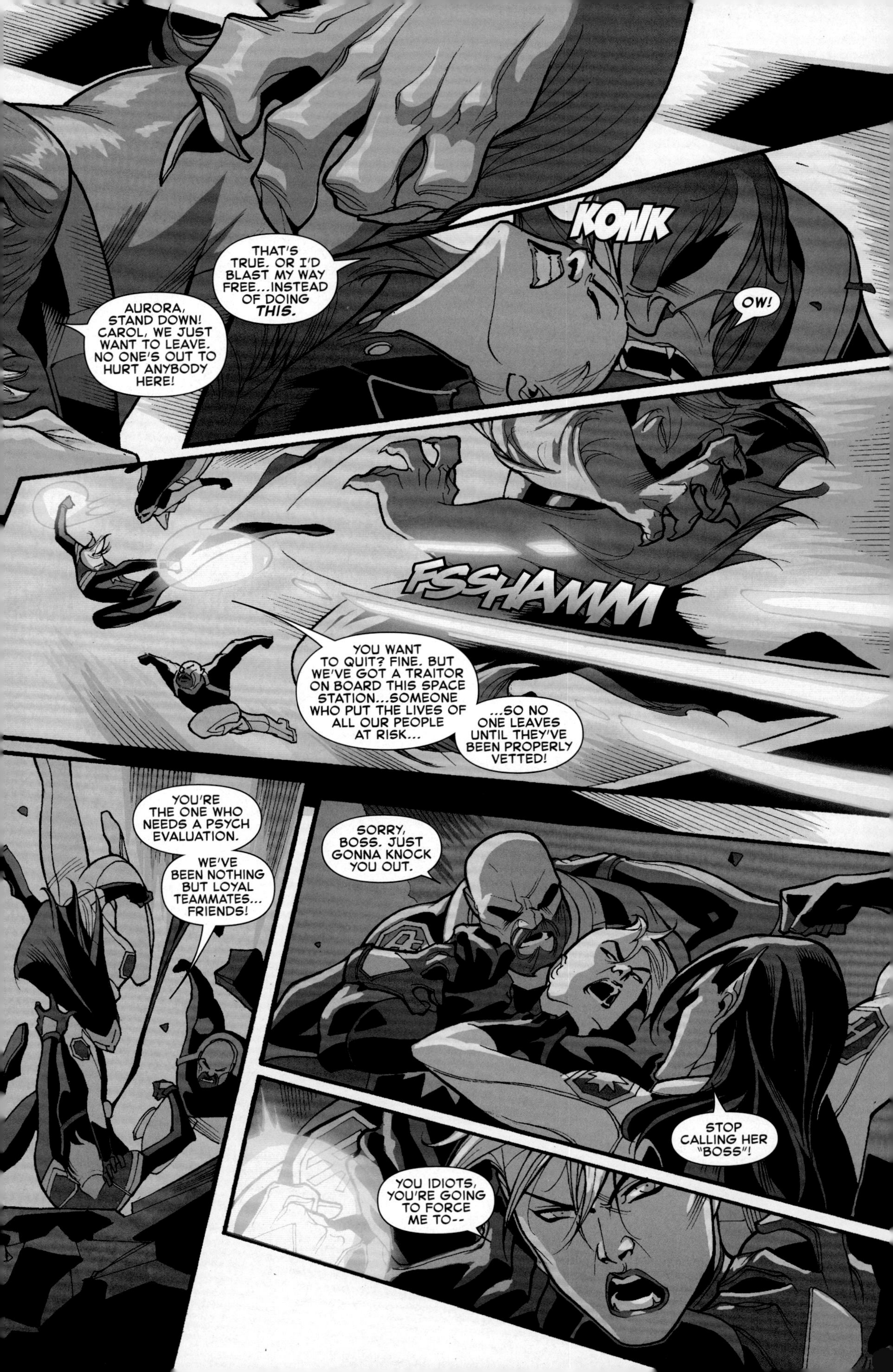
KONK
AURORA, STAND DOWN! CAROL, WE JUST WANT TO LEAVE. NO ONE'S OUT TO HURT ANYBODY HERE!
THAT'S TRUE. OR I'D BLAST MY WAY FREE...INSTEAD OF DOING THIS.
OW!
FSSHAMM
YOU WANT TO QUIT? FINE. BUT WE'VE GOT A TRAITOR ON BOARD THIS SPACE STATION...SOMEONE WHO PUT THE LIVES OF ALL OUR PEOPLE AT RISK...
...SO NO ONE LEAVES UNTIL THEY'VE BEEN PROPERLY VETTED!
YOU'RE THE ONE WHO NEEDS A PSYCH EVALUATION.
WE'VE BEEN NOTHING BUT LOYAL TEAMMATES... FRIENDS!
SORRY, BOSS. JUST GONNA KNOCK YOU OUT.
STOP CALLING HER "BOSS"!
YOU IDIOTS, YOU'RE GOING TO FORCE ME TO--

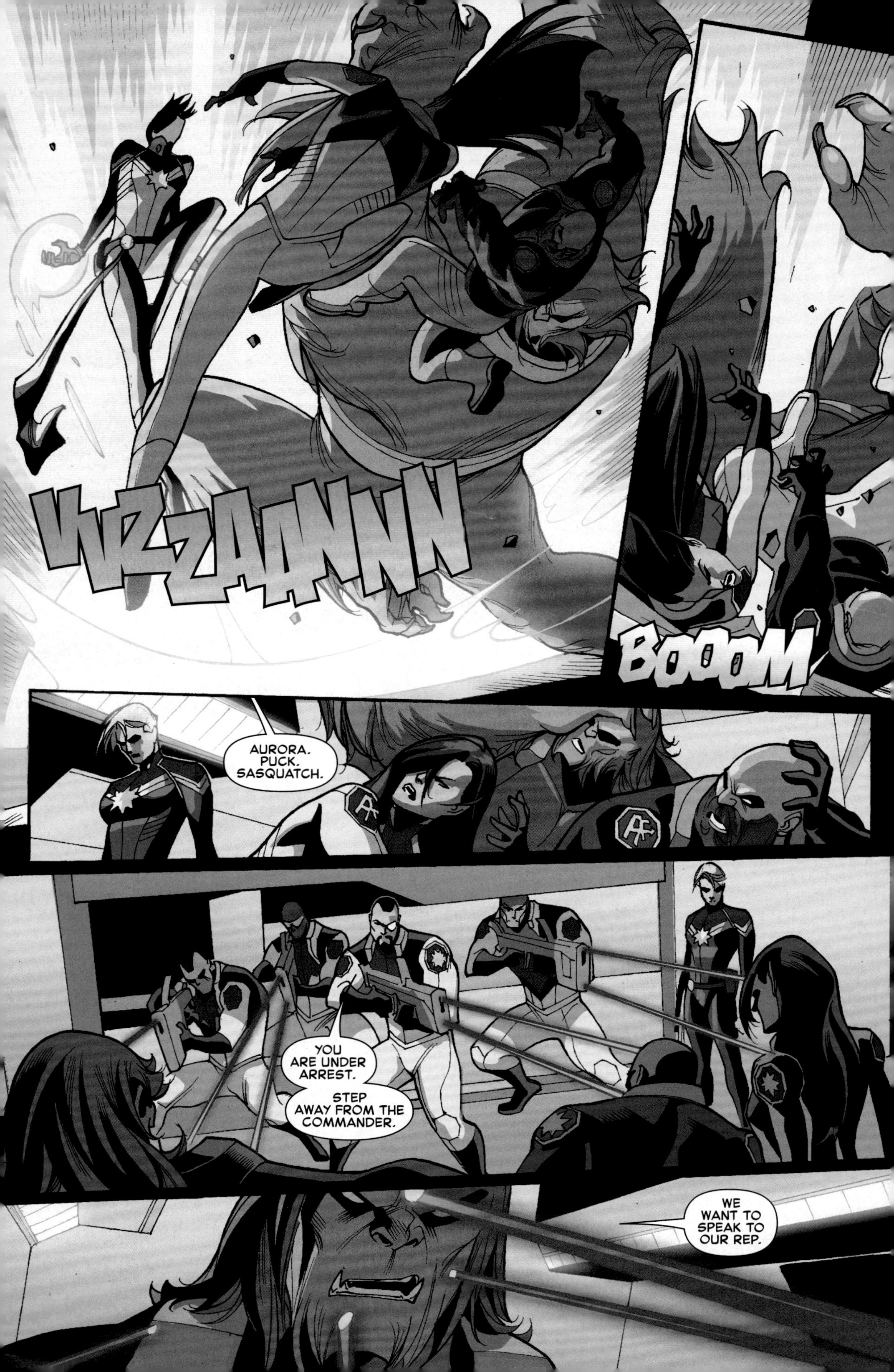
VVZZAANNN
BOOOM
AURORA. PUCK. SASQUATCH.
YOU ARE UNDER ARREST.
STEP AWAY FROM THE COMMANDER.
WE WANT TO SPEAK TO OUR REP.

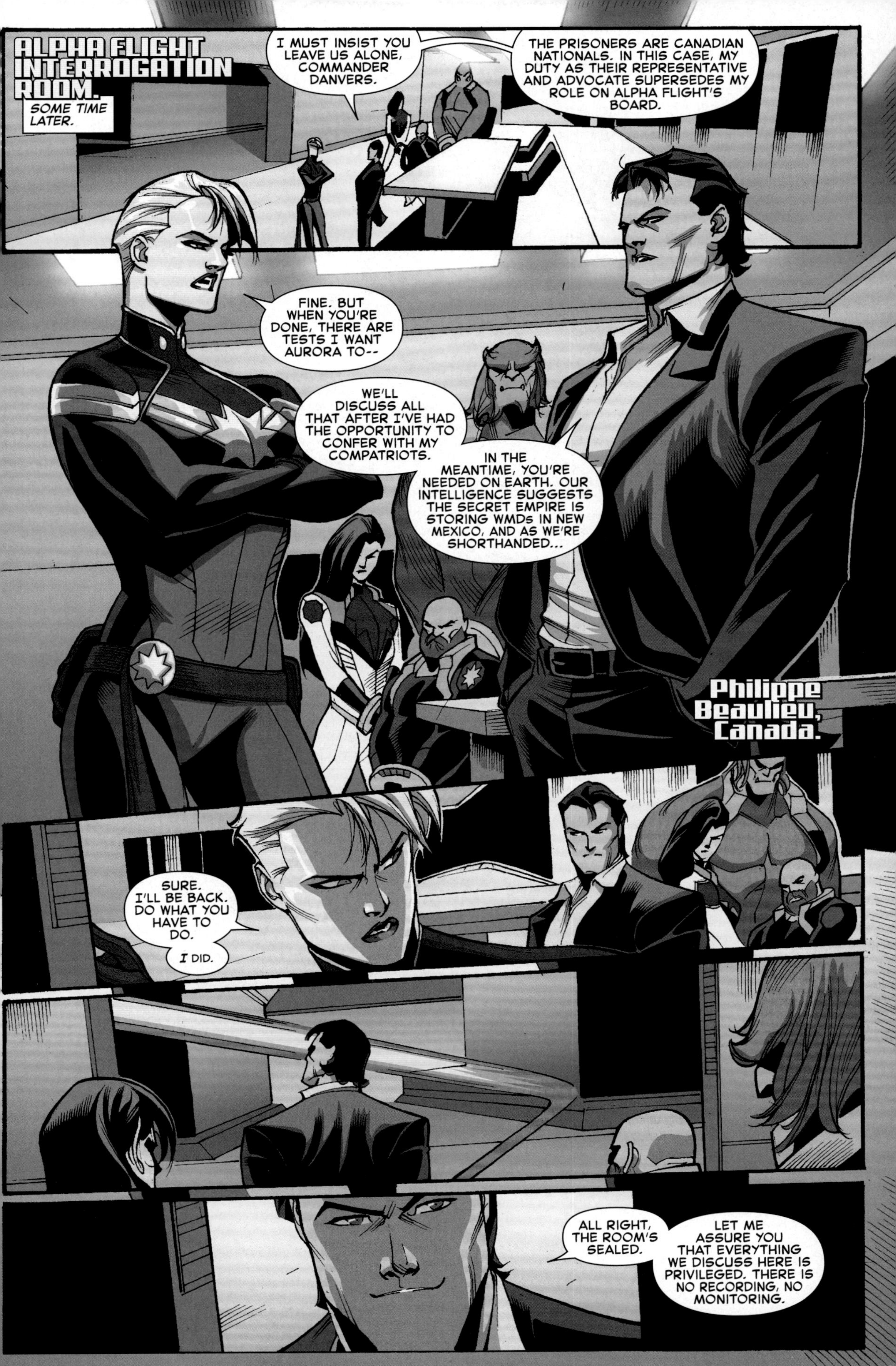
ALPHA FLIGHT INTERROGATION ROOM.
SOME TIME LATER.
I MUST INSIST YOU LEAVE US ALONE, COMMANDER DANVERS.
THE PRISONERS ARE CANADIAN NATIONALS. IN THIS CASE, MY DUTY AS THEIR REPRESENTATIVE AND ADVOCATE SUPERSEDES MY ROLE ON ALPHA FLIGHT'S BOARD.
FINE. BUT WHEN YOU'RE DONE, THERE ARE TESTS I WANT AURORA TO--
WE'LL DISCUSS ALL THAT AFTER I'VE HAD THE OPPORTUNITY TO CONFER WITH MY COMPATRIOTS.
IN THE MEANTIME, YOU'RE NEEDED ON EARTH. OUR INTELLIGENCE SUGGESTS THE SECRET EMPIRE IS STORING WMDs IN NEW MEXICO, AND AS WE'RE SHORTHANDED...
Philippe Beaulieu, Canada.
SURE. I'LL BE BACK. DO WHAT YOU HAVE TO DO.
I DID.
ALL RIGHT, THE ROOM'S SEALED.
LET ME ASSURE YOU THAT EVERYTHING WE DISCUSS HERE IS PRIVILEGED. THERE IS NO RECORDING, NO MONITORING.

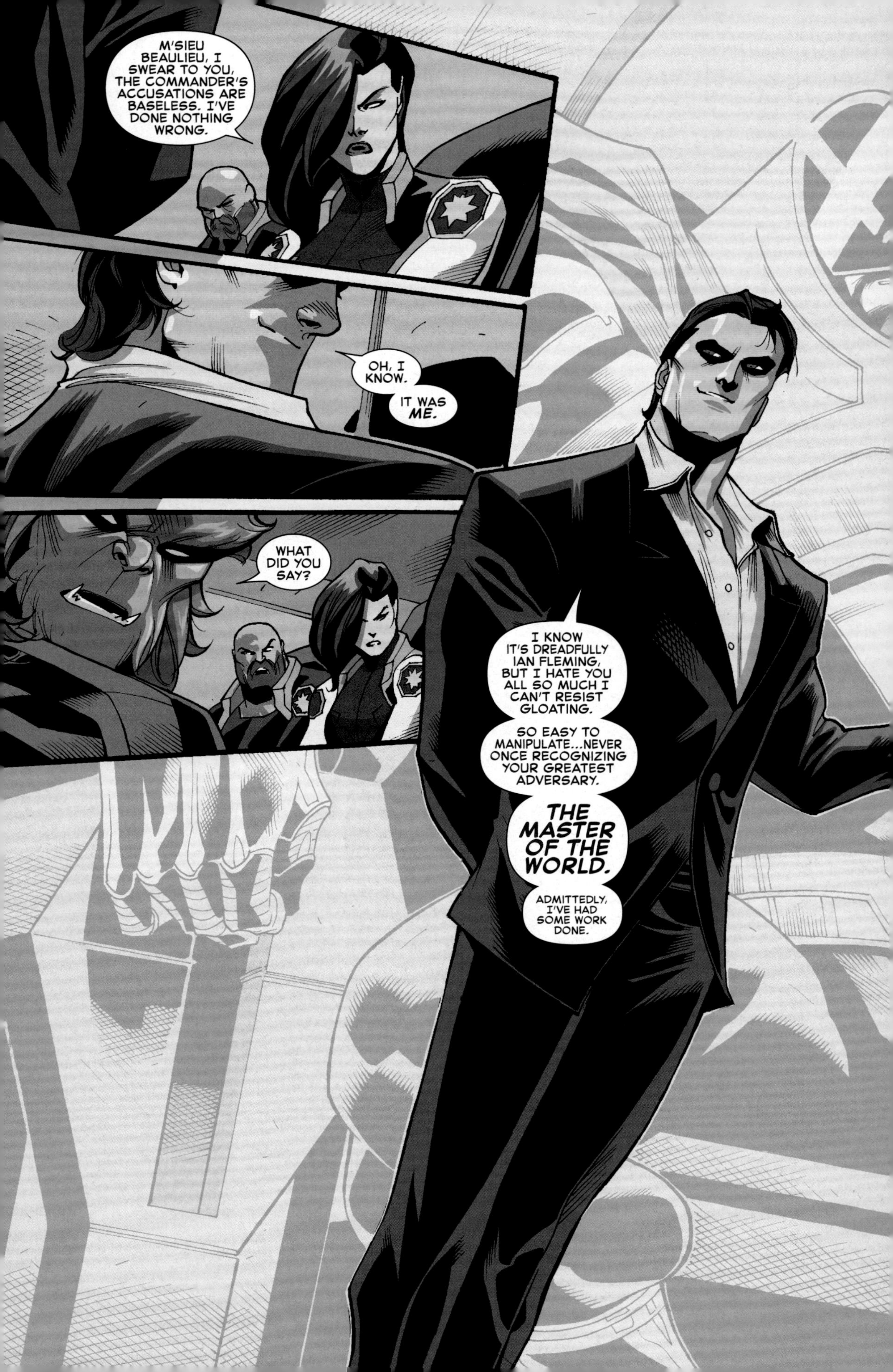
M'SIEU BEAULIEU, I SWEAR TO YOU, THE COMMANDER'S ACCUSATIONS ARE BASELESS. I'VE DONE NOTHING WRONG.
OH, I KNOW.
IT WAS *ME.*
WHAT DID YOU SAY?
I KNOW IT'S DREADFULLY IAN FLEMING, BUT I HATE YOU ALL SO MUCH I CAN'T RESIST GLOATING.
SO EASY TO MANIPULATE...NEVER ONCE RECOGNIZING YOUR GREATEST ADVERSARY.
THE MASTER OF THE WORLD.
ADMITTEDLY, I'VE HAD SOME WORK DONE.

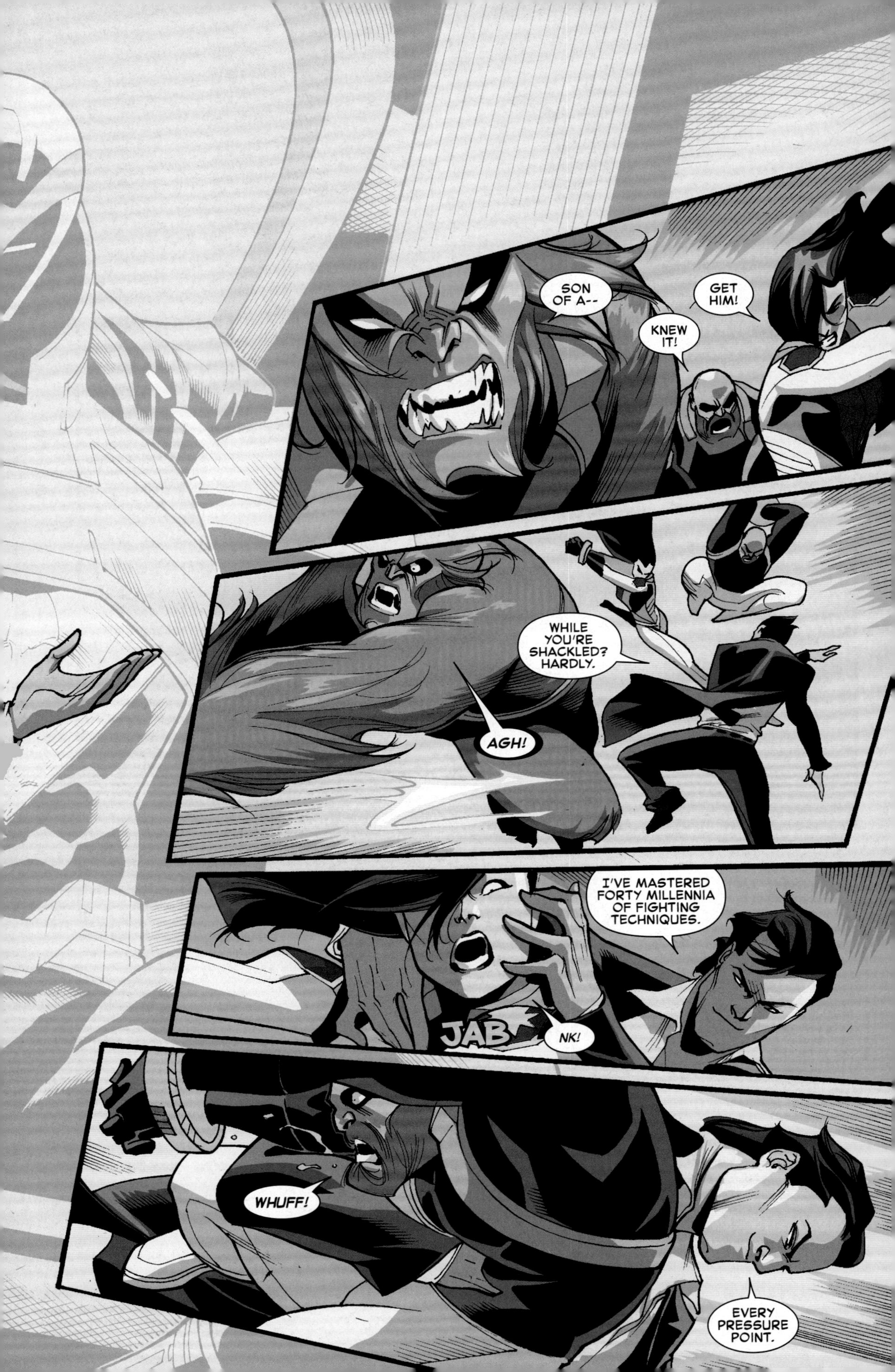
SON OF A--
GET HIM!
KNEW IT!
WHILE YOU'RE SHACKLED? HARDLY.
AGH!
I'VE MASTERED FORTY MILLENNIA OF FIGHTING TECHNIQUES.
JAB
NK!
WHUFF!
EVERY PRESSURE POINT.

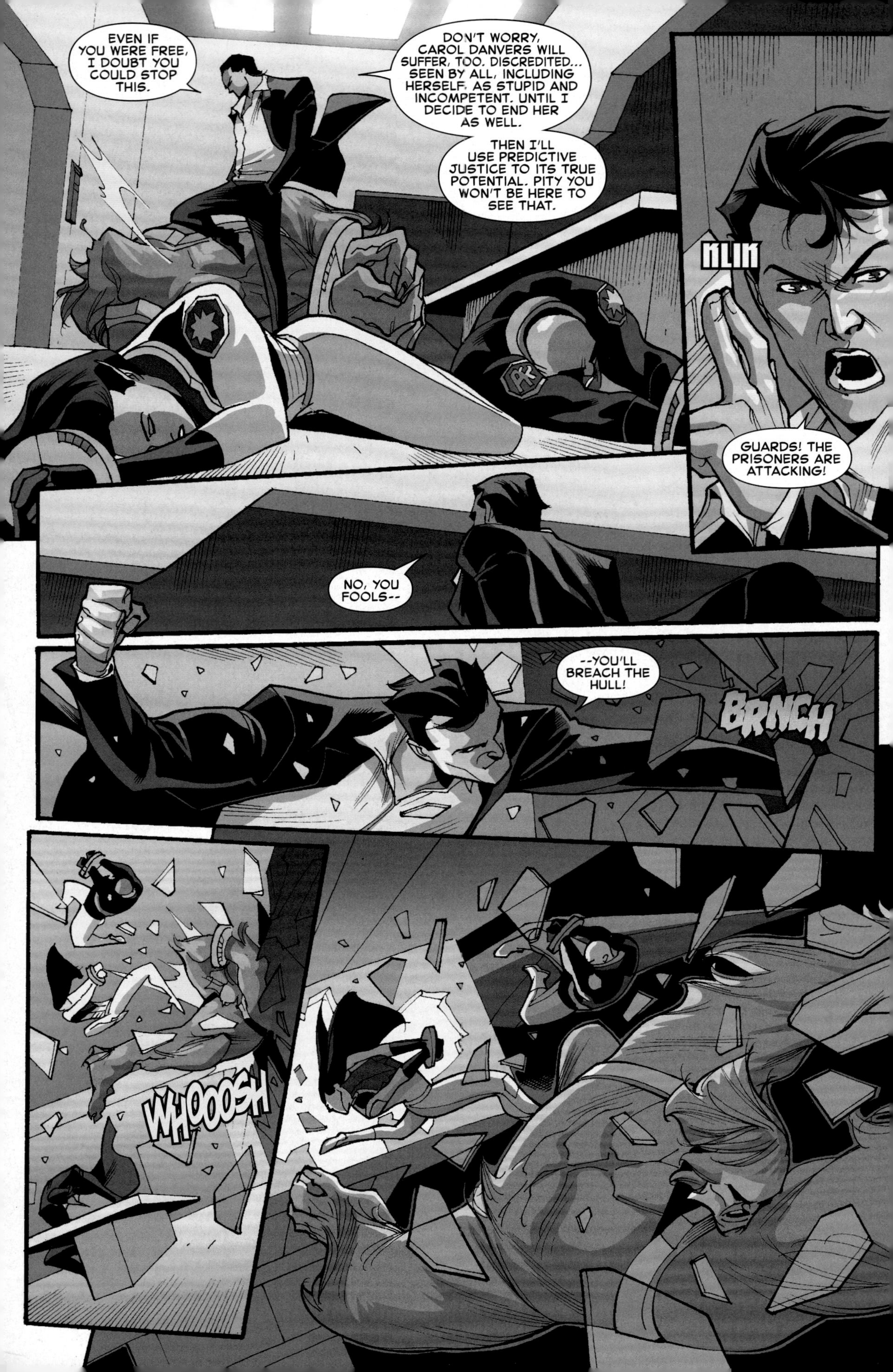
EVEN IF YOU WERE FREE, I DOUBT YOU COULD STOP THIS.
DON'T WORRY, CAROL DANVERS WILL SUFFER, TOO. DISCREDITED... SEEN BY ALL, INCLUDING HERSELF, AS STUPID AND INCOMPETENT. UNTIL I DECIDE TO END HER AS WELL.
THEN I'LL USE PREDICTIVE JUSTICE TO ITS TRUE POTENTIAL. PITY YOU WON'T BE HERE TO SEE THAT.
KLIK
GUARDS! THE PRISONERS ARE ATTACKING!
NO, YOU FOOLS--
--YOU'LL BREACH THE HULL!
BRNCH
WHOOOSH

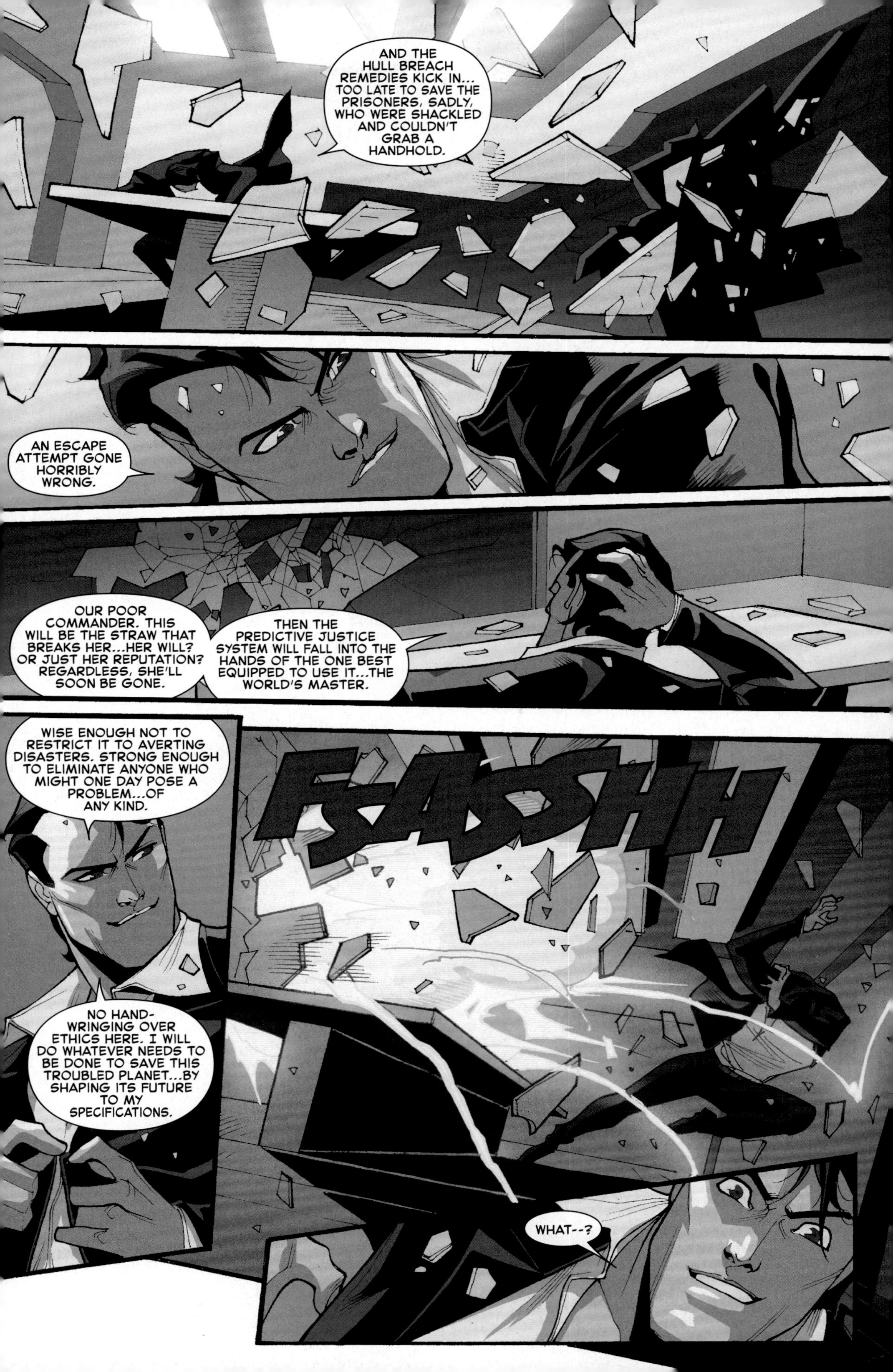

AND THE HULL BREACH REMEDIES KICK IN... TOO LATE TO SAVE THE PRISONERS, SADLY, WHO WERE SHACKLED AND COULDN'T GRAB A HANDHOLD.
AN ESCAPE ATTEMPT GONE HORRIBLY WRONG.
OUR POOR COMMANDER. THIS WILL BE THE STRAW THAT BREAKS HER...HER WILL? OR JUST HER REPUTATION? REGARDLESS, SHE'LL SOON BE GONE.
THEN THE PREDICTIVE JUSTICE SYSTEM WILL FALL INTO THE HANDS OF THE ONE BEST EQUIPPED TO USE IT...THE WORLD'S MASTER.
WISE ENOUGH NOT TO RESTRICT IT TO AVERTING DISASTERS. STRONG ENOUGH TO ELIMINATE ANYONE WHO MIGHT ONE DAY POSE A PROBLEM...OF ANY KIND.
FSASSHH
NO HAND-WRINGING OVER ETHICS HERE. I WILL DO WHATEVER NEEDS TO BE DONE TO SAVE THIS TROUBLED PLANET...BY SHAPING ITS FUTURE TO MY SPECIFICATIONS.
WHAT--?

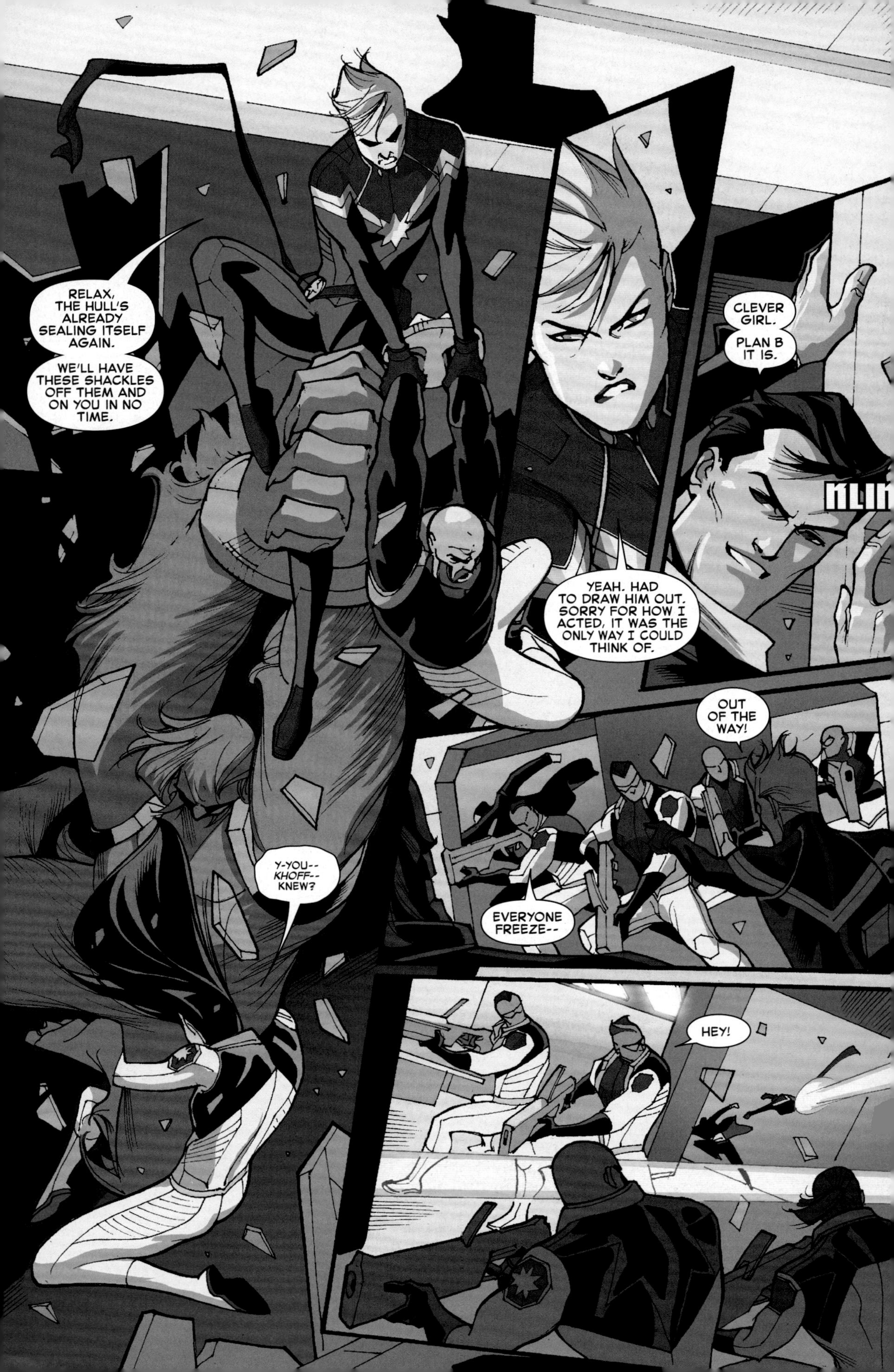
RELAX, THE HULL'S ALREADY SEALING ITSELF AGAIN.
WE'LL HAVE THESE SHACKLES OFF THEM AND ON YOU IN NO TIME.
Y-YOU-- KHOFF-- KNEW?
YEAH. HAD TO DRAW HIM OUT. SORRY FOR HOW I ACTED, IT WAS THE ONLY WAY I COULD THINK OF.
CLEVER GIRL.
PLAN B IT IS.
KLIN
OUT OF THE WAY!
EVERYONE FREEZE--
HEY!

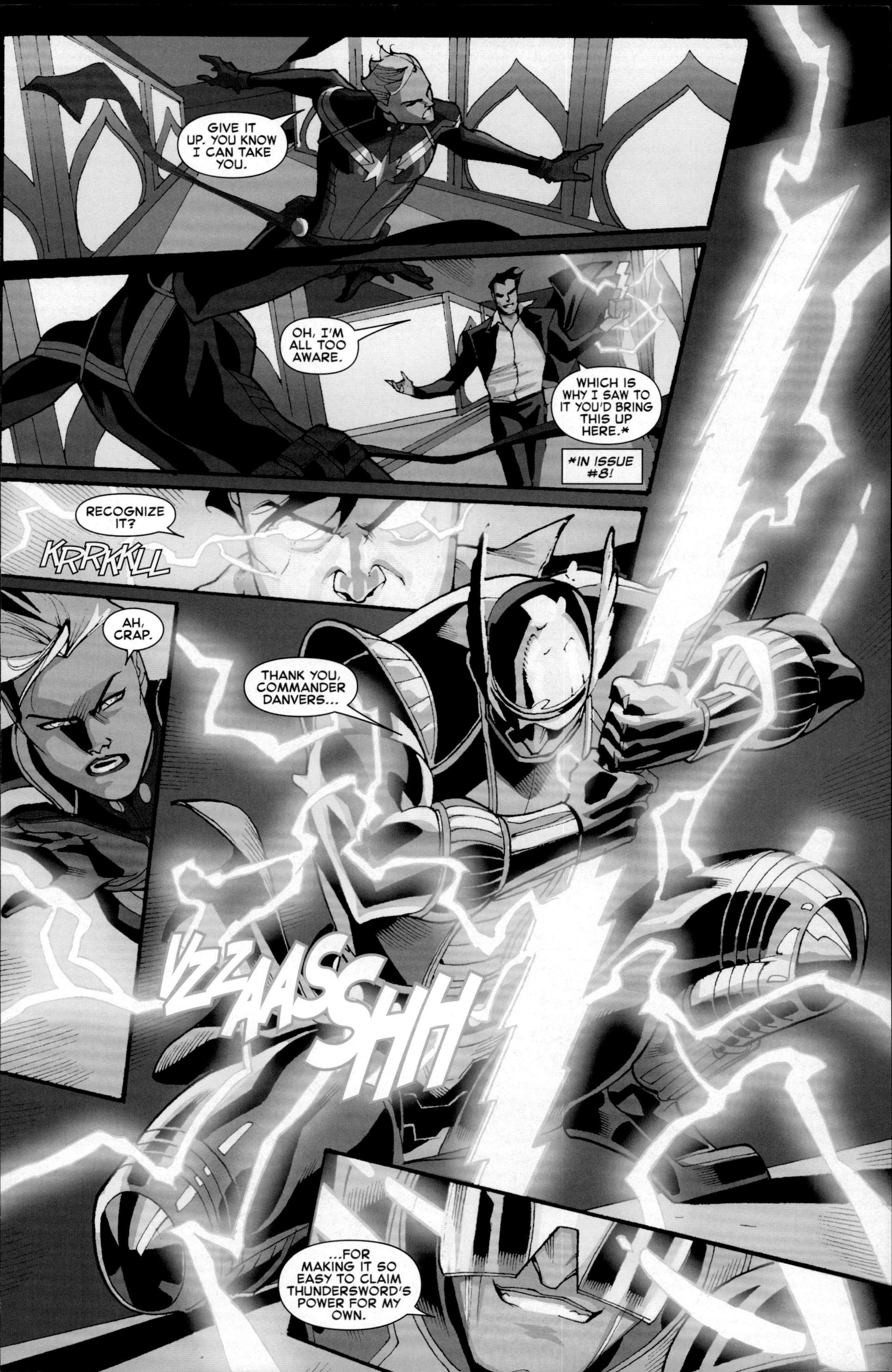
GIVE IT UP. YOU KNOW I CAN TAKE YOU.
OH, I'M ALL TOO AWARE.
WHICH IS WHY I SAW TO IT YOU'D BRING THIS UP HERE.*
*IN ISSUE #8!
RECOGNIZE IT?
KRRKKLL
AH, CRAP.
THANK YOU, COMMANDER DANVERS...
VZZAASSHH
...FOR MAKING IT SO EASY TO CLAIM THUNDERSWORD'S POWER FOR MY OWN.

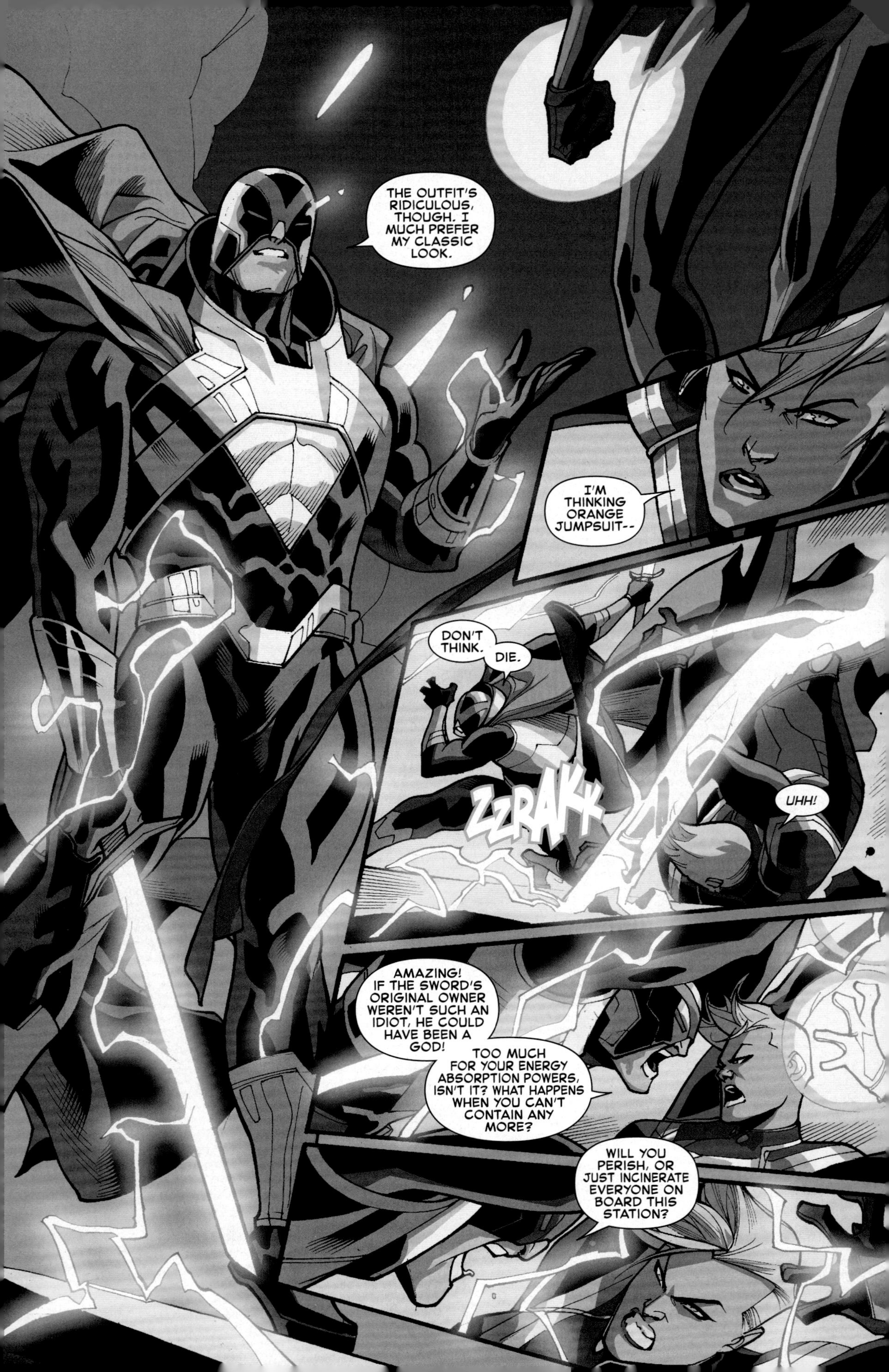
THE OUTFIT'S RIDICULOUS, THOUGH. I MUCH PREFER MY CLASSIC LOOK.
I'M THINKING ORANGE JUMPSUIT--
DON'T THINK.
DIE.
ZZRAKK
UHH!
AMAZING! IF THE SWORD'S ORIGINAL OWNER WEREN'T SUCH AN IDIOT, HE COULD HAVE BEEN A GOD!
TOO MUCH FOR YOUR ENERGY ABSORPTION POWERS, ISN'T IT? WHAT HAPPENS WHEN YOU CAN'T CONTAIN ANY MORE?
WILL YOU PERISH, OR JUST INCINERATE EVERYONE ON BOARD THIS STATION?

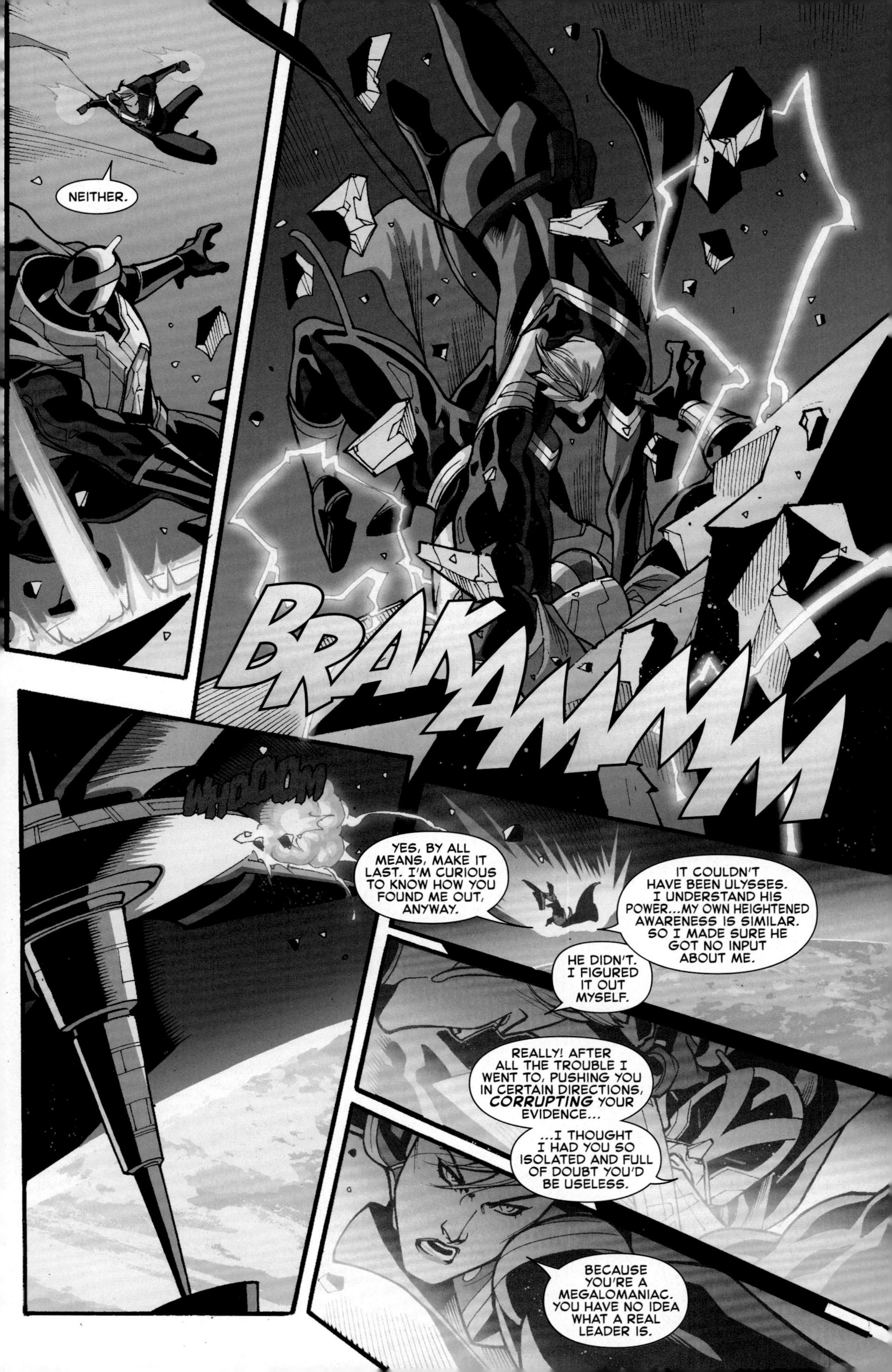
NEITHER.
BRAKAMMMM
WHOOOM
YES, BY ALL MEANS, MAKE IT LAST. I'M CURIOUS TO KNOW HOW YOU FOUND ME OUT, ANYWAY.
IT COULDN'T HAVE BEEN ULYSSES. I UNDERSTAND HIS POWER...MY OWN HEIGHTENED AWARENESS IS SIMILAR. SO I MADE SURE HE GOT NO INPUT ABOUT ME.
HE DIDN'T. I FIGURED IT OUT MYSELF.
REALLY! AFTER ALL THE TROUBLE I WENT TO, PUSHING YOU IN CERTAIN DIRECTIONS, *CORRUPTING* YOUR EVIDENCE...
...I THOUGHT I HAD YOU SO ISOLATED AND FULL OF DOUBT YOU'D BE USELESS.
BECAUSE YOU'RE A MEGALOMANIAC. YOU HAVE NO IDEA WHAT A REAL LEADER IS.

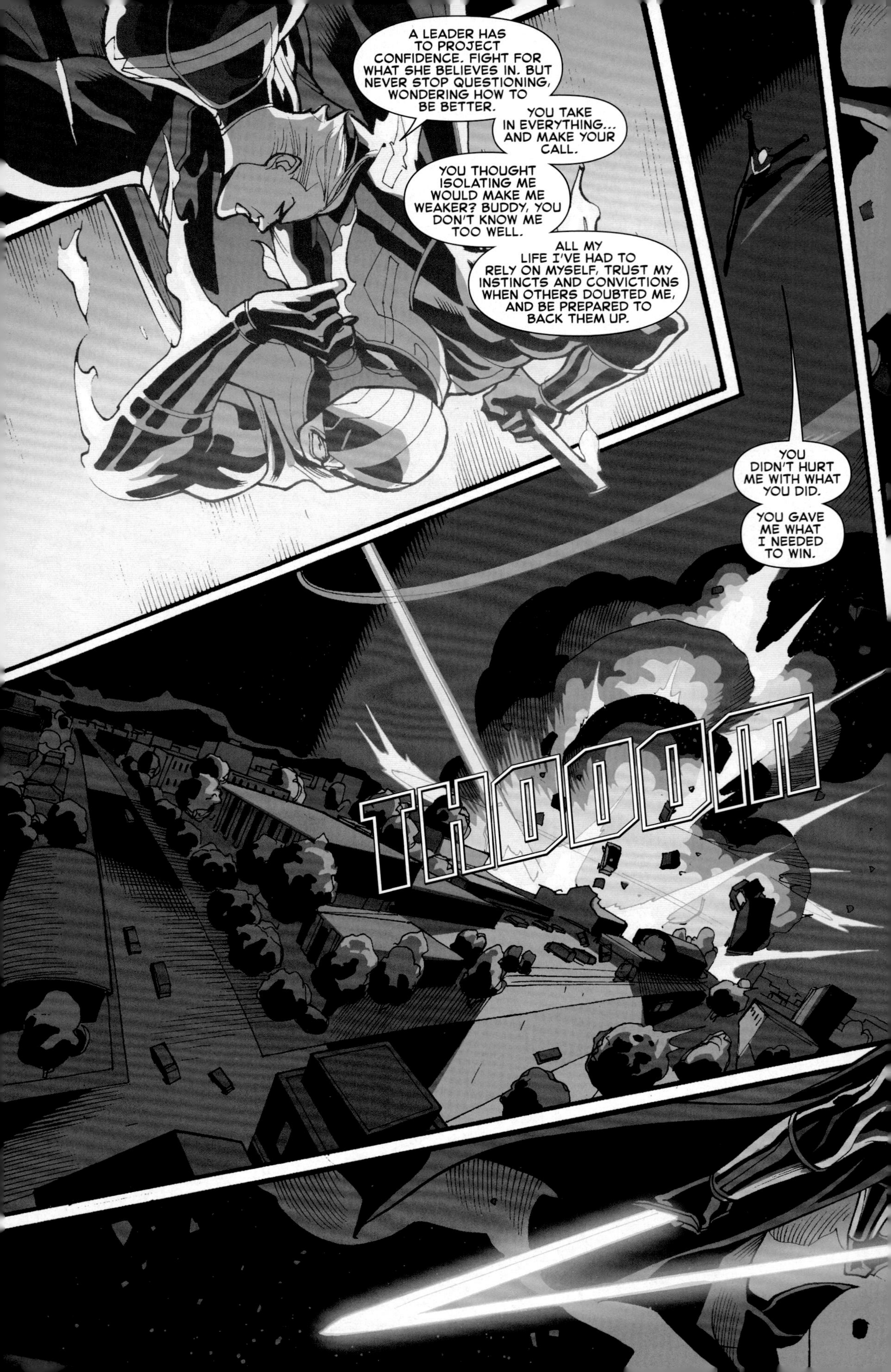
A LEADER HAS TO PROJECT CONFIDENCE. FIGHT FOR WHAT SHE BELIEVES IN. BUT NEVER STOP QUESTIONING, WONDERING HOW TO BE BETTER.
YOU TAKE IN EVERYTHING... AND MAKE YOUR CALL.
YOU THOUGHT ISOLATING ME WOULD MAKE ME WEAKER? BUDDY, YOU DON'T KNOW ME TOO WELL.
ALL MY LIFE I'VE HAD TO RELY ON MYSELF, TRUST MY INSTINCTS AND CONVICTIONS WHEN OTHERS DOUBTED ME, AND BE PREPARED TO BACK THEM UP.
YOU DIDN'T HURT ME WITH WHAT YOU DID.
YOU GAVE ME WHAT I NEEDED TO WIN.
THOOOM

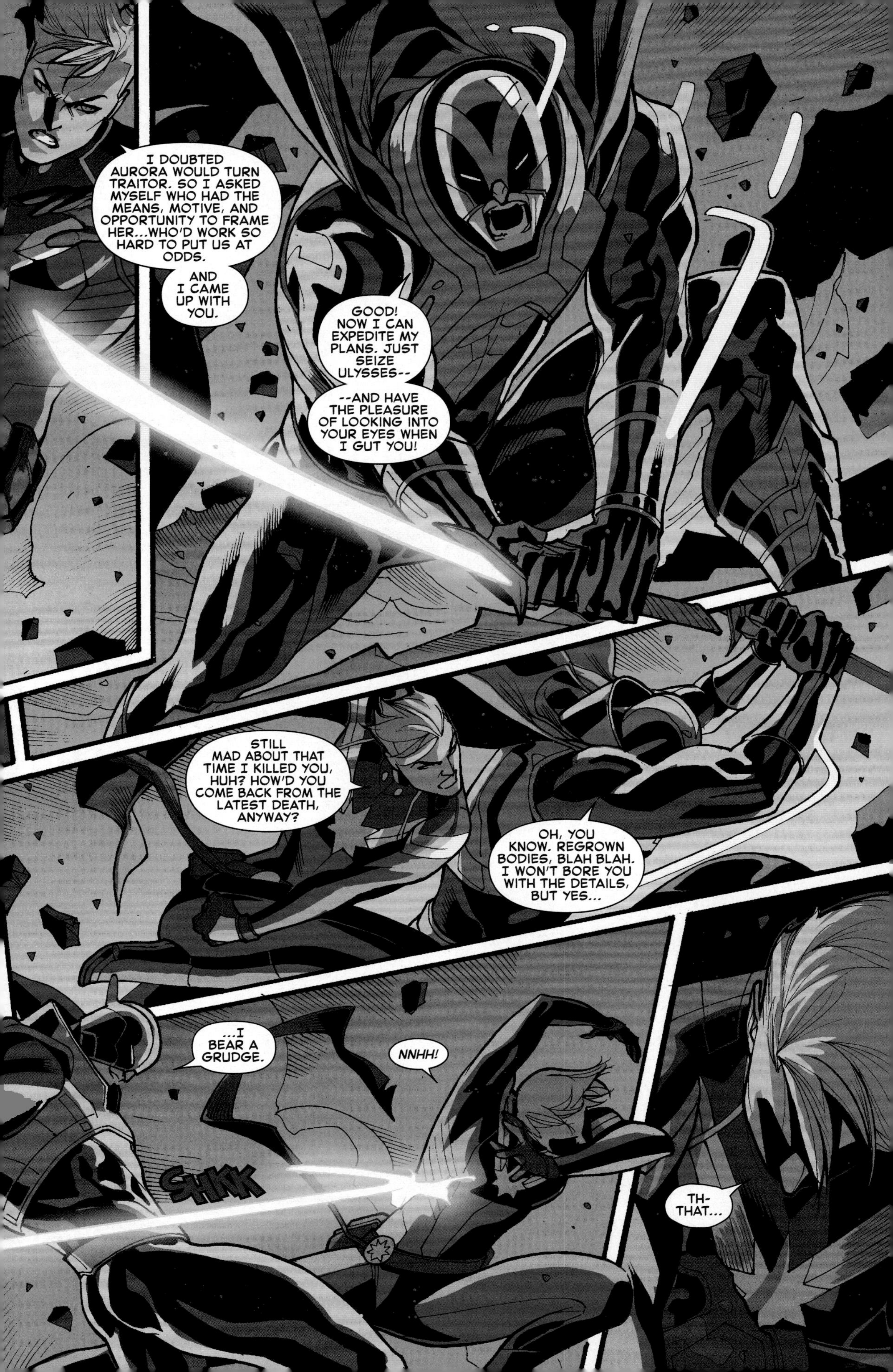
I DOUBTED AURORA WOULD TURN TRAITOR. SO I ASKED MYSELF WHO HAD THE MEANS, MOTIVE, AND OPPORTUNITY TO FRAME HER...WHO'D WORK SO HARD TO PUT US AT ODDS.
AND I CAME UP WITH YOU.
GOOD! NOW I CAN EXPEDITE MY PLANS. JUST SEIZE ULYSSES--
--AND HAVE THE PLEASURE OF LOOKING INTO YOUR EYES WHEN I GUT YOU!
STILL MAD ABOUT THAT TIME I KILLED YOU, HUH? HOW'D YOU COME BACK FROM THE LATEST DEATH, ANYWAY?
OH, YOU KNOW. REGROWN BODIES, BLAH BLAH. I WON'T BORE YOU WITH THE DETAILS, BUT YES...
...I BEAR A GRUDGE.
NNHH!
SHKK
TH-THAT...

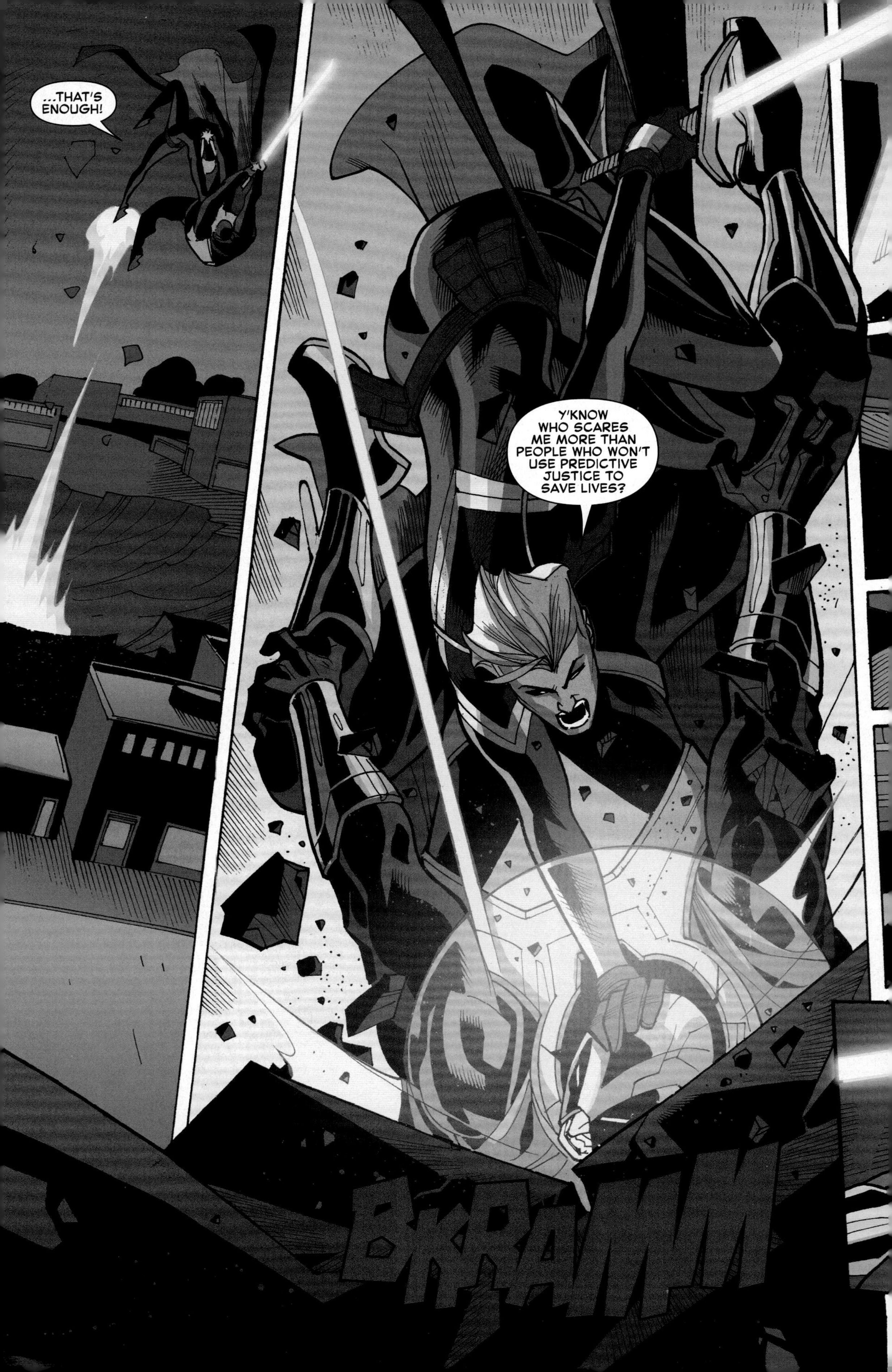
...THAT'S ENOUGH!
Y'KNOW WHO SCARES ME MORE THAN PEOPLE WHO WON'T USE PREDICTIVE JUSTICE TO SAVE LIVES?
BRRAMM

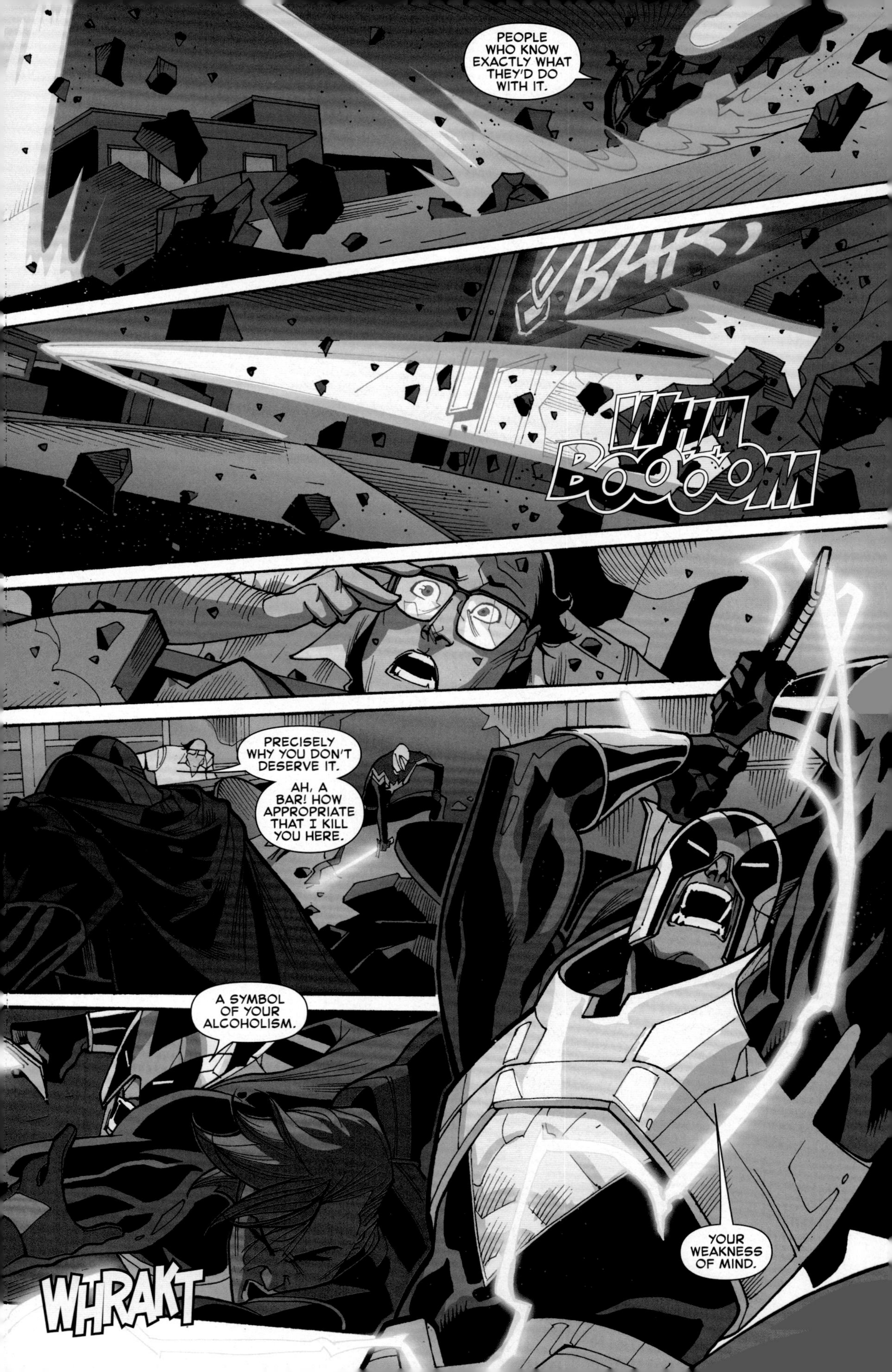
PEOPLE WHO KNOW EXACTLY WHAT THEY'D DO WITH IT.
WHA BOOOOOM
PRECISELY WHY YOU DON'T DESERVE IT.
AH, A BAR! HOW APPROPRIATE THAT I KILL YOU HERE.
A SYMBOL OF YOUR ALCOHOLISM.
YOUR WEAKNESS OF MIND.
WHRAKT

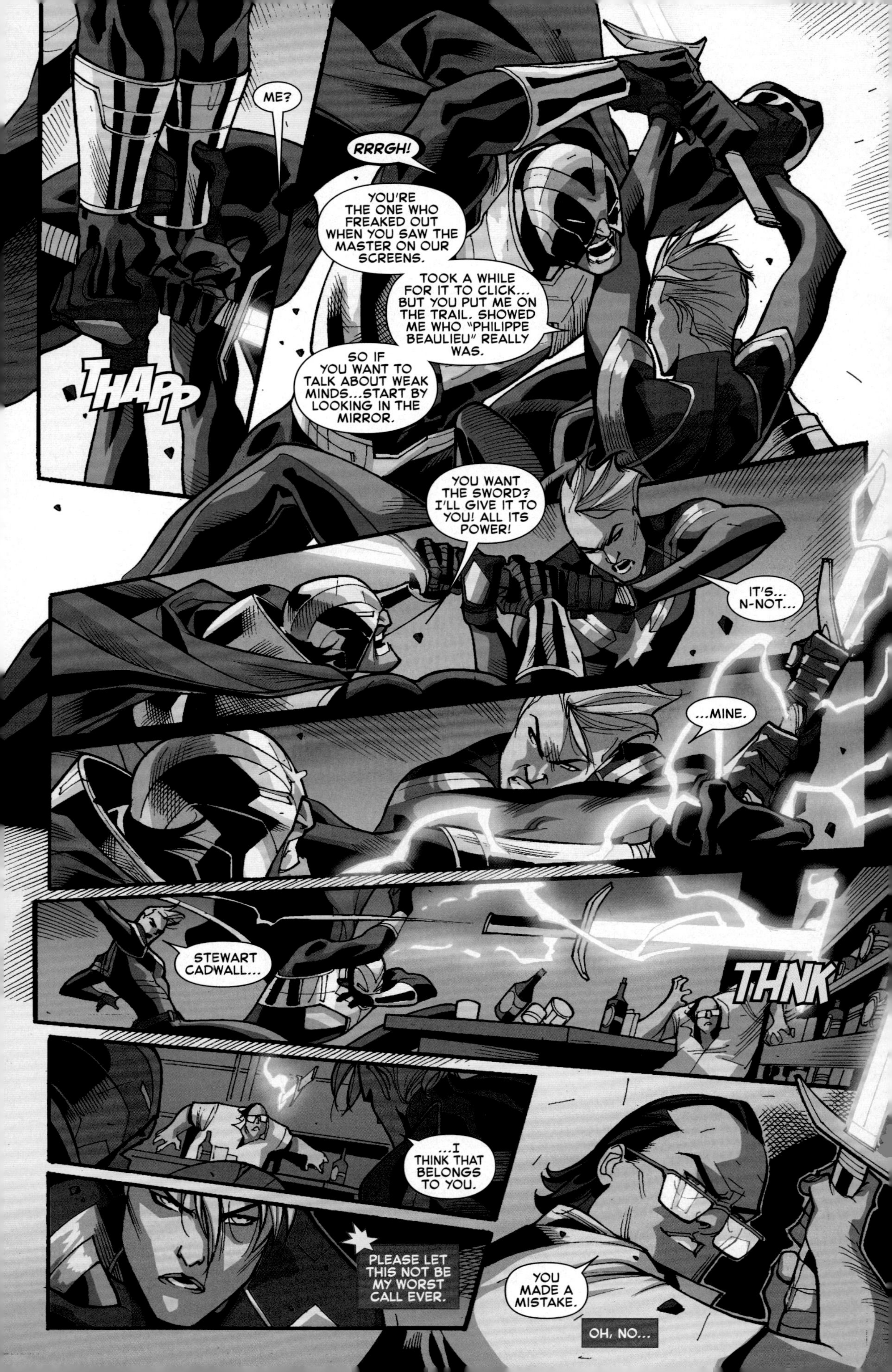

ME?
RRRGH!
YOU'RE THE ONE WHO FREAKED OUT WHEN YOU SAW THE MASTER ON OUR SCREENS.
TOOK A WHILE FOR IT TO CLICK... BUT YOU PUT ME ON THE TRAIL. SHOWED ME WHO "PHILIPPE BEAULIEU" REALLY WAS.
SO IF YOU WANT TO TALK ABOUT WEAK MINDS...START BY LOOKING IN THE MIRROR.
THAPP
YOU WANT THE SWORD? I'LL GIVE IT TO YOU! ALL ITS POWER!
IT'S... N-NOT...
...MINE.
STEWART CADWALL...
THNK
...I THINK THAT BELONGS TO YOU.
PLEASE LET THIS NOT BE MY WORST CALL EVER.
YOU MADE A MISTAKE.
OH, NO...

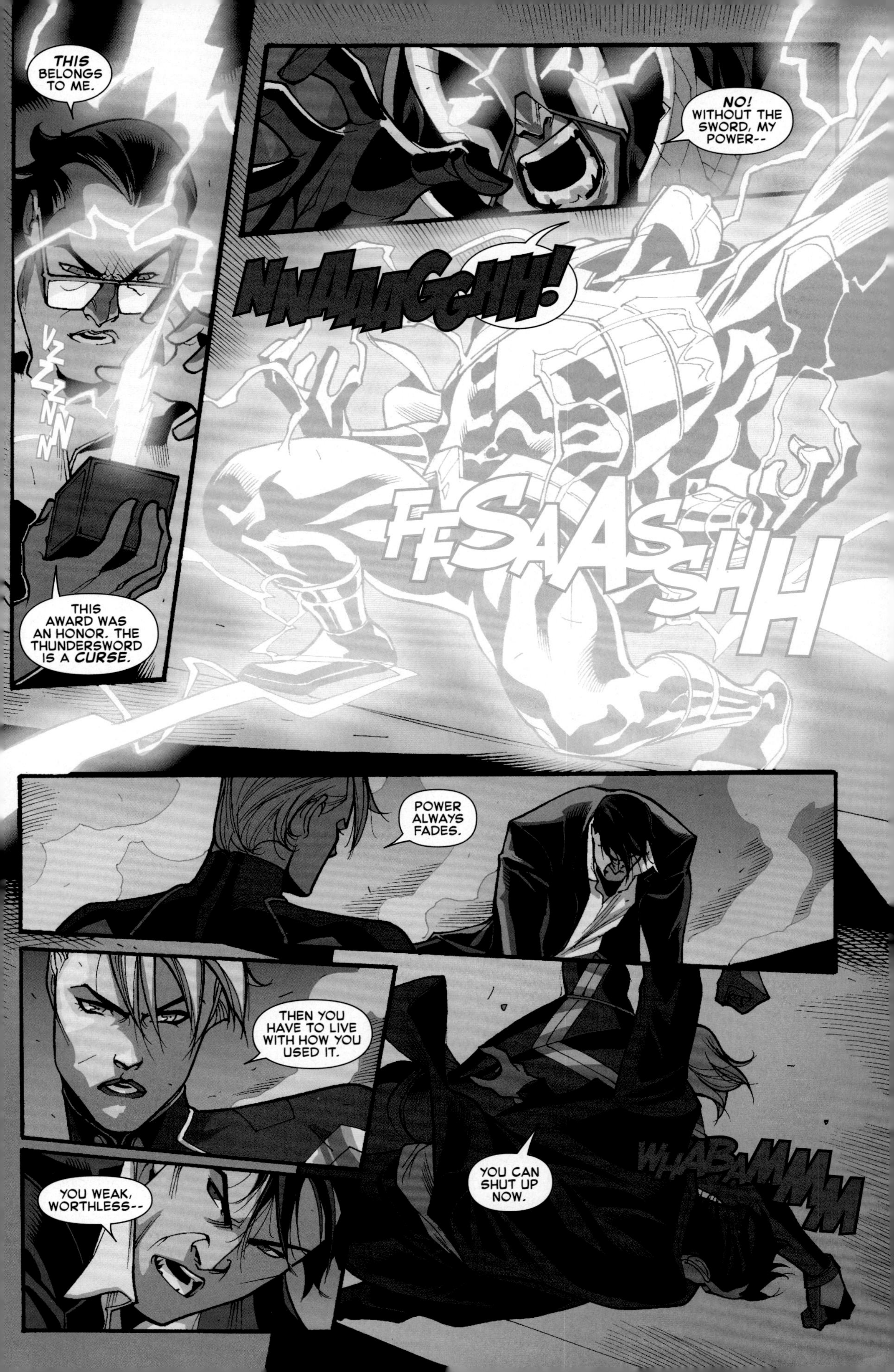
THIS BELONGS TO ME.
NO! WITHOUT THE SWORD, MY POWER--
NNAAAAGGHH!
VZZZNNN
FFSAASHH
THIS AWARD WAS AN HONOR. THE THUNDERSWORD IS A CURSE.
POWER ALWAYS FADES.
THEN YOU HAVE TO LIVE WITH HOW YOU USED IT.
YOU WEAK, WORTHLESS--
YOU CAN SHUT UP NOW.
WHABAMMM

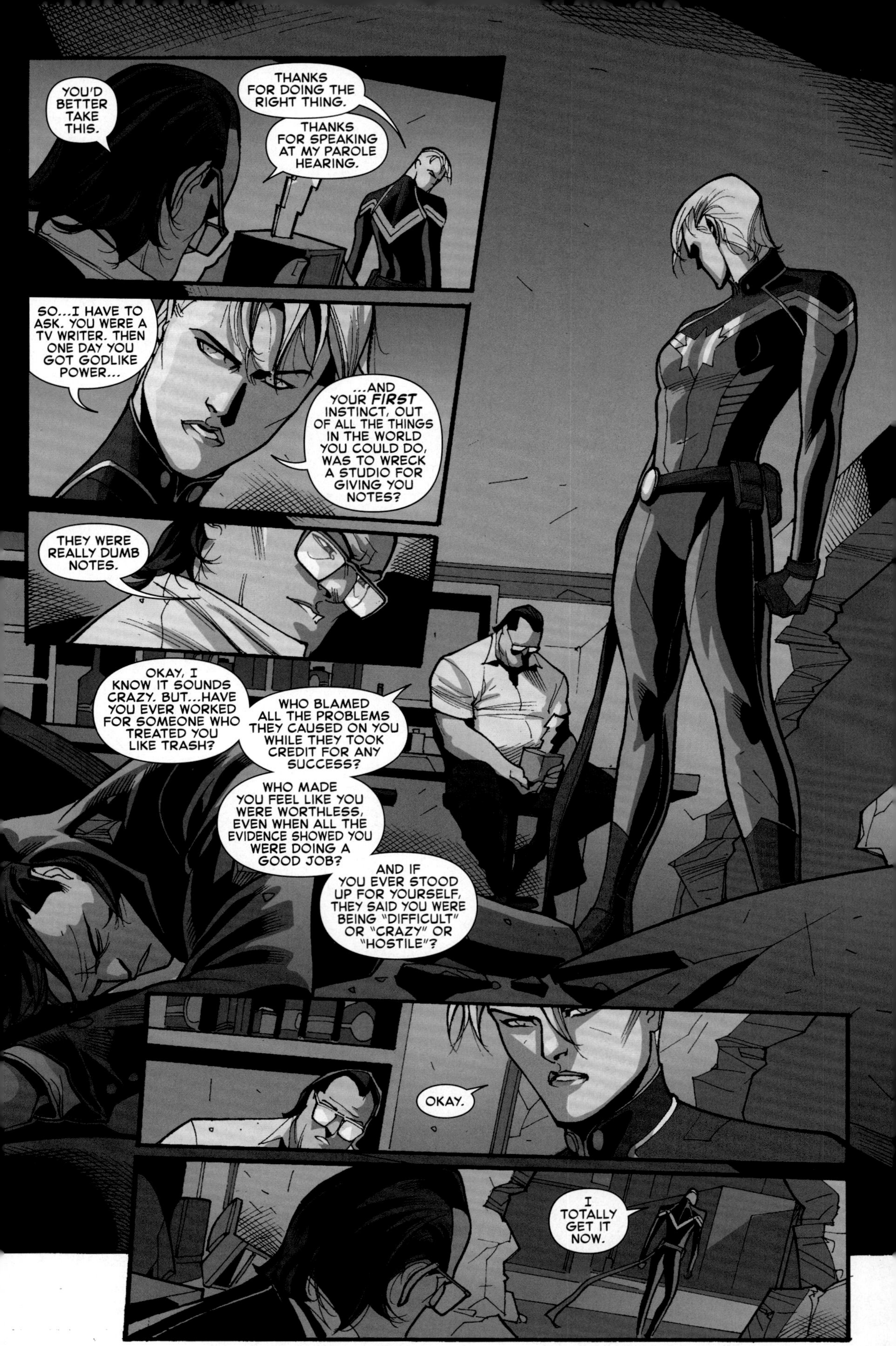
YOU'D BETTER TAKE THIS.
THANKS FOR DOING THE RIGHT THING.
THANKS FOR SPEAKING AT MY PAROLE HEARING.
SO...I HAVE TO ASK. YOU WERE A TV WRITER. THEN ONE DAY YOU GOT GODLIKE POWER...
...AND YOUR FIRST INSTINCT, OUT OF ALL THE THINGS IN THE WORLD YOU COULD DO, WAS TO WRECK A STUDIO FOR GIVING YOU NOTES?
THEY WERE REALLY DUMB NOTES.
OKAY, I KNOW IT SOUNDS CRAZY. BUT...HAVE YOU EVER WORKED FOR SOMEONE WHO TREATED YOU LIKE TRASH?
WHO BLAMED ALL THE PROBLEMS THEY CAUSED ON YOU WHILE THEY TOOK CREDIT FOR ANY SUCCESS?
WHO MADE YOU FEEL LIKE YOU WERE WORTHLESS, EVEN WHEN ALL THE EVIDENCE SHOWED YOU WERE DOING A GOOD JOB?
AND IF YOU EVER STOOD UP FOR YOURSELF, THEY SAID YOU WERE BEING "DIFFICULT" OR "CRAZY" OR "HOSTILE"?
OKAY.
I TOTALLY GET IT NOW.

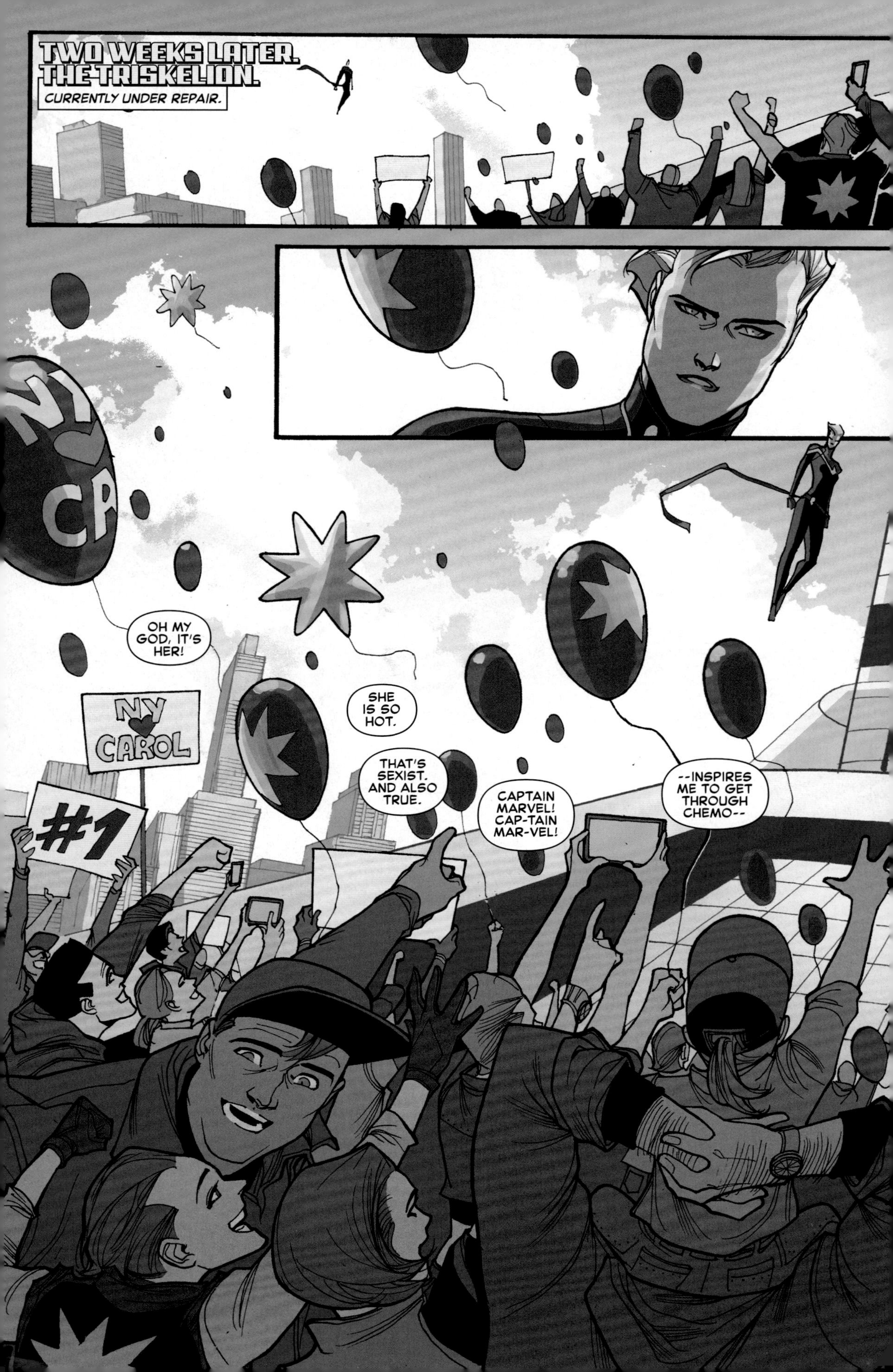
TWO WEEKS LATER. THE TRISKELION.
CURRENTLY UNDER REPAIR.
NY CAROL
#1
OH MY GOD, IT'S HER!
SHE IS SO HOT.
THAT'S SEXIST. AND ALSO TRUE.
CAPTAIN MARVEL! CAP-TAIN MAR-VEL!
--INSPIRES ME TO GET THROUGH CHEMO--

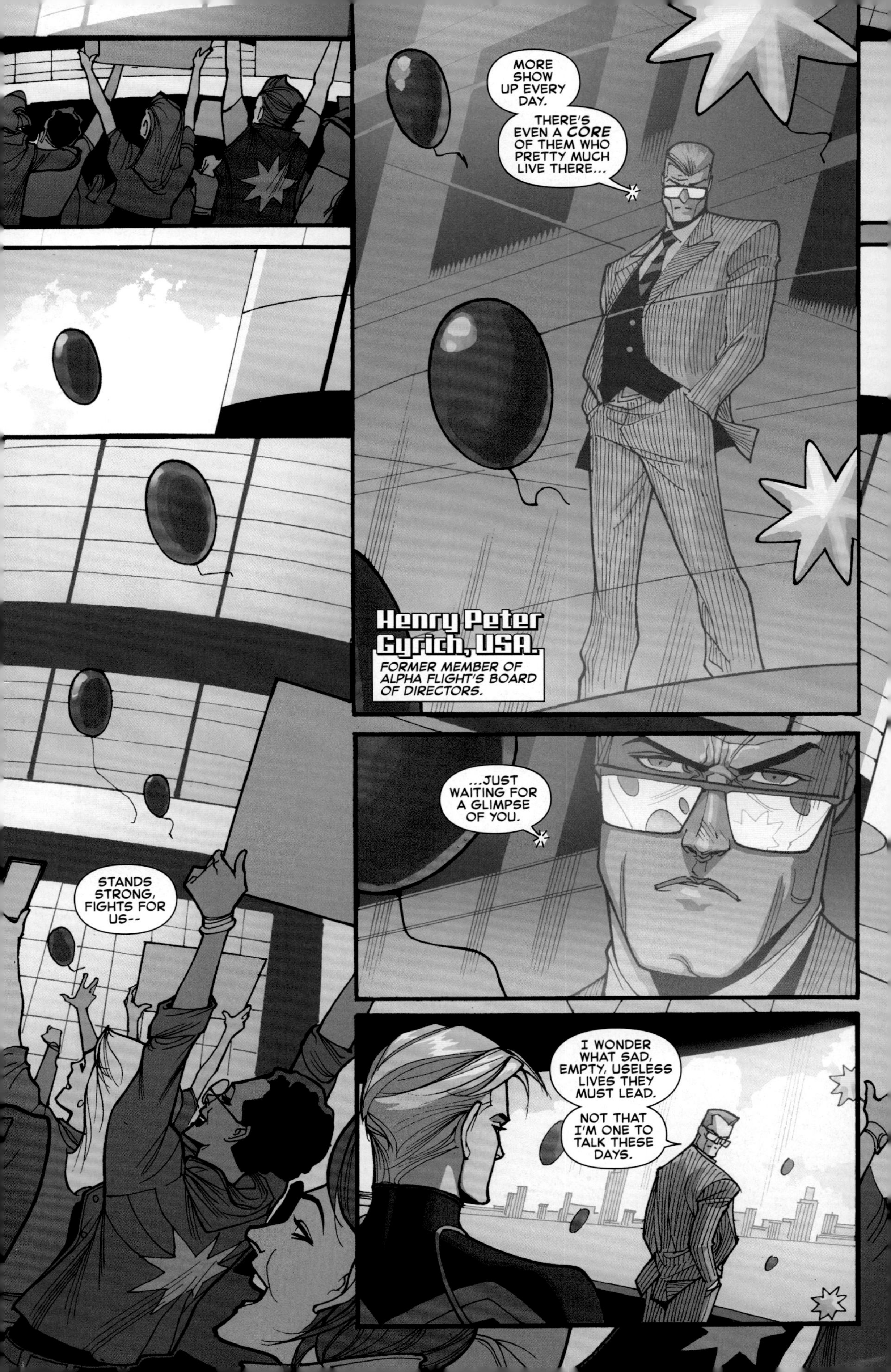
STANDS STRONG, FIGHTS FOR US--
MORE SHOW UP EVERY DAY.
THERE'S EVEN A CORE OF THEM WHO PRETTY MUCH LIVE THERE...
Henry Peter Gyrich, USA.
FORMER MEMBER OF ALPHA FLIGHT'S BOARD OF DIRECTORS.
...JUST WAITING FOR A GLIMPSE OF YOU.
I WONDER WHAT SAD, EMPTY, USELESS LIVES THEY MUST LEAD.
NOT THAT I'M ONE TO TALK THESE DAYS.

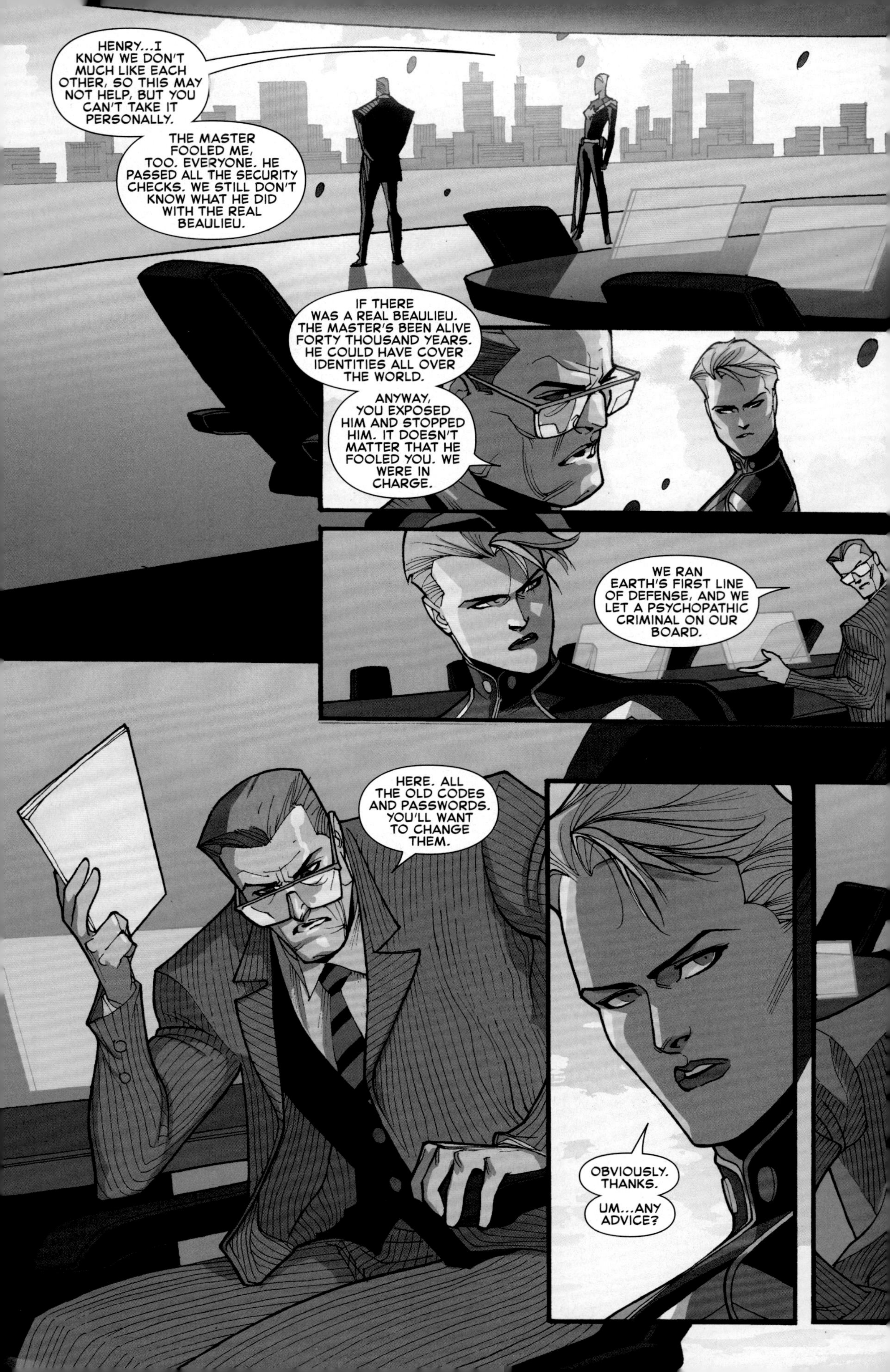
HENRY...I KNOW WE DON'T MUCH LIKE EACH OTHER, SO THIS MAY NOT HELP, BUT YOU CAN'T TAKE IT PERSONALLY.
THE MASTER FOOLED ME, TOO. EVERYONE. HE PASSED ALL THE SECURITY CHECKS. WE STILL DON'T KNOW WHAT HE DID WITH THE REAL BEAULIEU.
IF THERE WAS A REAL BEAULIEU. THE MASTER'S BEEN ALIVE FORTY THOUSAND YEARS. HE COULD HAVE COVER IDENTITIES ALL OVER THE WORLD.
ANYWAY, YOU EXPOSED HIM AND STOPPED HIM. IT DOESN'T MATTER THAT HE FOOLED YOU. WE WERE IN CHARGE.
WE RAN EARTH'S FIRST LINE OF DEFENSE, AND WE LET A PSYCHOPATHIC CRIMINAL ON OUR BOARD.
HERE. ALL THE OLD CODES AND PASSWORDS. YOU'LL WANT TO CHANGE THEM.
OBVIOUSLY. THANKS.
UM...ANY ADVICE?

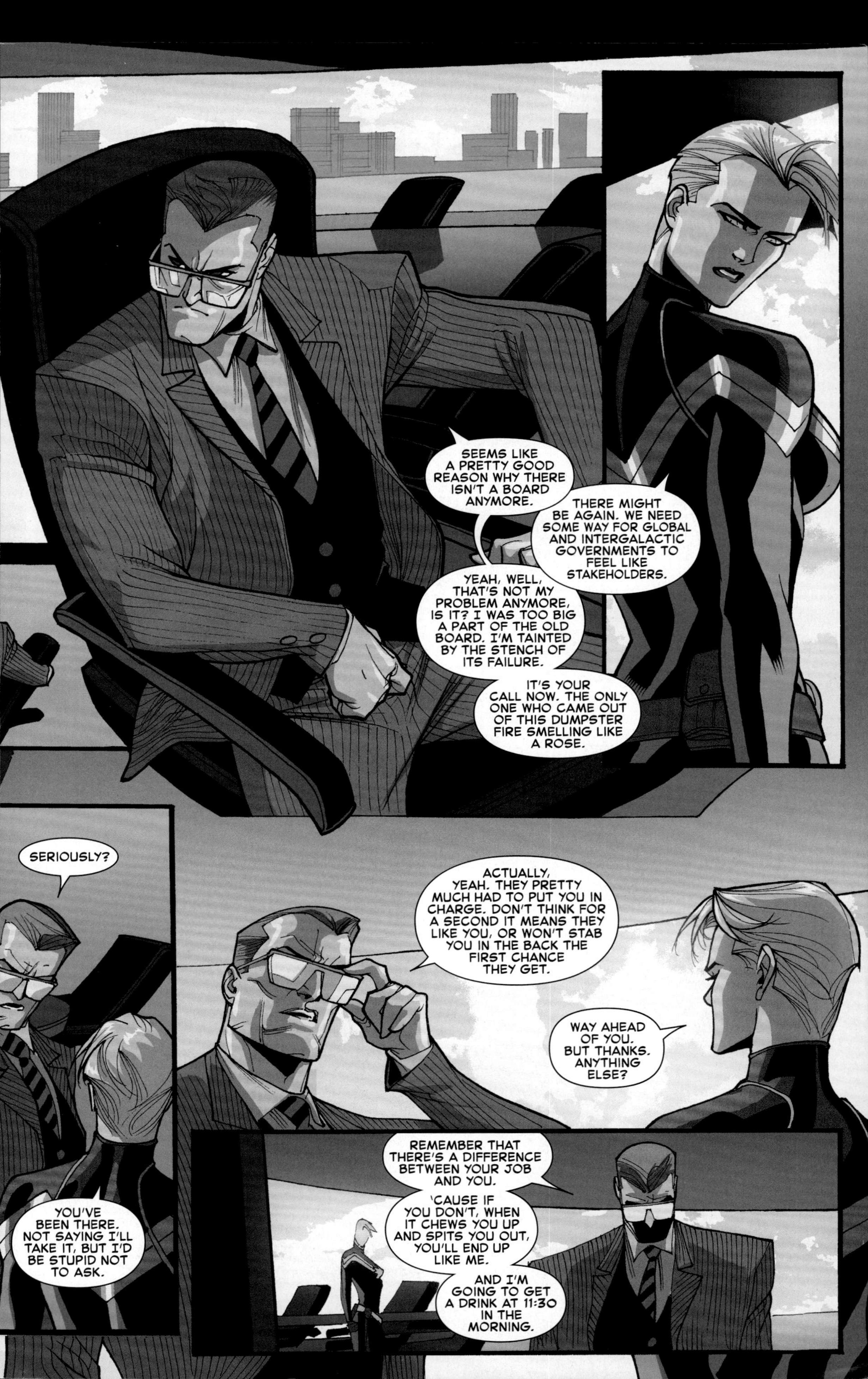
SEEMS LIKE A PRETTY GOOD REASON WHY THERE ISN'T A BOARD ANYMORE.
THERE MIGHT BE AGAIN. WE NEED SOME WAY FOR GLOBAL AND INTERGALACTIC GOVERNMENTS TO FEEL LIKE STAKEHOLDERS.
YEAH, WELL, THAT'S NOT MY PROBLEM ANYMORE, IS IT? I WAS TOO BIG A PART OF THE OLD BOARD. I'M TAINTED BY THE STENCH OF ITS FAILURE.
IT'S YOUR CALL NOW. THE ONLY ONE WHO CAME OUT OF THIS DUMPSTER FIRE SMELLING LIKE A ROSE.
SERIOUSLY?
YOU'VE BEEN THERE. NOT SAYING I'LL TAKE IT, BUT I'D BE STUPID NOT TO ASK.
ACTUALLY, YEAH. THEY PRETTY MUCH HAD TO PUT YOU IN CHARGE. DON'T THINK FOR A SECOND IT MEANS THEY LIKE YOU, OR WON'T STAB YOU IN THE BACK THE FIRST CHANCE THEY GET.
WAY AHEAD OF YOU. BUT THANKS. ANYTHING ELSE?
REMEMBER THAT THERE'S A DIFFERENCE BETWEEN YOUR JOB AND YOU.
'CAUSE IF YOU DON'T, WHEN IT CHEWS YOU UP AND SPITS YOU OUT, YOU'LL END UP LIKE ME.
AND I'M GOING TO GET A DRINK AT 11:30 IN THE MORNING.

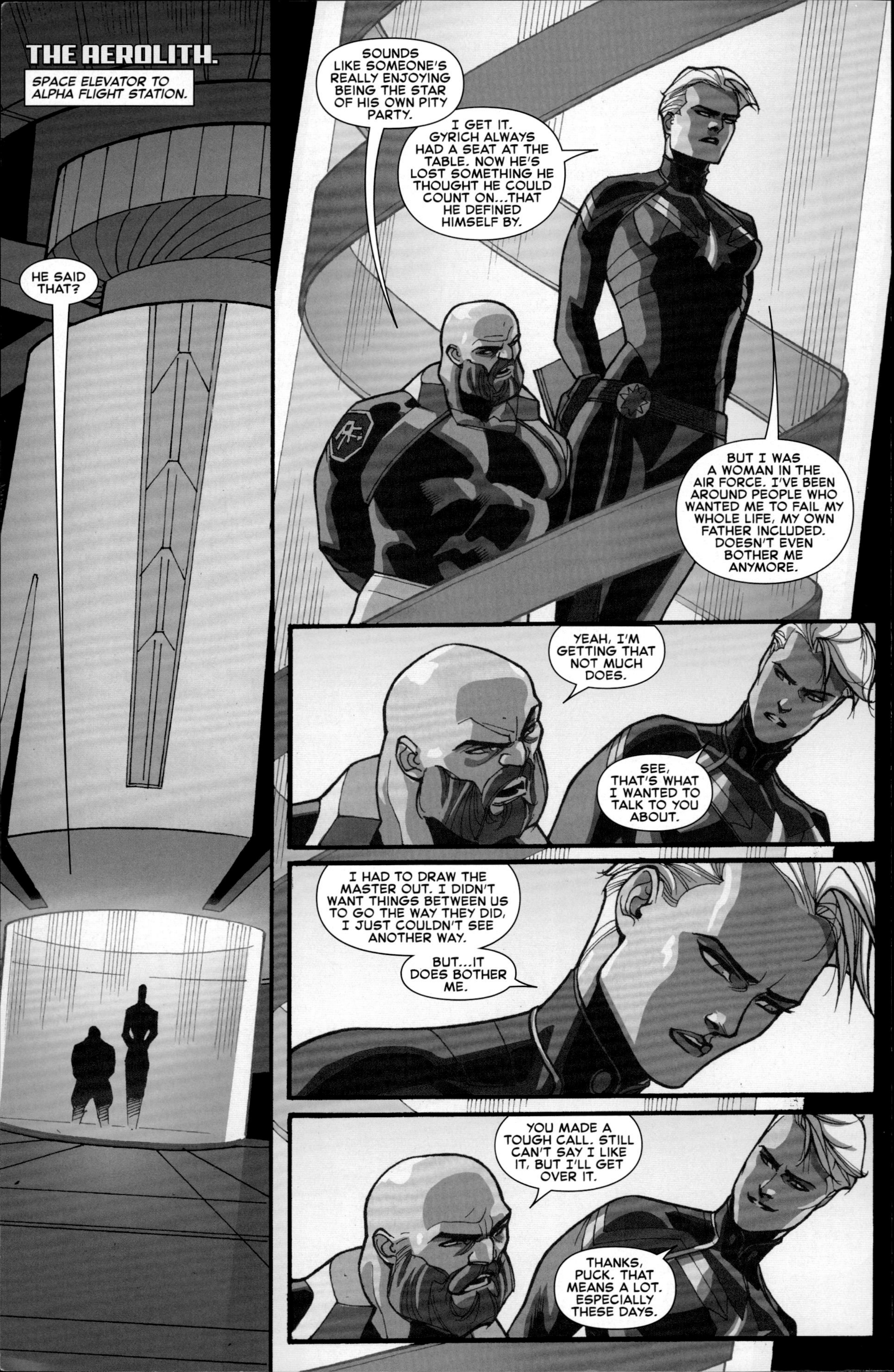
THE AEROLITH.
SPACE ELEVATOR TO ALPHA FLIGHT STATION.
HE SAID THAT?
SOUNDS LIKE SOMEONE'S REALLY ENJOYING BEING THE STAR OF HIS OWN PITY PARTY.
I GET IT. GYRICH ALWAYS HAD A SEAT AT THE TABLE. NOW HE'S LOST SOMETHING HE THOUGHT HE COULD COUNT ON...THAT HE DEFINED HIMSELF BY.
BUT I WAS A WOMAN IN THE AIR FORCE. I'VE BEEN AROUND PEOPLE WHO WANTED ME TO FAIL MY WHOLE LIFE, MY OWN FATHER INCLUDED. DOESN'T EVEN BOTHER ME ANYMORE.
YEAH, I'M GETTING THAT NOT MUCH DOES.
SEE, THAT'S WHAT I WANTED TO TALK TO YOU ABOUT.
I HAD TO DRAW THE MASTER OUT. I DIDN'T WANT THINGS BETWEEN US TO GO THE WAY THEY DID, I JUST COULDN'T SEE ANOTHER WAY.
BUT...IT DOES BOTHER ME.
YOU MADE A TOUGH CALL. STILL CAN'T SAY I LIKE IT, BUT I'LL GET OVER IT.
THANKS, PUCK. THAT MEANS A LOT. ESPECIALLY THESE DAYS.

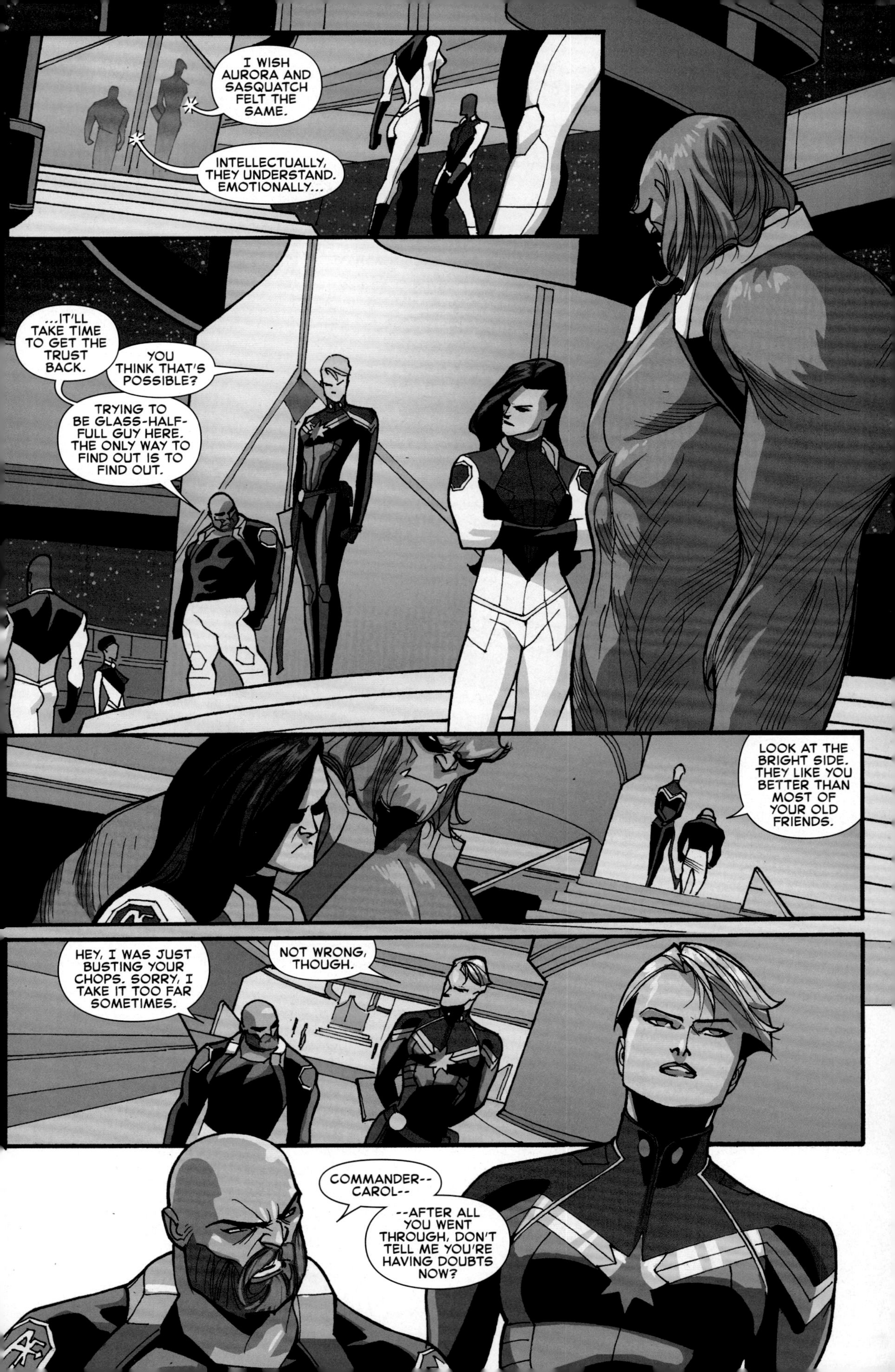
I WISH AURORA AND SASQUATCH FELT THE SAME.
INTELLECTUALLY, THEY UNDERSTAND. EMOTIONALLY...
...IT'LL TAKE TIME TO GET THE TRUST BACK.
YOU THINK THAT'S POSSIBLE?
TRYING TO BE GLASS-HALF-FULL GUY HERE. THE ONLY WAY TO FIND OUT IS TO FIND OUT.
LOOK AT THE BRIGHT SIDE. THEY LIKE YOU BETTER THAN MOST OF YOUR OLD FRIENDS.
HEY, I WAS JUST BUSTING YOUR CHOPS. SORRY, I TAKE IT TOO FAR SOMETIMES.
NOT WRONG, THOUGH.
COMMANDER--
CAROL--
--AFTER ALL YOU WENT THROUGH, DON'T TELL ME YOU'RE HAVING DOUBTS NOW?

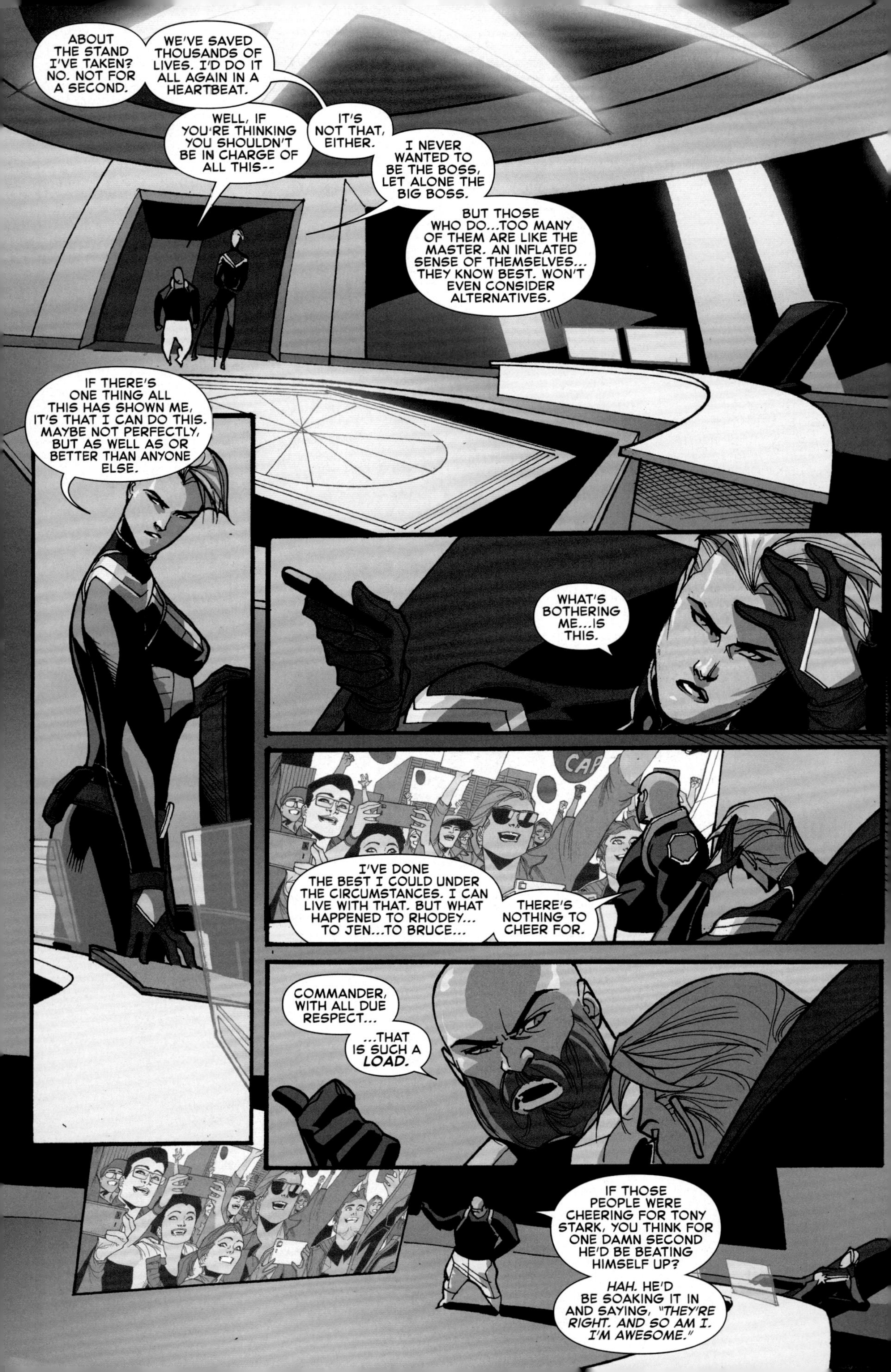
ABOUT THE STAND I'VE TAKEN? NO. NOT FOR A SECOND.
WE'VE SAVED THOUSANDS OF LIVES. I'D DO IT ALL AGAIN IN A HEARTBEAT.
WELL, IF YOU'RE THINKING YOU SHOULDN'T BE IN CHARGE OF ALL THIS--
IT'S NOT THAT, EITHER.
I NEVER WANTED TO BE THE BOSS, LET ALONE THE BIG BOSS.
BUT THOSE WHO DO...TOO MANY OF THEM ARE LIKE THE MASTER. AN INFLATED SENSE OF THEMSELVES... THEY KNOW BEST. WON'T EVEN CONSIDER ALTERNATIVES.
IF THERE'S ONE THING ALL THIS HAS SHOWN ME, IT'S THAT I CAN DO THIS. MAYBE NOT PERFECTLY, BUT AS WELL AS OR BETTER THAN ANYONE ELSE.
WHAT'S BOTHERING ME...IS THIS.
CAP
I'VE DONE THE BEST I COULD UNDER THE CIRCUMSTANCES. I CAN LIVE WITH THAT. BUT WHAT HAPPENED TO RHODEY... TO JEN...TO BRUCE...
THERE'S NOTHING TO CHEER FOR.
COMMANDER, WITH ALL DUE RESPECT...
...THAT IS SUCH A *LOAD.*
IF THOSE PEOPLE WERE CHEERING FOR TONY STARK, YOU THINK FOR ONE DAMN SECOND HE'D BE BEATING HIMSELF UP?
HAH. HE'D BE SOAKING IT IN AND SAYING, *"THEY'RE RIGHT. AND SO AM I. I'M AWESOME."*

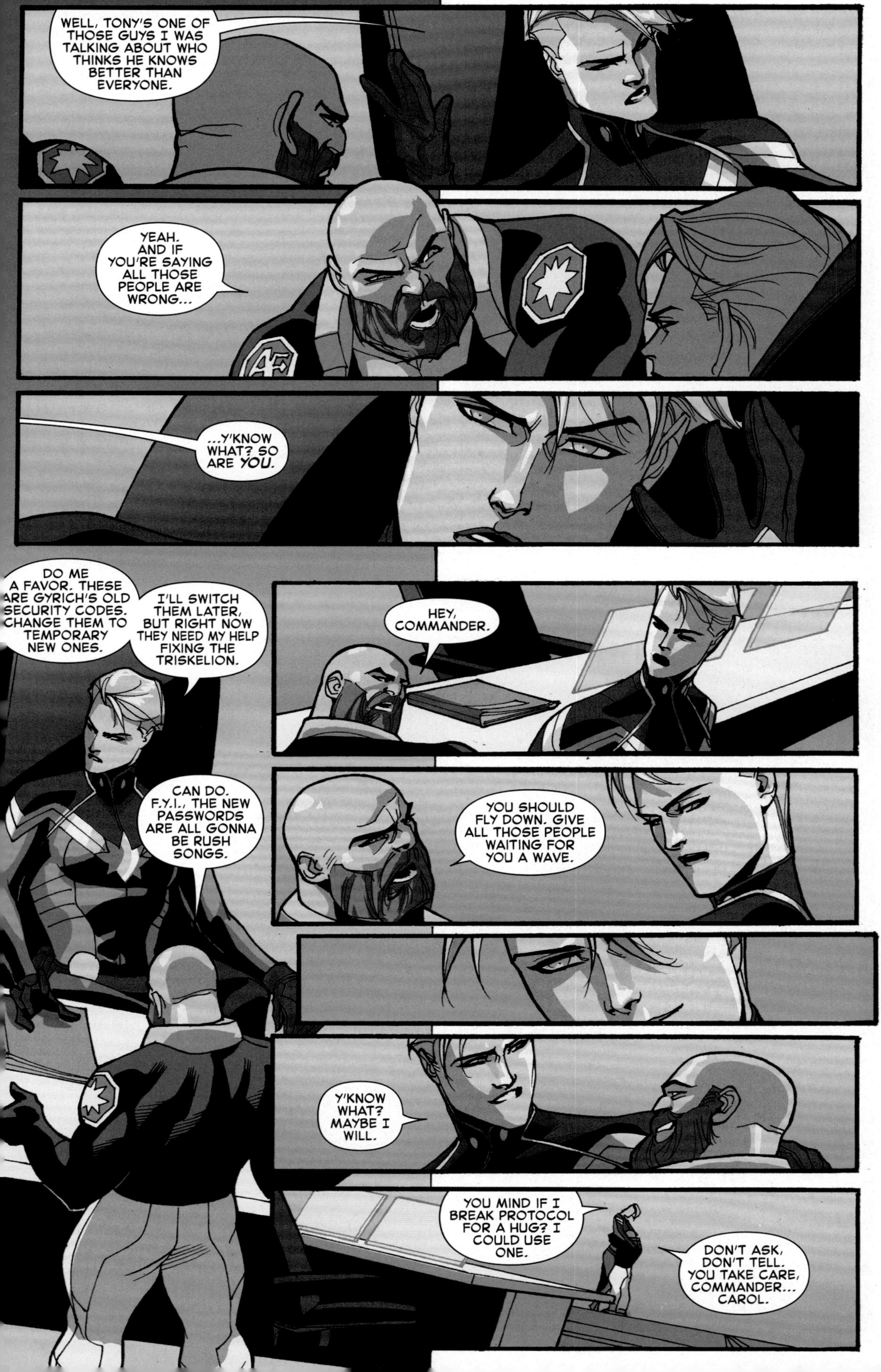
WELL, TONY'S ONE OF THOSE GUYS I WAS TALKING ABOUT WHO THINKS HE KNOWS BETTER THAN EVERYONE.
YEAH. AND IF YOU'RE SAYING ALL THOSE PEOPLE ARE WRONG...
...Y'KNOW WHAT? SO ARE *YOU*.
DO ME A FAVOR. THESE ARE GYRICH'S OLD SECURITY CODES. CHANGE THEM TO TEMPORARY NEW ONES.
I'LL SWITCH THEM LATER, BUT RIGHT NOW THEY NEED MY HELP FIXING THE TRISKELION.
CAN DO. F.Y.I., THE NEW PASSWORDS ARE ALL GONNA BE RUSH SONGS.
HEY, COMMANDER.
YOU SHOULD FLY DOWN. GIVE ALL THOSE PEOPLE WAITING FOR YOU A WAVE.
Y'KNOW WHAT? MAYBE I WILL.
YOU MIND IF I BREAK PROTOCOL FOR A HUG? I COULD USE ONE.
DON'T ASK, DON'T TELL. YOU TAKE CARE, COMMANDER... CAROL.

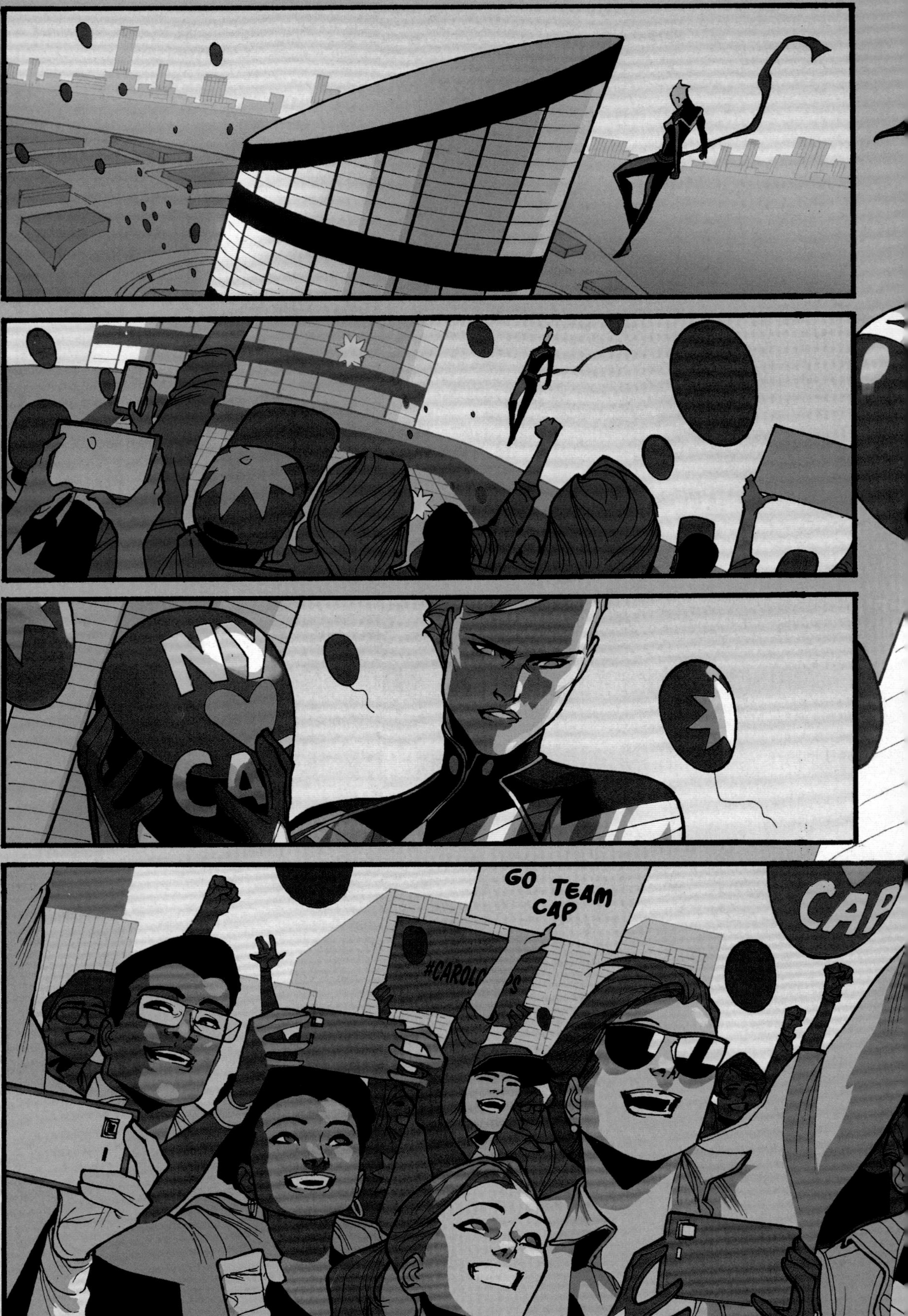
GO TEAM CAP
NY
CAP

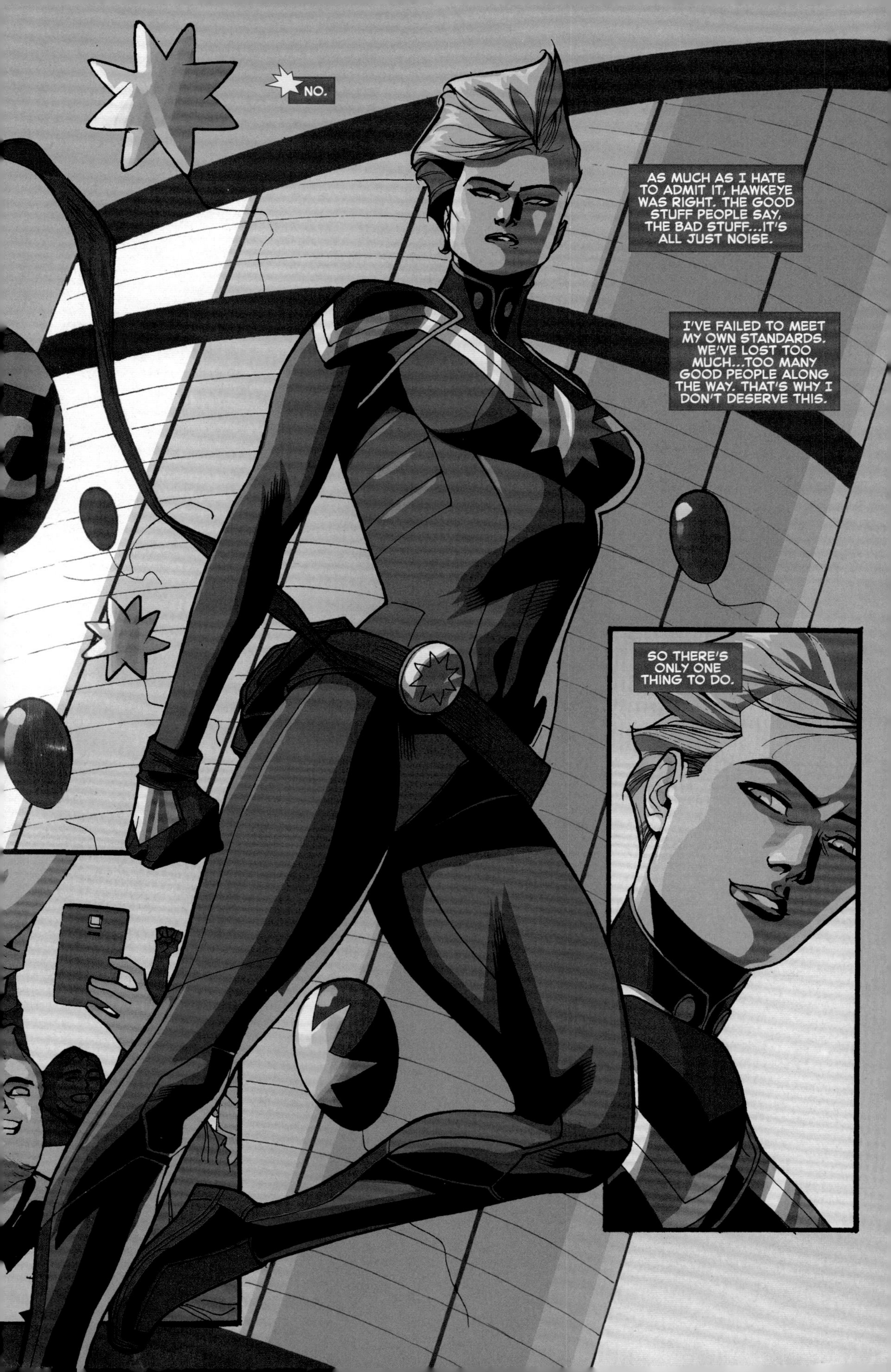
NO.
AS MUCH AS I HATE TO ADMIT IT, HAWKEYE WAS RIGHT. THE GOOD STUFF PEOPLE SAY, THE BAD STUFF...IT'S ALL JUST NOISE.
I'VE FAILED TO MEET MY OWN STANDARDS. WE'VE LOST TOO MUCH...TOO MANY GOOD PEOPLE ALONG THE WAY. THAT'S WHY I DON'T DESERVE THIS.
SO THERE'S ONLY ONE THING TO DO.

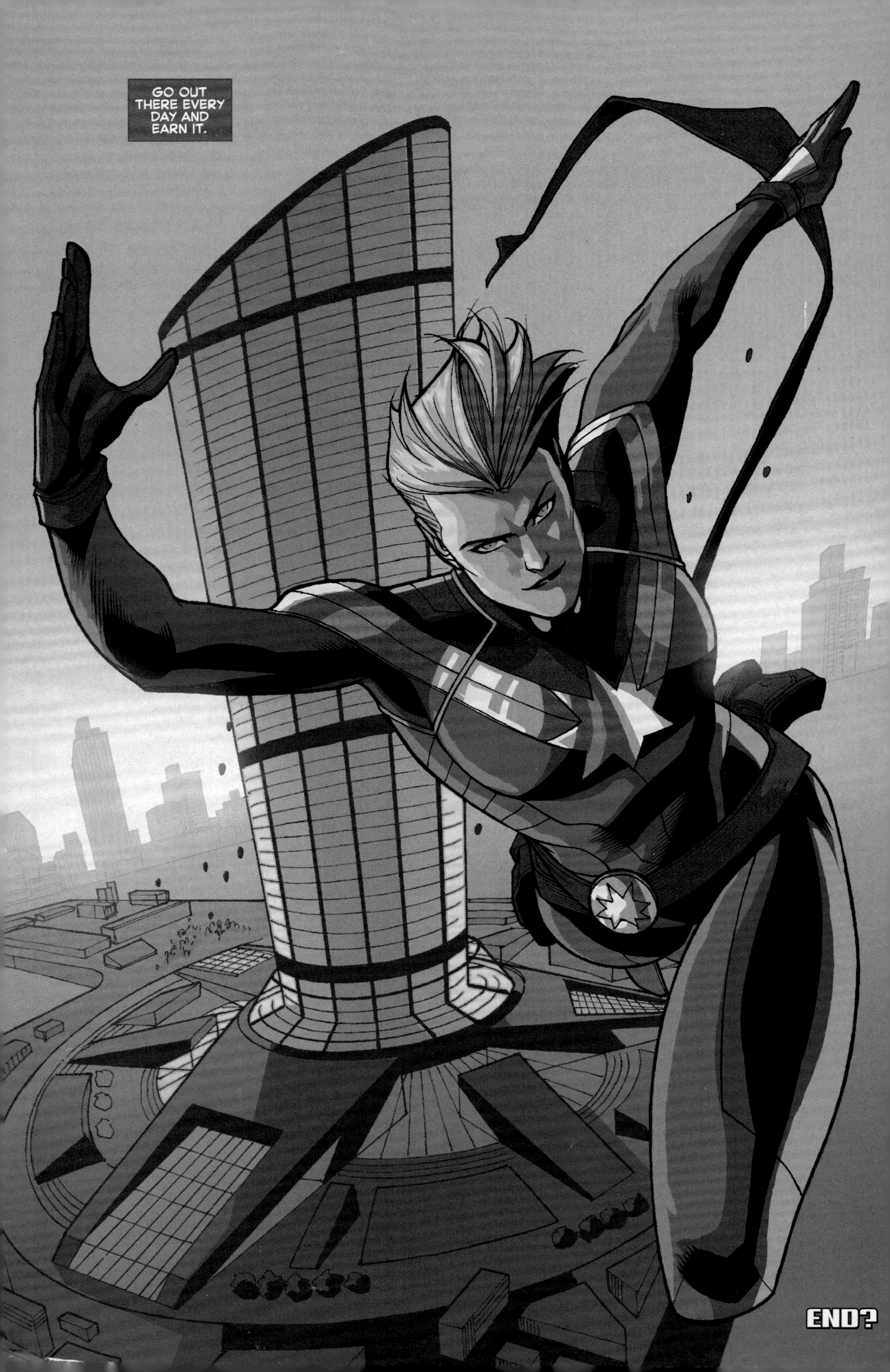
GO OUT THERE EVERY DAY AND EARN IT.
END?

I remember . . .

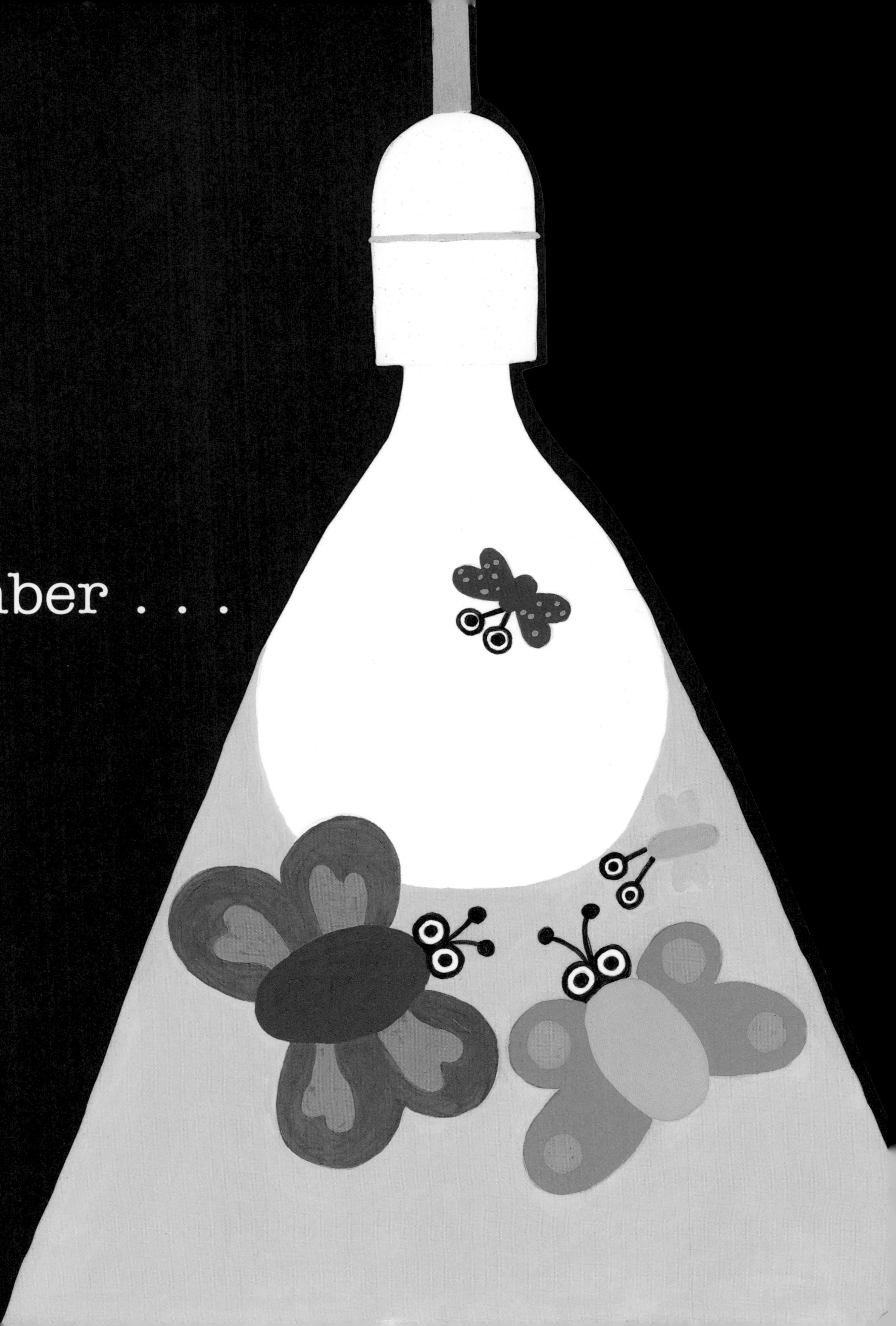

to turn off the light
when I leave the room.